THE PAYMASTER

Also by Tom Bower

Blind Eye to Murder – The Pledge Betrayed
Klaus Barbie: The Butcher of Lyons
The Paperclip Conspiracy
Maxwell: The Outsider
The Red Web
Tiny Rowland: The Rebel Tycoon
Heroes of World War II
The Perfect English Spy: Sir Dick White
Maxwell: The Final Verdict
Blood Money: The Swiss, the Nazis and the Looted Billions
Fayed: The Unauthorised Biography
Branson

Tristan   Loss Love   Gillie
xxx

Happy Birthday

The Paymaster

Geoffrey Robinson,
Maxwell and New Labour

Tom Bower

SIMON & SCHUSTER
A VIACOM COMPANY

First published in Great Britain by Simon & Schuster UK Ltd, 2001
A Viacom Company

1 3 5 7 9 10 8 6 4 2

Simon & Schuster UK Ltd
Africa House
64–78 Kingsway
London WC2B 6AH

Simon & Schuster Australia
Sydney

A CIP catalogue record for this book is available from the British Library

ISBN 0-7432-0689-4

Typeset by SX Composing DTP, Rayleigh, Essex
Printed and bound in Great Britain by Butler & Tanner Ltd, Frome and London

To Veronica, Alexander, Sophie, Oliver and Nicholas

CONTENTS

INTRODUCTION

During the months before the May 1997 general election, Tony Blair, the leader of the Labour Party, pledged that his new government would exterminate sleaze and introduce a government of utmost purity – 'purer than pure' were his words.

Seven months after the election, Geoffrey Robinson, the paymaster-general, was accused of deception. From December 1997 until his resignation twelve months later, Robinson denied a succession of allegations that he was dishonest. In his defence, Tony Blair repeatedly vouched that Robinson was a 'high-calibre' businessman and a 'brilliant minister' who had 'done everything according to the rules'. The paymaster, insisted the prime minister, was honest. This book shows the prime minister to have been mistaken.

During 1999, the year after Robinson's resignation, the prime minister's mistake was strangely compounded by what appears to be concealment and a cover-up.

The life and career of a hitherto shadowy politician who unsuccessfully sought his fortune as a tycoon became the litmus test of New Labour's probity.

PROLOGUE

The voice was weak, quite desperate. 'Virginie! Viens!' Those were the last words.

Virginie Bourquin, the secretary, rushed from the kitchen through the large penthouse apartment, brushing past the heavy Spanish furniture, to her employer's office. The traffic streaming along the Croisette on the Cannes seafront was audible through the open window.

The coiffured eighty-one-year-old woman was slumped over a leather-topped desk. Her afternoon cup of tea was surrounded by mountains of letters and brochures, the detritus of an active businesswoman. Trembling, Virginie cradled the murmuring millionairess in her arms. The large green eyes were closed. Her gasps were unforgettable. Attempts at revival by the summoned paramedics failed. At 5.30 p.m. on 9 October 1994, Joska Bourgeois died. Gently, the strangers carried the corpse to her bed and with polite, professional condolences bade her farewell.

By then others, summoned by the loyal Spanish housekeepers, had arrived. Well-groomed women, professing friendship, had flocked to the spectacle. In their midst, an Arab man was wailing.

Gradually, Saad Boudamagh, the young Algerian companion of the deceased woman, was becoming hysterical. For many years, the gigolo had loyally obeyed the summons to her bed. Well into her middle age, the autocrat had been a sexual predator, and in old age she had refused to surrender her lust for young men.

In the early evening, a tall, elegant Englishman arrived from Monte Carlo. Momentarily, the cacophony inside the penthouse ceased. John Morgan, a retired executive of Jaguar cars, had known Joska Bourgeois for forty-seven years. Introduced by their mutual love of Jaguars, the gentle Englishman had become a reliable friend. His final favour was to calm the chaos and organise the final rites. With disdain he observed the visiting women, bewailing the loss of a friend as a prelude to mentioning the deceased's promise that her furs, couture clothes and jewellery would be their inheritance. Like vultures, Morgan cursed, they had descended to snatch baubles from the warm corpse. In their midst, the wailing had intensified. 'The Arab,' Morgan fulminated, 'is the worst. He's worried about his source of money.'

'Have you called Geoffrey?' Morgan asked the sobbing secretary. 'Nieves has,' replied Virginie, referring to the Spanish domestic. 'He's coming.'

At one o'clock in the morning, Morgan was waiting in the forlorn general aviation building at Nice airport for Geoffrey Robinson to arrive from England in a private jet. The fifty-six-year-old member of parliament for Coventry, Morgan knew, would be distraught. Over the previous twenty-one years, the socialist politician had assumed the role of the millionairess's indispensable adopted son. Every day, at any time, anywhere in the world, Robinson had taken her telephone calls asking for advice and reassurance. In Geneva, Cannes, Paris and her rented flat at the Grosvenor House Hotel, London, Robinson behaved like the son of the house. 'I manage Joska Bourgeois's fortune,' Robinson told Roland Urban, another of her circle. Robinson, it seemed, enjoyed being the 'big chief'. Frequently, he had accompanied Joska Bourgeois to the safe-deposit box at her Geneva bank where she gazed at her jewellery and plucked a wad of cash from the bricks of notes in the steel box. The reward for his diligence had been her guarantees for bank loans to finance his ambition to become a tycoon, to own some magnificent properties, and the promise of great wealth after her death.

Morgan grasped the proffered hand of the grieving politician, whom he had known for twenty-four years. Their conversation during the thirty-minute drive from Nice to Cannes soon switched from condolences to practicalities. 'The Arab's behaving badly,' Morgan volunteered. 'I'd get rid of him as quick as possible.'

'What shall I do?' asked Robinson.

'Change the locks. Seal the flat. Protect everything of value. Keep Saad out' was Morgan's practical advice. Joska Bourgeois's lover had been classified as an interloper by the two Englishmen.

Robinson's arrival in the penthouse just before three o'clock in the morning was fraught. His emotion was genuine. Tearfully, he entered Joska Bourgeois's bedroom, closed the door and for thirty minutes sat with the woman who had been his lover, friend and surrogate mother. They had met when he was thirty-four and she was fifty-nine, but age had never been a barrier. He had willingly succumbed to all her requirements and in return had been well rewarded. The financial relationship suited her. Only money, she knew, would attract young men to old women, and her hunt for indulgence and companionship had been shameless.

Emerging into the huge salon, Robinson spotted Saad, Virginie and Morgan. In the background were the Spanish housekeepers, a married couple.

'The funeral's here, I suppose?' Robinson asked Morgan, pointedly ignoring the Arab.

'Oh, no,' replied the Englishman. 'I'm sure she said she wanted to be buried in Brussels.'

Saad moved forward. 'Brussels,' he insisted, with the certainty of an intimate.

At daybreak, Robinson telephoned Jacques Mounier, Joska Bourgeois's former employee in Brussels. 'Joska's dead,' he revealed. 'A heart attack. Sudden and painless. Can you arrange

the funeral?' Mounier had helped construct Joska Bourgeois's
£15 million fortune, first as the Jaguar agent in Belgium and
then, more lucratively, as the agent for Toyota cars. With a sense
of obligation, he agreed to organise the last rites. Ever since she
had fled the country after the sale of her business to evade about
£6 million in taxes, Mounier had rarely spoken to the woman. She
had settled in Geneva, a tax haven, and spent the summers in
Cannes, and she had never returned to Brussels. But there were
many in the capital who recalled the tigress and would want to say
adieu. Robinson uttered his gratitude. To his relief, Morgan
immediately agreed to make the arrangements in Cannes for the
shipment of the corpse.

'What will you do?' asked Morgan.

'I'm flying to Geneva,' replied Robinson.

'Take the Arab with you,' suggested Morgan in English,
knowing that the third man could not understand. 'We need to
get him out of here.'

Robinson nodded. Saad, he knew, would insist on coming. Both
had forged a relationship based upon dependence. Like himself,
the Arab had certainly been promised an inheritance. To
guarantee friendship and attract admirers, Joska had habitually
promised, 'You'll have something when I die.' Like a puppet
master, she had revelled in dangling enticements before those who
in other circumstances might have shunned her company. The
most gullible were invited to gaze at her huge collection of jewels
– she possessed enormous pearls, emeralds and diamonds – in the
vaults of her Swiss bank and were satiated by her bait. Both
Robinson and Saad were understandably nervous. Behind their
backs, she had suspiciously professed to others, 'I don't want one
person to have all the keys to my papers.'

As day broke, Robinson was not entirely innocent of a desire to
know how her promises had materialised. An unprompted comment from Virginie Bourquin – 'Only recently Madame said she
wanted to go to Geneva to change her will, but she didn't go' –
aggravated his curiosity. The enviable view from the penthouse of
the sun shining on the Mediterranean infused the mourners with

relief at their own survival. The departed would certainly have included her desires for the funeral in her last testament deposited with her Swiss lawyer. That was the perfect reason for racing to Geneva.

The forty-minute flight in the private jet was surreal. The two passengers, one born near Algiers and the other born in Sheffield, were united by grief and greed. They shared an apprehension about an uncertain legacy which was guaranteed to conspicuously alter the remainder of their lives.

In Geneva, Robinson had resolved, he would not allow Saad under any circumstances to remain in Joska's flat. He could not prevent Saad making one last visit but he would be told to stay in a hotel. The expensive *pietra d'oro* furniture, the exquisite Chinese porcelain figurines and vases and the rich carpets and tapestries might resemble a museum but would invite fears for its safety. 'I'll give them all to my friends,' he could recall Joska Bourgeois predicting, but Robinson expected to inherit everything. His suspicion of Saad, he felt, was justified. Frequently, Robinson had been irritated by the Arab's arguments with Joska and he recalled his concern when she occasionally locked herself in a room to avoid the Arab's rage. Naturally, Robinson forgot Saad's anger towards himself when he was drunk, a frequent occurrence. For his part, Saad could understand Robinson's resentment that a chance meeting in the lift at the Plaza Athenée hotel in Paris had transformed a poor Arab's life.

Saad Boudamagh had been carrying the luggage for a playboy Arab prince visiting the five-star hotel. Living on his wits, the Algerian was a popular clown, renowned for entertaining the rich. Joska Bourgeois had arrived in Paris for a knee operation and, during that brief encounter, Saad volunteered to visit her in hospital. Faster than Robinson, he had spotted Bourgeois's passion to spend money. As usual, she was travelling with nine suitcases filled with the most expensive clothes which had once, to her anger, featured in an Alan Whicker television documentary about the fabulously rich sailing on the luxury QE2 liner. Before her departure from Paris, Bourgeois had offered Saad a proposition:

'Stay with me and you'll be rich.' For the money, Saad agreed to become an old woman's adornment. Although he lived in Algeria, he responded over the following years to her summons to become her driver, poodle, jester and lover. In return, he received very little cash but was inundated with entertainment, clothes, forty watches, furniture including kitchen appliances for his Algerian home, and eventually a factory to manufacture sweets. The absurdity of life as Joska's playboy was justified by earning a real income from that childish desire.

Robinson had benefited similarly. Thanks to Joska Bourgeois, he possessed two beautiful Lutyens houses, in Godalming and Stockbridge, and an estate in Tuscany; he lived in her rented flat at the Grosvenor House Hotel in Park Lane; and he was a large shareholder in an industrial company quoted on the London stock exchange. Like Saad, whenever he had eaten with his benefactress at the best restaurants in London, Paris, Geneva and the Côte d'Azur, he had chosen the most expensive food and wines but her credit card had settled the account. Unlike Saad, he knew details of their benefactress's wealth. In their regular telephone conversations, she monotonously asked his advice about her investments and the price of gold, which she possessed in considerable quantities.

Before visiting the lawyer, Robinson and Saad were driven to Parc Plein Soleil A in the Chemin de Pommier, Bourgeois's apartment, where they were greeted by Emmanuelle Davoigne, her Swiss secretary. Joska Bourgeois had ordained that on her death, Emmanuelle would supervise the distribution of her fortune. Robinson had other ideas. Saad asked for cash from the safe – as usual, Bourgeois had left him without any money – and in the metal box there were certain to be bundles of Swiss and French banknotes in large denominations. Robinson refused. He had decided not to open the safe in Saad's presence. They would certainly dispute the fate of the other contents, including the jewels. Saad was dispatched to a hotel. In his absence, but with Emmanuelle present, Robinson as executor opened the safe and gave the secretary some cash and jewels. The remainder would be safeguarded by himself.

At the end of that long day, Robinson locked the flat, abandoned Saad in the city and returned to Britain in the private plane. Shortly afterwards he received a telephone call. 'I'm stuck in a hotel and I've got no money,' complained the Arab. 'If you don't send me some money, you'll regret it. And there'll be trouble if I don't get my inheritance.'

Only the beneficiaries ever saw the will, and each saw only that part referring to their bequest. 'Joska Bourgeois did it that way,' said Mounier, 'so nobody could be jealous.' Her friends estimated that Bourgeois had left over $60 million, divided as $40 million for Saad and $20 million for Robinson, who also received all her property and their contents which were shipped to England. Robinson says he received £9 million. Emmanuelle Davoigne received a small bequest. Bourgeois's jewellery was bequeathed to the Institut Pasteur in Paris.

'You're right about the funeral,' Geoffrey Robinson told John Morgan. 'She wanted to be buried in Brussels.' By then, Morgan had chosen an expensive coffin and arranged for a 'lying-in-state'. To his disgust, not one of the female vultures whose tears had accompanied their demands for an inheritance visited their 'friend'. Nor did they volunteer to attend the funeral. Crafty, manipulative Joska Bourgeois had few genuine friends in her exile.

In her native city there was no resentment. Over a hundred mourners were personally welcomed by Robinson for the two-hour afternoon service at L'Eglise Saint-Lambert. Among them were John Morgan and her three staff from Cannes. Saad, abandoned by Robinson without a visa, had been smuggled into the country in the car of Roland Urban, an amusing companion of Joska Bourgeois in Geneva and Cannes. Urban, a retired film stuntman, like so many others, had been surprised to hear that her promises to himself of a generous bequest had not been honoured.

Those entering the church saw the coffin in the centre, bedecked with flowers placed by Robinson with the inscription 'Thank you Joska' in English. Tearfully, dabbing his eyes, Robinson read in French during the service from Matthew,

Chapter 25: the parable of the wealthy master who divided his gold between his servants and charged them to invest wisely. Marie Elena, his Maltese wife, stared dry-eyed and unemotional. Their turbulent marriage attracted some bewilderment but little speculation. Few could recall a memorable conversation with the permanently aspiring opera singer, except John Morgan. 'Can you imagine all these Arabs with Joska?' Morgan had once joked. 'She's so old. It's all hanging out.' Marie Elena could not resist a jocular riposte: 'Well, she wouldn't want to go to bed with Geoffrey. He's so small and no good in bed.'

At the wake that afternoon in the Château St Anne, an international club in St Pierre, Robinson fulfilled his duties as the adopted son, reassured by his fellow mourners' sympathies. Pointedly, he ignored Saad, who already planned to buy a tax exile's residence on Monaco's waterfront, a yacht in Cannes, a facelift, treatment for hair replacement and a playboy's lifestyle chasing young women. For his part, the British politician and proud owner of five homes anticipated a flamboyant lifestyle, buying himself influence and status disguised by subterfuge.

1

THE BUTTERFLY

Simultaneously coveting affluence and influence were confusing ambitions for a traditional socialist in the Seventies, but for Geoffrey Robinson, the son of a furniture manufacturer, born in Sheffield on 25 May 1938, the journey from Labour's left wing was unusually comfortable.

The second of four children of an unhappy marriage, Robinson had excelled at school as a superb sportsman, an excellent academic and a popular prefect; was a success as a student of economics and history at Clare College, Cambridge; and shone during a fellowship at Yale. In a period of great Conservative prosperity under Harold Macmillan, he joined the Labour Party in 1958, a fractious movement championing punitive taxation, widespread state control and the nationalisation of Britain's principal industries. The inspiration for joining the left, he remarked, was his fiery mother and, later, his involvement with the civil rights protesters in Mississippi. Travelling with friends from Yale, Robinson was shocked by the deprivation and prejudice suffered by black Americans in the southern states. Living in America at the time of John F. Kennedy's assassination, a time when the right offered slow solutions to remove inequalities and was deploying CIA officers across the globe to destabilise communist sympathisers, he was inspired to become an activist.

The agent of his recruitment to work for the Labour Party was Harold Wilson, leader of the opposition, during a visit to Yale. Wilson, an outstanding Oxford academic who promised to revolutionise Britain, was easily attracted to intelligence and sycophancy, and by then Robinson had perfected a vivid performance towards those he sought to impress. His charm, gregariousness and engagement in politics and economics triggered Wilson's interest. The graduate was invited to join the Labour Party's research department at Transport House, the incubator for Wilson's 'one hundred day' revolution promising to transform Britain by 'the white heat of technology'. The twenty-six-year-old arrived in 1964 with notable qualifications and high expectations, anticipating automatic progression to the House of Commons.

Fluent in German and French and with an engaging self-confidence after national service in the army's Intelligence Corps, Robinson suffered no doubts about his destiny. Unlike his parochial colleagues in the department, he was a man of action, combining political zeal with a passion to earn money, a preoccupation inherited from his father, a dedicated businessman. Within weeks, Robinson was noted as an intelligent researcher able to present good arguments on paper, yet nervous that his high expectations might not materialise. Assigned to the international section under David Ennals, damned by many as an uninspiring dullard, he was frustrated by the Labour government's support of America's developing war in Vietnam. His vehement opposition to the war aligned him with the party's far-left MPs, especially Tony Benn, Frank Allaun and even Ian Mikardo, an East End MP who, unlike the others, did not warm to Robinson. Courting those opposed to Harold Wilson outraged Gwyn Morgan, the director of the international section, who criticised Robinson's alignment with the party's neo-Marxist left as 'gross disloyalty'. In the ensuing rows, Morgan ordered Robinson not to associate with

Benn and others classified as fellow travellers. Although Robinson eventually conceded with a smile, 'OK, you're the boss', Morgan's dislike extended beyond his subordinate's politics to his personality.

Some at Transport House recognised Robinson's amiability, appreciating a man who had achieved some fame within their small community for his remarkable ability to beguile older women, especially Mary Wilson, the prime minister's wife. Some joked that Robinson switched on his coquetry so automatically that he occasionally forgot the identity of his target. Many were amused by the energetic raconteur and bon vivant. Others were irritated, especially Gwyn Morgan. In Morgan's opinion, Robinson's efforts to please were the machinations of a 'greasy, over-flattering, insidious and ingratiating operator working for his own agenda'. Being nice, Morgan concluded, reflected Robinson's constant search for contacts to satisfy his political ambitions, a quality common among those seeking election to the House of Commons.

Others were impressed by his utter self-confidence. Not a hint of self-doubt or a word of self-criticism was ever heard. 'He never thinks he does wrong,' smiled Mike Lewis, an admiring school-friend and Labour activist. 'No, you're wrong,' was Robinson's abrupt termination of any discussion. Naivety, self-delusion and dishonesty were the characteristics suggested but never admitted. That repeatedly reinforced Geoffrey Robinson's mystery.

At Transport House, Geoffrey Robinson's ideology appeared confused. He supported the left, convinced of the importance of state intervention to remedy and control capitalism, yet he clearly sought personal wealth, if only to finance his political ambitions. Unlike his contemporaries, who were steeped in the dense literature written by prophets and agitators analysing the tor-mented history of socialism, revolution and the People's Struggle against capitalism, Robinson avoided the endless meetings sum-moned to debate an agreed path towards Paradise. His interest in politics did not extend to passionate immersion in the political world. Living in an attractive flat in Earls Court, financed, it was assumed, from his father's resources, he was not committed to financial self-sacrifice for socialism, while his desire for political office appeared suddenly to be weaker than his desire for money. In 1968, at the age of thirty, denied those intimate relationships within the party necessary to secure a seat in the Commons, and forewarned that he would not be sponsored as a special candidate, Robinson spotted his gratifying salvation.

The Industrial Reorganisation Corporation, the IRC, was Harold Wilson's agent to revolutionise British industry and radicalise British management. Besotted by the idea that 'Big is Beautiful', Wilson created a state bank to stimulate mergers and invent British Goliaths to compete against the new multi-nationals. Although the IRC's bankers were unable to cure 'the sick man of Europe' of the trade unions' restrictive practices and constant strikes, Wilson lured some of the dynamic players in the City and industry to realise Labour's dream of urging Britain's myopic managers to embrace the 'white heat of a technological revolution'. Robinson joined an organisation which had recruited future leaders of Britain's economy. In the confused ideals of socialist sentiments and capitalist objectives, Robinson was introduced to industry, business, finance and the relationship between the private sector and the government by Frank Kearton, Ronnie Grierson, Graham Hearne, John Gardiner and Alistair Morton – later chief executives of major British corporations. Some had good qualities while others were flawed. Under the supervision of Roger Brooke, he became involved in the reorgan-isation of Britain's mining-machinery industry and the merger of Britain's three major manufacturers of electrical equipment. There were only eulogies for his energy, intelligence, diligence and practicality. Although he was no more talented than others, he was blatantly more ambitious. To some, Robinson was 'clearly on the make', searching for success, no longer political but commercial. His invaluable opportunity was an assignment with Geoffrey Owen, a future editor of the *Financial Times*, to negotiate the merger of Britain's several motor manufacturers into one company under Donald Stokes, chairman of British Leyland, a manufacturer of coaches and trucks.

Harold Wilson had taken a personal interest in the reorganisation of the motor industry. At a lunch at Chequers in 1968, he sought with Tony Benn, minister of technology, to persuade Sir George Harrison, chief executive of the British Motor Corporation, the manufacturer of Austin and Morris cars, to merge with Leyland. 'Work together,' Wilson urged Stokes and Harrison, convinced that the industry's sole salvation against world competition was unification. 'Over my dead body,' retorted Harrison. Wilson was undeterred. 'If you pull it off,' he promised Stokes later, 'you'll get a peerage.'

Stokes, a member of the IRC board, could not succeed without finance and the only source was the IRC. One intermediary between Leyland and the bank was Robinson. 'Do everything for him,' Stokes ordered John Morgan, assistant to the managing director of Leyland International. 'Take him wherever he wants.' Morgan, the same age as Robinson, was instantly impressed by the visitor: 'His brain was far ahead of everything I was saying.' Soon afterwards, the IRC awarded Leyland a generous grant and the merger of the British motor industry began. During that complicated process, Stokes often met – and became impressed by – Robinson, a man who had no difficulty repeating the jargon and reflecting the attitudes impregnated by the City types within the IRC. The transformation of Robinson from left-wing firebrand into putative tycoon had commenced. His instinct was to earn money. Barriers, however, remained. The manufacturing process and financial controls were unfamiliar sciences. The priority in business was profits, a truism he, like many socialists, preferred to ignore. The extremists in the trade unions, Britain's industrial curse, were his political allies. He was a committed disciple of state intervention but he also ached for a champagne lifestyle. While others might be vexed by the irreconcilable struggle between political and commercial ambitions, by 1970 Robinson found it easy to compartmentalise his philosophical aspirations.

Immediately after the election of the Conservative government in 1970, the IRC was closed. Most outsiders condemned the institution as disastrous, except for the few who had personally benefited. Robinson was among that minority. Few were surprised when he, searching for a new employer, proposed to Lord Stokes, 'I got you the money; how about a job?' Stokes, the self-confident salesman of Leyland buses, promoted far beyond his ability to save the British motor industry, was happy to oblige.

Stokes was generous. In 1971, Robinson was appointed 'staff executive, facilities planning' at Leyland, an anonymous post in a confusing bureaucracy. Months later, he was promoted to a senior financial controller at the company's headquarters in Berkeley Square, an exceptional position for someone with no qualifications in accountancy. The thirty-three-year-old's arrival in Mayfair caused a flutter among the more insular car men. Robinson was good-looking, energetic and articulate, and his background – a direct-grant public school, Cambridge, Yale, Transport House and the IRC – cast him as Stokes's chosen son. The reliable gossip that he regularly wrote speeches for Stokes and senior Labour politicians, and maintained close relations with Harold Wilson and Marcia Williams (later Lady Falkender), the prime minister's political assistant, silenced those complaining about his unpredictable nature and unpunctuality. Few did not comment about his habit of cultivating contacts but nurturing few friendships. Robinson, they noticed, was a butterfly, alighting on somebody useful and soon departing for someone better.

There was good reason for Robinson to feel secure. In 1967, he had married Marie Elena Giogo, a Maltese whom he had met at a reception for Commonwealth students. By 1970 they were living in Kensington with a newborn daughter, Margot-Véronique. At first, the marriage seemed a pleasant contrast to his turbulent childhood in a flat above an off-licence in Sheffield and in Balham, south London. Robinson occasionally reminisced about his quarrelling parents and the repeated scolding from his unhappy mother. After his parents' divorce and his father's remarriage, he became distant from his mother while remaining close to his father. The unstable relationship with his mother was duplicated with his new wife. Marie Elena, Robinson told acquaintances, possessed a volcanic temper, provoking furious arguments. 'We've lost three alarm clocks in three months,' he moaned. 'I just duck and run.'

The marriage was unstable when he travelled in 1972 with John Morgan to Milan, Italy. Morgan was accompanying Leyland's financial controller to inspect the company's latest acquisition, Innocenti, a small manufacturer of Leyland's successful Mini.

'Why have you bought it?' asked Robinson.

'Because it makes the Mini Cooper,' explained Morgan. 'Although they make them better than us.'

'Who's going to run it?' Robinson asked, clearly intrigued.

'Filmer Paradise,' replied Morgan referring to a New Yorker.

'Why him?' asked Geoffrey Robinson.

'Because he ran Ford in Italy and he's got a girlfriend in Lugano,' said Morgan, with deliberate eccentricity.

Their tour of the small, clean and efficient factory provoked Robinson to declare, 'I want to run this.' Innocenti was an opportunity to escape the anonymity of Berkeley Square and run his own show. The change would be the gift of Donald Stokes. To satisfy Robinson's desire would show considerable faith: he had neither industrial experience nor any knowledge of car design and production. Yet Stokes was smitten with a favoured son who argued persuasively that he had mastered financial controls, industrial production, labour relations, marketing and international negotiations. 'And I speak fluent Italian,' he added. Stokes not only agreed to arrange Paradise's immediate resignation but also promised Robinson an extraordinarily lucrative contract with a high salary, generous bonus payments and unusual living expenses. The transformation was remarkable.

Four years earlier, Robinson had been a protester against the war in Vietnam, a member of CND and a socialist committed to nationalisation of industries and confiscatory rates of taxation. In the intervening years, his politics had not changed. Like many in that era, he remained a socialist, but wanted to enjoy the rewards of capitalism.

During his next flight to Milan, Robinson was deeply engrossed in a dog-eared, second-hand copy of *Teach Yourself Italian*. On arrival, he asked for a translation of a short speech he had written during his journey. One hour later, he was reading phonetically from a document and speaking with passion to many of Innocenti's four thousand employees, convincing his audience of his managerial skills and deep understanding of their culture. His audience, surprised by the arrival of a thirty-three-year-old political appointee rather than an experienced car expert, were content to welcome a man clearly willing to accept a factory burdened by crippling costs and dictatorial trade unions which fiercely protected their restrictive practices and had forced the Innocenti family to sell their beloved company for just £4 million to escape bankruptcy.

Robinson was unfazed by the scanty scrutiny of Innocenti's accounts conducted by Leyland's financial controllers, which included himself. Innocenti was his opportunity, to emulate other graduates from the IRC, to rank among Britain's industrial Titans. He assumed that his informal 'American-style' manner and socialist principles would win converts among the workers, and that his managerial flair would resolve Innocenti's financial predicament. After eight years of subordination since Yale, he intended to behave like a king. Settling into a furnished apartment in the Via Cusani without his wife and child, he adopted an unorthodox lifestyle. Most evenings he spent eating, drinking and night clubbing. Often, Paolo Caccamo, the factory's technical director and the only Italian appointed to the board of directors, carried his employer home only to discover, the following morning, the same man drinking whisky in his office and even stepping slightly drunk into the production area.

Initially, Robinson's habits were discounted as an Englishman's eccentricity. His enthusiastic endorsement of socialism, his warmth towards the local communists, and his glad-handing of workers along the assembly line, in the shops and schools, aroused popularity, especially among the 1500 militant communist workers whom he recruited from southern Italy. On his small foreign stage, Robinson enjoyed being the admired centre of attraction. One Sunday, he even joined a communist rally of the Parti d'Unità outside Milan. The fraternal image was contradicted by his comments during his return journey to the city. 'God, I'm fed up with all that,' he told Caccamo in the exhausted gasp of a professional actor. The obvious dangers were ignored and, during that journey, the hypocrisy was exposed. The following day, Caccamo mentioned he planned to teach engineering at Turin University. 'Are you paid?' asked Robinson. 'No,' replied the Italian. 'Then drop it,' advised the socialist. Unpaid community service did not appeal to Robinson. Evading British exchange controls and avoiding taxes was more appealing. With Caccamo's knowledge, Robinson had arranged with the local Leyland accountant that his salary would be transported in cash to Switzerland and deposited in a Swiss bank.

In London, there was only praise for Robinson. Enthused by his protégé's mastery of Italian and his evidently good relations with the notorious Italian trade unions, Lord Stokes was amenable to Robinson's request to exhibit his presence. His totem would be the Regent, a new car designed by Bertone and Allegro, to replace the British-designed Mini. Despite the paucity of Robinson's market research and technical specifications, Stokes approved the necessary finance. That lackadaisical decision roused Robinson to augment his ambition and expand production until the new car was launched.

Robinson was learning in a business school reliant upon a wing and a prayer. With pride, he summoned the Innocenti workforce to hear a speech of self-congratulation intended for consumption in London as well as Milan. Both audiences were impressed by a mind 'running at twice the normal speed', displaying an apparent feel for finance. Wiser hands like Paolo Caccamo grasped Robinson's technical ignorance. He was an actor rather than a diligent number-cruncher. To that minority, Robinson's plan was ill-conceived. But the cautious were brushed aside. Robinson, they discovered, smiled at advice and ignored it. The king was impatient and hated criticism. Thereafter, he was a rebel, proudly disdainful of rules, preferring not to refer anything to London for approval. 'Don't worry, Paolo,' he smiled to his new friend. 'He doesn't want to learn,' Caccamo told Bruno Jotti, the director of corporate relations.

The impromptu decision to build a new car proved disappointing. Despite Robinson's impatience for rapid results, the new car's launch was delayed. As a temporary substitute, he ordered the redevelopment of the old Mini but the premature launch of the redesigned vehicle, cramped at the back, persuaded the experienced technicians at Innocenti that Robinson's mission to turn their company into a respectable manufacturer was floundering. At sales conferences, the dealers departed convinced that Robinson did not understand marketing. Robinson appeared oblivious of that criticism and of the impression he was creating. In his social life, he was emerging as a man whose character had sharply changed since leaving London.

'Put it on your expenses,' Robinson regularly slurred to Paolo Caccamo at the end of a raucous dinner with the Englishman's latest girlfriend. Helping Robinson home, Caccamo wondered about his employer's accountancy habits and particularly about his womanising. At every business meeting and social event, Robinson's eyes were fixed on women, regardless of age or status, a surprise in Catholic Italy to those who knew he was married. Old, young, married and single women were propositioned by Innocenti's chief. 'Women are his hobby,' Caccamo and Jotti agreed, hearing about the many telephone calls from various conquests, including beautiful actresses and models, to his office and the problems caused by his pursuit, especially, of married women whom he met at parties and dinners. Many, including Annabella Incontrera, one beauty he vowed not to abandon, were introduced as 'Signora Robinson'. Incontrera was irritated. 'I was a well-known actress,' she protested, 'so I was already known by my real name.'

Robinson's activities, especially his weekend excursions, irritated Marie Elena, his wife, who was living alternately in Malta and at a school for opera singers in Asolo, north of Venice. Regularly, late at night, Marie Elena telephoned around Milan, searching for her husband.

'Is Geoffrey with you?' she asked Caccamo.

'Yes,' he replied, smiling at his employer sitting with his latest prize.

'Can I speak with him?'

'He's busy now.'

'Tell him, I'm coming to Milan.'

Flying from Malta, the strange woman seemed burdened by jealousy, anger and by the conviction of her beauty. Despite their dinner-time arguments, which suggested they had little in common, Robinson professed his loyalty and travelled to local theatres in Palma and other small towns to hear his wife sing in her good but weak voice. His diffidence suggested a man of wavering sincerity, indulging in games with people, as confused about his relationships as about his politics.

By early 1973, the result of Robinson's management was undisguised. Innocenti's high costs had not been reduced and the communist trade unions had strengthened their grip over the company's fate. Robinson's enthusiasm for expansion had produced thousands of unwanted Minis. They had been either sold to Leyland in Belgium for £850 each, a considerable loss, or 'sold' to a shadow company and parked in a field near the factory. Innocenti's internal accounts did not reflect those losses. In less than two years, Robinson had steered Innocenti further towards bankruptcy and industrial anarchy but his dubious achievement had been disguised from Leyland's headquarters in Britain. Chaotic internal accounts within the whole corporation made the discovery of any financial truths practically impossible. No one even knew the actual cost of producing the successful Mini in Britain, which, it later transpired, was being sold at a loss. In those circumstances, Lord Stokes had been easily persuaded by the smooth-talking manager that Innocenti had become profitable with a record return on capital. The moment was opportune, Robinson decided, to depart. His parting legacy was his appointment of Bruno Bella, director of purchasing, as his successor.

'Geoffrey, please,' begged Caccamo. 'Bella is no good. You've been fooled because he always arrives in your office with big files. He's a useless showman.'

'Don't worry, Paolo,' smiled Robinson, pleased to have made a decision. 'You'll see.' He bade *arrivederci* to his colleagues and returned with an enhanced reputation to London. By the time the truth and the terrible consequences of Robinson's management had emerged, he had attracted the epithet, the 'ultimate butterfly'.

Stokes had rewarded Robinson's Italian success by his appointment as the chief executive of Jaguar, a seemingly enviable position but recognised among real car men as a poisoned chalice.

In early 1973, the world demand for Jaguars, a symbol of glamour, was insatiable. In America and Europe, the inability of Jaguar's managers to produce sufficient cars had spawned a black market: new Jaguars were resold by customers for more than the showroom price.

The halcyon image belied the reality of Robinson's new kingdom at Brown's Lane in Coventry. Turbulent industrial relations and constant strikes were the principal reasons for the shortage but the unpublicised vices were shoddy production and faulty components. 'Jaguar's quality is no good,' John Barber, managing director of Leyland, told Robinson. 'Improve it.' Robinson was blessed with one advantage. Within Leyland, renamed BL, Jaguar was a protected, niche operation immune from the perpetual crisis infecting the principal company after the IRC's interference. Constant reorganisation of BL, to overcome the staggering obstacles of producing one million cars every year amid industrial turmoil and shortage of finance, promised Robinson some freedom from supervision.

The challenge was enormous. Brown's Lane was a sweatshop of old buildings for low-paid, occasionally hard-working people slowly shedding the benign philosophy of William Lyons, the former owner: 'If a bucket has a hole, I'll repair it. I won't buy a new one.' Old-fashioned machines and production methods had not been discarded. Improvisation was the gospel. The Jaguar's metal panels were stitched together rather than pre-assembled on big frames; the electrical parts supplied by Smith's and Lucas were faulty; the chassis, manufactured in Castle Bromwich, had rusted by the time the bare metal was delivered on open trucks to Brown's Lane; and customers regularly found their new car's paintwork on their fingertips.

In the arcane world Robinson inherited, Jaguars were built and sprayed with one coat of paint before a fifteen-mile road test around Coventry. On its return, the completed car was given a final coat of paint by hand in one of four colours, Cotswold Yellow, Regency Red, Royal Blue or white. Metallic paint was not an option. That bizarre, expensive procedure compared badly with Mercedes and Porsche, which offered twenty colours applied by modern sprays, and whose customers did not risk the headliners – the fabric sheets fitted internally underneath the roof – dropping on to their heads while driving. To assuage its customers' anger, Jaguar was paying after delivery huge compensation to make each car fit for the road. For the man who had supposedly transformed Innocenti, success was a realisable challenge.

Robinson's appointment was generally applauded. Self-assured and reminding his subordinates of his IRC pedigree, Robinson presented himself as the redeemer, convinced that his 'brilliant mind and quick thinking' perceived the heart of the problem before others did. Those who answered slowly would be discomfited by the impatience of an aspiring superman working aggressively without respite.

Robinson, the benign agreed, did not possess an original mind but he was not a fool. Even the sceptical spoke of an intuitive leader prepared to learn from the professionals. All identified a man in a hurry to make his mark and unlikely to stay for long. Instead of renting or buying a home in Coventry, Robinson occupied a double room at the Post House Hotel, commuting most weekends to Milan ostensibly to monitor Innocenti's development and employing Paola Amorosa, his secretary at Innocenti, as his secretary in Coventry, although her English was poor. None, including Robinson, pondered the incongruity of a socialist producing a luxury item for the rich despite the increasing price of petrol. The new chief executive was untroubled by the incompatibility of his political and commercial ambitions, a familiar trait among Labour's wealthier supporters. During the resumption of his relations with Labour's leaders, he was intent on establishing himself as the party's industrial star. In the ideological split between Harold Wilson and left-winger Tony Benn, no disagreement was more bitter than that over industrial policy. Benn argued for wholehearted government intervention in the ownership and management of Britain's key industries involving a revived IRC called the National Enterprise Board. He favoured renationalisation of most industries in a state-organised partnership between the trade unions and the Labour Party, replacing industry's managers with workers' co-operatives. Robinson was attracted by some of those ideas and, in terms familiar to communist governments in Eastern Europe, sought personal stardom by announcing his bid for 'record production' at Jaguar.

Robinson's plan was to build sufficient cars to satisfy market demand. Production would rise, he announced, from the historic maximum of 23,000 cars every year to 60,000 and then more. To establish his decisiveness and the benefit of his Italian experience, he commissioned an immediate facelift to produce the XJS Series 3, a good-looking success. A more substantial improvement was his replacement of Jaguar's twenty-five-year-old paint-shop.

The customers' complaints about Jaguar's soft paint finish, which dulled quickly in bad weather, were costing astronomical sums in warranties to repaint cars. BL's traditional managers would have awaited formal approval by the board for the new expenditure, but Robinson was unconventional. Nothing would deflect him. He chose to assume that John Barber's expression of 'interest', following an 'obscure' mention at a board meeting, implied formal approval. Barber subsequently complained that Robinson was 'an impatient man who ignored rules'. Robinson countered to friends that he had 'got the wink' from Stokes without bothering with the board. 'I got the board's approval,' he insisted. The tender for Project 2641, a new paint-shop, was sent out in early 1973. Although every major British producer, including Ford and Rover, was supplied by British manufacturers, Robinson chose Interlack of Milan, a small company managed by his friend Georgio Cattani. Under their contract, the new paint-shop would be operating in July 1976. Robinson assigned Robert Lindsay, director of manufacturing with responsibility for placing major contracts, as his liaison with Cattani.

Two weeks after Robinson's arrival, an unofficial strike for more pay stopped production. Strikes bedevilled Coventry like all of the British motor industry. In Bill Lyons's era, strikes had been bitter confrontations, with managers refusing to negotiate until the strikers returned to work. Robinson disdained confrontation. As an overt socialist, he sought to implement the credo of Labour's latest proposals for partnership in industrial relations. Regularly, he walked along the production track at Brown's Lane, joking with the assembly workers, and he occasionally ate in the works canteen. He was not embarrassed to knock on his employees' front doors while campaigning for Labour in elections. 'One of my skills,' he enjoyed saying, 'is that I am not bad at leading people.'

At monthly dinners in his rooms at the Post House, Robinson succeeded, during memorable parties, in developing better personal relations with the union leaders. His guests of honour were Bill Lapworth, a district official of the Transport and General Workers' Union, and the most aggressive shop stewards. Drinking copiously, Jaguar's chief executive mouthed 'progressive' ideas about the rights of workers. To achieve 'constant production' – a euphemism for ending strikes – before tackling overmanning and the union's restrictive practices, he enthused about creating a collaborative, happy workforce by promising to maintain full employment. 'I'll meet them more than halfway' was the wisdom of a manager eager to be acknowledged as humane and understanding. 'It worked in Italy and I am confident it will work at Jaguar,' he explained. The symbol of the new philosophy was the construction of new lavatories for the workers, starting with the foremen's, and Robinson's promise to pay high prices to secure the trade unions' agreement to change. His charm, he believed, would win converts. The unions were certainly encouraged by his enthusiasm and hospitality, and he later boasted that there were no further strikes during his management. There was, however, a price.

Geoffrey Whalen, the company's personnel director, arrived in Robinson's rooms at the Post House to find the chief executive, to everyone's embarrassment, barely able to stand. Their host was being cheered. Later it was said that the shop stewards had been 'permanently lent' Jaguar cars. Robinson had discovered a novel mode of winning converts and friends: gargantuan hospitality. Generosity, he believed, was an emulsifier, although he seemed oblivious of one side effect. His own excess drinking had become noticeable to visitors, one of whom mentioned that the executive, during a tour of the factory, was 'well lubricated but safe on his feet'. His charity towards the union officials and his personal behaviour attracted some criticism from other executives. 'You're mad,' he was told by the old guard. 'You're caving in.' 'It's the only way,' he replied, oblivious of the consequences of buying support but certain that his courtship of the trade unions and Labour politicians would satisfy more than one goal.

Robinson's approach thrilled Labour's leaders. Regularly, he travelled to London to speak to James Callaghan, Michael Foot, Harold Wilson and, especially, Tony Benn, the putative secretary of state for industry. Pleasing Labour meant much to a man embarking on a crusade. In turn, Tony Benn praised the 'go-ahead' Jaguar executive and lamented Robinson's frustrations about expansion. 'Geoffrey is an active, energetic, sympathetic man, which is more than you can say for most of the directors in the British car industry. If only others would follow his lead,' recorded Benn in his diary after succumbing to the engaging self-salesmanship directed by Robinson at all Labour's competing ideologues.

Benn's praise coincided with problems at Jaguar caused by his hero's limitations. Jaguar's reliability was crippled by the supply of faulty electric components, but the technical detail confused Robinson. Negotiating improvements required exhaustive discussions. Robinson preferred to delegate that chore to others, matching his self-promotion as an energiser of subordinates. Those he had selected, however, were proving incompetent. Robinson appreciated engineers but did not understand their science. While relying on design engineers, his relationship with those engineers responsible for the detailed intricacies required for quality was markedly casual. 'He's too parochial,' complained John Barber, originally a supporter of Robinson but who gradually recognised that his technical ignorance and impatience with detail were flaws. The only project Robinson appeared to supervise personally was the purchase of the new paint plant in Italy. None of his senior managers was formally consulted about the £8,650,000 contract by then awarded to Georgio Cattani. Nor were they consulted during the further negotiations for additional work as the price rose to £9,877,000. Within weeks, Cattani invoked an escalator clause in the agreement and the price rose to £10,994,000.

Robinson appeared undisturbed. His single goal, resembling that of his period at Innocenti, was higher production. Like a Stalinist, the standard-bearer of Harold Wilson's latest blueprint for Britain's Soviet-style industrial Gosplan was intent on fulfilling a production forecast. As the numbers of Jaguars produced rose from 23,000 towards 39,000, the price of oil soared in the wake of the 1973 Yom Kippur war and the sales of Jaguars in America, like those of all luxury cars, collapsed. The crisis required a solution. 'Cut production immediately,' urged Bob Berry, Jaguar's sales and marketing director. 'No,' snapped Robinson. 'Sell the cars in Britain.' Berry was puzzled. The market for Jaguars in Britain had also evaporated. There was deadlock.

At 9.30 one Sunday morning in mid-1974, Berry arrived at Robinson's bedroom at the Post House Hotel. Robinson was clearing up the debris of the previous night's party. Berry's reports were grim. Henley's, Jaguar's major distributor in Britain, was on the verge of bankruptcy and even Stokes had said, 'This can't go on.'

Berry was emphatic: 'British dealers can't take all these cars. They can't even take one tenth of output. Britain has the same problems as America.' Robinson was impassive. Berry continued: 'If you build them, we can't sell them.'

'I will build them and you will sell them,' declared Robinson. 'By the end of 1975, I want to be selling 60,000 cars a year.' As he spoke, the Labour government was on the verge of issuing coupons to ration petrol for motorists.

Their meeting broke up at 6 p.m. Overnight, Berry resolved to resign. At 7 a.m. on Monday, he arrived in the office to await Robinson. A magnum of champagne stood on his desk. 'I appreciate you more than you'll ever know,' read the attached note; tears welled in Berry's eyes. The telephone unexpectedly rang. 'Come to my office at ten o'clock,' said Robinson. The chief executive had no intention of retreating. He refused to change his mind. Extravagance, he believed, induced sympathy towards himself.

'What are we going to do with the cars?' asked Berry at ten o'clock.

'That's your problem,' smiled Robinson.

'I'll have to store them,' suggested Berry.

Robinson shrugged.

The position was surreal. Robinson would never query the cost or the condition of the cars stored in the rented hangar in Wellesbourne, near Warwick. So long as they were removed from his sight, he could focus on producing cars regardless of whether they could be sold. Even Belgium was, for the moment, not a profitable market, although that small country had become an important influence in his life.

The invitation to meet Jaguar's Belgian representative in 1973 had plainly not excited Robinson. The suggestion by Bob Berry, 'Let's give her dinner at the Warwick Castle' (a hotel in Leamington Spa), had not encouraged Robinson to curtail his game of squash and arrive punctually. For Jaguar's old guard however, Joska Bourgeois was a living legend steeped in adventure, mystery and sensuality.

The Belgian's struggle to secure an introduction to Bill Lyons in 1947 had proven her mettle. In the months after the Second World War, to obstruct European refugees entering Britain, travel across the Channel for non-military personnel was practically impossible. Joska Bourgeois had set her mind on becoming the Belgian representative of Jaguar, a car which she adored and which could be effortlessly sold for huge prices to Belgium's wartime profiteers.

Money was not a problem for Bourgeois. Her father, a diplomat, had earned a fortune before the First World War by importing precious stones, carpets and furniture from Iran. Every year, from Bourgeois's birth until her twenty-sixth birthday in 1939, her father had given her and her sister additional gold so that they possessed their exact weight in the precious metal. On his death, his own fortune was divided between the sisters. That wealth was concealed during the four years of German occupation.

Joska Bourgeois did not suffer during the war. Contrary to the daring tale she spun about fighting for the resistance while operating from a bar frequented by Germans – and once escaping capture by driving her Jaguar through a hail of bullets – she occasionally drove an ambulance and was decorated for bravery in 1945 because she was once arrested by the enemy. Her British admirers later surmised that her wartime years were eased by discreet affairs with German officers.

One reason for that speculation was her ruse to cross the Channel in 1947. Picking up a handsome Canadian officer, she promised to sleep with him, 'but only in England'. The officer arranged a flight to Bovingdon in Hertfordshire. On landing, Joska Bourgeois stipulated that bed would have to wait until he arranged transport to Coventry. On arriving in the town in the evening, the hapless officer was told to wait while Bourgeois sought the home of Bill Lyons. Even the confident Lyons was surprised by the sight of an attractive, tall blonde with huge hands, long legs and big feet on his doorstep in the twilight.

'I want the dealership in Belgium,' she announced resolutely. 'I love the new XK 120.'

Although naturally impressed, Lyons proffered an immediate condition. 'You'll need a lot of money. You have to pay for the cars in cash, in advance.'

'No problem,' replied the woman.

'You'll also need a British partner,' he stipulated.

'No problem,' she again replied. 'The Canadian's my partner. He's British.' (Citizens of the old British Empire – the Dominions – were automatically British subjects.)

The five-year agreement, hurriedly patched together by a local solicitor, between Jaguar and the new Anglo-Belgian Motor Company was signed at Bovingdon airfield on Lyons's behalf by John Morgan. Before she returned to Belgium, Bourgeois guaranteed the dealership by initiating a brief affair with Lyons and fixed her reputation in Britain as a sexual predator. Six months later a new contract was drafted. 'Cut out the Anglo,' Bourgeois told John Morgan. 'I'm the only director now.' The Canadian had been obliterated.

Over the following twenty years, Joska Bourgeois sold between four hundred and five hundred Jaguars every year. Like dealers throughout the world, she screamed frustration about insufficient supplies in a market desperate to buy the cars and limiting her income. In 1968, Frank 'Lofty' England, a lifelong Jaguar man and the chief executive, hosted a twenty-first-anniversary party for his seductress. Lofty mischievously asked the fifty-five-year-old married woman, 'Why do you always chase young boys?' The predator replied, 'Old men chase young girls, so why shouldn't old women chase young men?'

Three years later, in 1971, Lofty returned to Brussels. There were substantiated doubts about Bourgeois's honesty. A spot-check on her warranty claims proved that many were false.

'This is a very serious business,' said Lofty. 'We could get rid of you for this.'

'Let's go out for lunch,' implored Bourgeois.

'No, let's see all the documents first,' insisted Lofty.

The fraud was exposed. 'You're right,' said Joska Bourgeois. 'My staff are outrageous. Let's go out for dinner.'

That night's sex removed the threat of losing her franchise. Sex, Joska Bourgeois believed, always delivered her requirements. On her visit to Coventry in 1973, she was embroiled in another financial imbroglio and a threat to terminate her franchise for dishonesty. Robinson, the new chief executive, she hoped, might accept her solution.

The lobby of the Warwick Castle was not an ideal location to wait with Bob Berry. Robinson arrived late, wearing a sweatshirt,

shorts and plimsolls. A few minutes after the three entered the
restaurant Robinson announced, 'I've just to go somewhere.'
Fifteen minutes later, he had not reappeared. 'Better go and look
for him,' suggested Bourgeois. 'Look in the toilet. Perhaps he's
drunk.' Berry returned puzzled. Robinson, according to the
receptionist, had walked out of the dining room, out of the hotel
and stepped into his waiting car. 'Get me a toothbrush,' ordered
Joska Bourgeois. 'I'll stay here for the night.'

The next morning, Berry entered Robinson's office. 'What
happened to you?' Robinson smiled and offered no explanation.
Some speculated that, after looking at the middle-aged woman,
Robinson decided he preferred to spend the evening with a
younger consort from Jaguar's pool of typists. Joska Bourgeois was
undeterred. Her business was in jeopardy. BL was terminating all
contracts with foreign distributors of Jaguar without compensation, and although Lofty England, as an act of friendship for past
favours, had promised an eighteen-month extension, her position
was precarious. Naturally, she had tried to exploit the chaos and
the misdemeanours committed by the British company. To evade
import duties, Leyland was dispatching assembly packs to
Belgium with two invoices, while some Jaguars had been
mysteriously delivered without the relevant documents.
Bourgeois had asserted that the cars had never been delivered and
demanded compensation. There was no alternative but to settle
her claim, albeit not in full. Bourgeois wanted more. She wanted
to retain the Jaguar franchise and hoped to secure help from Lofty
England's successor, Geoffrey Robinson.

Among the executives in Britain's beleaguered motor industry,
Joska Bourgeois found Robinson unusual. Not only were his
intellect and manner superior to any other car man's, but his
ambitions were unusually overt. His lust for money and fame was
breathtaking. His enthusiasm for life and personal warmth were
magnetic. Time spent with Robinson was fun. The sixty-year-old
woman was not crass. She might be too old to compete with all his
beautiful girlfriends in Milan, Coventry and London, where he
was often seen at the parties of Mary Hope, a young widow, but

she was quite prepared to offer her money in return for his assistance and companionship. In the circumstances, anything more than an occasional liaison would be inappropriate.

Joska Bourgeois, on the verge of divorce and childless, was in the midst of a fourteen-year affair with Spiro, a good-looking Greek who obeyed the regular summons to her bed and the occasional demand that he accompany her around the world, especially to the Far East. Together, they bought expensive artefacts for shipment to Belgium. But recently those trips were being ruined by Spiro's habit of disappearing with younger women and regularly abusing his Paymaster.

Joska Bourgeois did not resent her role as Paymaster to secure those she desired and she sensed that Robinson enjoyed her hospitality. Before returning to Brussels, Robinson had agreed to seek an extension of her franchise although by then Jaguar was but a small percentage of her income. Her principal business was a dealership for Toyota, a franchise which she had astutely secured long before the car's popularity. Sales permanently soared. To retain that lucrative contract, Robinson soon afterwards flew to Japan to negotiate on Bourgeois's behalf an enhanced arrangement. By any standard, theirs had quickly become an unusual relationship.

The following year, 1974, Robinson was seen at the Geneva and Turin motor shows with his wife and Joska Bourgeois alternately. Paolo Caccamo, his Italian friend, was in no doubt that Robinson was enjoying a sexual relationship with Bourgeois. Wearing tight trousers and tight pullovers and behaving like a twenty-year-old bimbette, she occasionally aroused the Englishman's irritation. 'Joska, please don't dress like that,' Robinson urged in front of his friends, but the Paymaster ignored the entreaty. In their relationship, even when ordering food in a restaurant, he was obliged to defer. Although Robinson had been unable to arrange a permanent extension of her franchise, John Morgan was not surprised to discover that there were no legal grounds to compel Bourgeois to return £1 million to Jaguar for her unsubstantiated claims on warranties. The evidence, Morgan was told by the accountants, was insufficient. That was the last favour Jaguar could bestow on its Belgian representative.

At the very moment in September 1974 when Jaguar's sales were stagnating and BL's board was battling to prevent a financial meltdown, Robinson confessed another problem to the directors. The interim cost of the paint-shop had risen to £13.7 million, a 58 per cent increase in nine months. Donald Stokes was embarrassed. His protégé had privately admitted that, without approval, he had committed a further £3 million to the plant, whose total cost had escalated to £15,644,000 – almost double the original estimate – but terminating the contract would cost a further £5.5 million. Amid the sensitivity of negotiations with the banks and government to determine BL's entire future, Stokes agreed that the latest bills could be paid on the understanding that no further money was available and the project was to remain frozen until BL's fate was resolved. In anger, Robinson asked Stokes to release £1 million to secure delivery. Stokes refused. Robinson ignored the refusal and secretly committed Jaguar to paying a further £2,056,000 to Georgio Cattani.

Robinson felt inviolate. Senior ministers in the new Labour government were encouraging his maverick behaviour. Inspired by those politicians and his own self-promotion, newspapers were describing Robinson as 'the fastest rising star in British Leyland's firmament'. Tony Benn, in particular, was leaning on Robinson for advice and assistance, planning for the new socialist economy run from Whitehall in co-operation with the trade unions. In particular, Benn wanted government funds for a new industrial legion 'sweeping the country . . . the most exciting thing since the war'. Those were workers' co-ops in defunct industries producing unwanted products from obsolete designs. Benn was especially excited by the prospect of a co-op at the Triumph motorbike factory in Meriden, manufacturing bikes designed twenty years earlier in a dilapidated factory. Meriden became a Mecca for Labour's left wing, including Robinson.

The British motorbike industry had once supplied 70 per cent of the world's demand, but strikes and restrictive practices among

the workers, old factories and redundant designs had propelled
Triumph towards bankruptcy and extinction. The managers'
solution was to amalgamate various factories, invest in modern
machinery and remove unhelpful workers. Their announcement of
1700 redundancies at Meriden had provoked a workers' block-
ade, crippling the production of bikes in other subsidiaries. No
solution had been found to save jobs by the Conservative government before the Labour election victory in February 1974. Once
appointed secretary of state for industry, Tony Benn gratefully
accepted Robinson's offer to negotiate an agreement between the
owners and Triumph's workers, and eventually to establish a
workers' co-operative.

Many in Jaguar and Leyland were surprised that their chief
executive, with so many problems in Brown's Lane, appeared to
spend more time serving his political interests than managing
Jaguar. That displayed a misunderstanding. Robinson envisaged a
political advantage in presenting himself as a socialist committed
to industrial regeneration. Reconciling the contrast between the
champion of the workers and the high-living Jaguar executive
might have presented difficulties for many, but Robinson either
inhabited a world of make-believe or was a sharp hypocrite.

By April 1975, his efforts at Meriden had failed to negotiate a
solution which either offered sufficient compensation to the
factory's owners from government funds or produced a workers'
proposal which would justify a government grant. That deadlock
coincided with the accumulation in the Brown's Lane car park of
tons of steel girders and panels. Curious workers spoke with
astonishment about a paint-shop shipped from Italy, contrary to
the board's instructions, without any groundwork done for its
construction.

Robinson's paint-shop had become a scandal. Robert Lindsay,
the director of manufacturing responsible for negotiating the
contract in Italy, had fallen under suspicion of accepting bribes. In
entirely separate contracts worth £600,000, three cheques for
£2,400 had been passed to him by Centri-Spray, a manufacturer of
specialised assembly equipment for car production, in return for

Jaguar's order. In Lindsay's expression, he accepted the money 'for advice given'. As the car park filled with steel, Jaguar's managers and the directors of BL began suspecting that Lindsay had obtained bribes from Interlack, Cattani's company, for the unauthorised paint-shop.

Eric Gregory, a former assistant chief constable of Thames Valley Police employed as Leyland's security manager, was ordered to investigate not only the paint-shop's history but all Geoffrey Robinson's activities. An audit of Innocenti had revealed the deposit of his salary in the Swiss bank and the purchase of twelve pairs of women's gloves, charged to Innocenti. In Britain, it was assumed the gloves were for his wife. In Italy, the gloves' owners were presumed to be his Italian girlfriends. But those were trifles compared to his enduring legacy in Milan.

Months after Robinson's departure, Bruno Bella, his chosen successor, was dismissed amidst allegations of incompetence. The second of Robinson's legacies, his generosity to the trade unions, throttled Bella's successors. Explosives demolished Innocenti's showrooms and the lives of Italian and British directors were threatened by the militant trade unions who had enjoyed Robinson's nurturing. Amid growing anarchy, his successors required armed guards for protection until they abandoned the factory. 'We bought Innocenti really for nothing,' Robinson boasted in 1976, referring to the original £4 million. The cost to Leyland for leaving in redundancy payments, taxation and accumulated losses was £100 million. That, though, was not why Robinson's voice was unusually strained when he told Paolo Caccamo on the telephone, 'I've got problems. I don't know if we'll meet again.'

Eric Gregory had been told that the completed paint-shop would cost £24 million, compared to the original estimate of £8.6 million, an unjustifiable contract for a small Italian company lacking experience in Britain. Suspicious that only one company appeared on the original tender list, Gregory began investigating rumours of bribes paid by the Italian company to someone other than Robinson. His target was Robert Lindsay, director of manufacturing with responsibility for placing major contracts, and Robinson's subordinate. Although Lindsay had no experience in paint-plants, he had accepted Robinson's instructions to conclude a contract with Interlack. Gregory assigned ten investigators to follow Lindsay. Within a short time, his team discovered how the director had been 'set up by the Italians with a flat filled with food and drink, lots of floozies, a car and a lot of money'. Lindsay, the investigators suspected, had enjoyed a holiday in Italy paid by Cattani who regularly stayed at the Post House near Coventry with Lindsay and Robinson. At the end of his investigation, Gregory had telephoned Lindsay at his home and they met at a lay-by on the main road near Banbury. Gregory's allegation was conclusive: 'You've been paid by Interlack to vote for them.' By the end of an hour, Lindsay had confessed to accepting excessive hospitality from Cattani. After reporting his conclusions, Gregory was ordered not to approach Robinson, but inserted into the security officer's final report, presented to the board by Arthur Large, the company secretary, were further allegations about Robinson's secret bank deposits in Switzerland during his employment at Innocenti and his excessive entertain-ment expenses. The accusation against him was corporate indiscipline.

Robinson refused to be cowed. 'We need the damn thing [the paint-shop],' he told the board of directors. At a critical moment in his career and the fate of the motor company, he found no sympathisers. The paint-shop was the breaking-point but the antagonism was fomented by criticism of his self-interested courting of Labour and the trade unions. There were too many reports of deals concluded with Bill Lapworth, the trade unionist, too often inspired by alcohol, which had benefited Robinson's reputation but not Jaguar's. There was prevalent criticism round the boardroom table of insincerity; of a man appearing to offer friendship but disappearing after achieving his needs.

At the Labour government's request, Lord Ryder, the former manager of a paper and publishing company, had submitted a plan for the reorganisation of BL. In that era, it was normal for the inexpert to decide the fate of an industry, contrary to the advice of experienced insiders. Ryder recommended the amalgamation of all BL's car companies, destructively including Jaguar, within one division under one director. Among his peers, Robinson was tipped as the favourite candidate to run BL's car division, the senior appointment, with 180,000 employees. His rival was Derek Whittaker, his uncharismatic and limited subordinate. Robinson was desperate for the post but Whittaker succeeded. The decision against Robinson was influenced by distrust. Robinson was doubly upset. His trajectory was halted and he would be subordinate to his former deputy. He was not compelled even to consider that distasteful humiliation. In early May 1975, the board requested his resignation after considering Gregory's report on the paint-shop fiasco. At the board meeting, Ronald Lucas, the company secretary, recorded the board's acceptance of Robinson's resignation following his 'censure', but Lucas understood the directors had agreed on his 'dismissal'. Many said that his personality, good looks and relationship with Labour ministers forestalled those minded to issue a public rebuke. Instead, he was compensated with £50,000 and silence.

News of his departure provoked astonishment. Summoned to the canteen by the shop stewards, Robinson entered to rousing cheers by workers who approved the stewards' eulogies of his management style.

To smudge the reasons for his departure on 11 May 1975, Robinson told inquirers, 'I was offered a job under Derek Whittaker and I declined.' He added, 'I fought hard against Ryder and now that I have lost, I prefer to leave.' The accusations of incompetence and mismanagement were concealed. Those directors who remained – his critics, who condemned him as a charlatan looking for the main chance – were irritated by his adroit public performance. One newspaper credited Robinson with 'successfully turning Innocenti into one of BL's few profitable overseas subsidiaries'; another reported how he 'quit' because of unhappiness with BL's business strategy; and Robinson described his departure as part of 'the great Leyland tragedy'. In his analysis,

Robinson blamed the 'chaos' and 'disaster' on everyone but himself. There was 'trench warfare', he accurately complained, between the management and workers about overmanning, strikes, differentials and restrictive practices which destroyed productivity. He squarely fixed the blame on the managers. There had been, he said, an 'indulgence [and] failure to deal . . . ruthlessly . . . with the battle-weary line management of British Leyland'. He was silent about the tons of steel which were to rust in the Brown's Lane car park for several years before disposal as scrap metal, and the unsold Jaguars stored in a hangar. Both piles were testament to his own failure to provide solutions.

Few who remained at Jaguar spoke unqualifiedly favourably about Robinson. Many were irritated by his boast 'My ambition is to be Labour's first millionaire prime minister.' Without a corporate expense account, they thought, his life would be dreary and austere. 'Like the Cheshire cat,' grumbled a contemporary who had watched his entry to and exit from Innocenti and the repeat performance at Jaguar. 'Only the smile remains after he invisibly slides out.'

Robinson left Jaguar unsure of his future but grateful to be hired as Joska Bourgeois's consultant and adviser. Over the following months, he spent time with her in Brussels, lectured at a management college and continued to advise the workers at Meriden while pondering his future. In December 1975, his limited prospects were transformed. Like generals in battle, putative tycoons rely upon luck, and Robinson's good fortune was the death of Maurice Edelman, Labour MP for Coventry North West. Edelman's majority in 1974 had been 7488. Many aspiring candidates sought that safe seat in a constituency where 60 per cent of the workforce was employed in manufacturing, but none enjoyed the popularity that Robinson, a committed anti-European, had cultivated among local activists. The recompense for his hospitality to trade unionists at the Post House Hotel, the unsubstantiated rumours of loaned Jaguars for the shop stewards, and his efforts for the workers' co-operative at Meriden, placed Robinson as the runaway favourite to be declared Labour's candidate on 5 February. Unlike others, not only was he popular with Labour voters but his middle-class background might also attract some Conservatives.

Victory for Labour at the by-election was crucial not only for the candidate. Harold Wilson's overall majority in the Commons was a single seat and was jeopardised by the government's huge unpopularity caused by a deep recession, suicidal wage demands and inflation racing towards 30 per cent. Nevertheless, Robinson was confident of his future. Since the government's fate depended upon his victory, party workers were recruited from the whole country for the campaign and, to maintain their good humour, lodged at his expense in hotels rather than the usual boarding-houses.

Election campaigns often expose candidates' unseen character-istics, but Robinson proved inscrutable to normal judgement. He was popular in the constituency although noticeably unpassionate about politics. His simultaneous support for Denis Healey's destructive economic policies and his sympathy for business co-existed oddly with his vocal commitment to the state ownership of Britain's major industries and high taxation. Whichever side he supported, his pedigree classed him as an outsider in the Labour Party, especially among the local far-left activists. Peter Snape, a newly elected MP appointed as his escort, complained that the candidate was an enigma. While affable and effective on the door-step, he was noticeably lazy, always looking for an opportunity for a drink or an excuse for 'a meeting' at the nearest restaurant, although only the best restaurants were acceptable. Robinson appeared untroubled by any categorisation.

In a turgid contest against Jonathan Guinness, an unsuitable Tory candidate supported by all his party's leaders, Robinson wooed the working-class women on council estates in the morn-ing as a well-dressed enchanter, and arrived every lunchtime in his brother's mustard Jaguar XJ6 to address workers outside factories. The introduction was glowing. Robinson was hailed as an exceptional candidate, a whizz-kid certain of appointment to the cabinet within one year. 'This is no backbench utility model,'

blared his propagandists, suppressing an embarrassing condemnation of Robinson by the Italian Socialist Party for 'creating
cloud-cuckoo-land' at Innocenti. Labour's efforts also concealed
another of their candidate's explicable sensitivities, his marriage.

Sympathetic journalists had been asked by the party to subject
Robinson to a mock press conference. The candidate, it was felt,
required tuition in how to repel embarrassment. Robinson arrived
unaware of the fake conditions for what Simon Hoggart, the
journalist, called 'a grilling far worse than anything he was likely
to have to suffer during the real campaign'. The first question
bewildered the candidate: 'As a boss, did you not make life
miserable for so many decent, hard-working people?' The second
was equally troubling, despite the gross exaggeration: 'Why
should an immensely rich man also seek to be powerful?' But it
was the third question that drove Robinson to storm out: 'Have
you left your wife?' For Robinson, it was too close to the truth.
That emerged on 12 March 1976, the morning after he won the
election with a majority of 3694.

Marie Elena, the new MP's wife, had not been seen in Coventry
throughout the campaign or even on election night. Party workers
had realised that she 'hated' politics and that the marriage was
precarious. A few days before the election, Marie Elena had
admitted, with dangerous honesty, 'Things are not perfect in our
marriage. I would not say it is in difficulties, but the situation is
not perfect, either,' and had confirmed her uncertainty about
Robinson's return to his home, except 'when he's sure that everyone else is happy'. At Labour Party headquarters, her disparage-
ment caused concern. Two days after the election, Kathy Ham, a
press officer, was dispatched to Surrey to await Robinson's arrival
and arrange a 'happy family' photo call. 'I'm not ready,' shouted
Marie Elena, slamming the door. 'Wait outside. He's not here yet.'
When the new MP arrived and stepped smiling from the car, Ham
dived through the front door. 'The whole house is a stage set,'
she thought, looking at the crimson-velvet-upholstered furniture,
heavy velvet curtains and rococo sofas. The eventual photograph,
she reflected, matched the setting and was completely phoney.

Shortly after Kathy Ham departed, Mrs Robinson emerged from the house and admitted with excruciating candour, 'My career is music, his is politics. I am just not interested in politics. I don't think I should follow like a little dog.' Asked about their relationship, she answered, 'I can't say yes or no about divorce.'

Such honesty was unusual but it was the inevitable consequence of Robinson's affairs, especially his growing attachment to Joska Bourgeois. For any other novice backbench MP the publicised rages of an irate wife would have been embarrassing, but Robinson was strangely insensitive to criticism or conventional expectations. Flush with self-admiration, he disparaged anyone failing to accept unquestioningly his interpretations of events. That was both a source of strength and a weakness. Pursuing his interests with fevered sanctimony, he would not be swayed by consideration for others or ponder whether their judgement was valid. Rich in contradictions and glorification, the admirer of Shakespeare offered himself as a servant of the people selflessly seeking the common good. Few were convinced except Robinson, who appeared to be utterly persuaded by his own performance. His weakness was the unusual hauteur which Peter Snape observed during the election campaign and described as 'laziness'. The frenetic Robinson would have been baffled by that description, because Snape's observation was incomplete. The 'laziness' was Robinson's proclivity to cut corners, ignore rules and sustain secrecy about some sensitive activities, especially his commercial life.

Robinson had no intention of adopting the lifestyle of a traditional MP earning £5750 per annum. Although he was not wealthy, Robinson had received £50,000 compensation from BL and had earned some fees from Joska Bourgeois. There was no sign that his Italian earnings, deposited tax-free in Switzerland, had been repatriated, although after the devaluation of sterling the value of those foreign savings had been protected. Like his predecessor, who spent much of the year in the South of France writing romantic novels, Robinson chose to be an absentee MP. There would not be a permanent home in the constituency;

instead he would either stay at the Post House or lodge with
Brenda Price, his new assistant, whom he had met at Meriden.
Nor would he encourage the local party to rent permanent
headquarters for political meetings. Instead of rousing the public
to enrol as party members, he would establish alliances with
friendly councillors and trade-union leaders and seek to dis-
enfranchise the critics and the left-wing activists by limiting the
number of meetings.

Blessed with that easy self-assurance, Robinson entered the
Commons convinced of early promotion by Harold Wilson.
During his first days, no one was unaware that the self-confident
victor was uninterested in the customary parliamentary life of a
backbencher and was searching for an immediate place in
Whitehall. 'I have a contribution,' he repeated. 'With my business
knowledge and common sense, I have a lot to offer to the
government.' The brash message jarred with the politics and
atmosphere of perpetual crisis within the party. Although the
government was about to renationalise the aircraft and ship-
building industries, forge a servile Social Contract with the trade
unions and bow to the IMF's humiliating terms to prevent Britain
being declared bankrupt, Robinson was discouraged only by the
creeping paralysis caused by the militant left. His message that
Labour should co-operate with business and not fight against the
market was sincere but, he noticed, incomprehensible to most of
his new colleagues. Adroitly, he modified his arguments and, after
Wilson's resignation, appeared to align himself with Michael
Foot, minister of employment and deputy leader of the party, and
Tony Benn.

For Benn, in particular, the Meriden workers' co-operative was
a nirvana. The occupation of the factory by workers since 1974
had become a high-profile socialist cause, repeatedly attracting
public attention to the strident demands of the anti-capitalist
extreme left. Although the workers were producing only 250
bikes a week based on twenty-two-year-old designs, Meriden
represented for the left the ideal of workers' self-management.
Survival and success depended upon obtaining adequate funds

from the government and the guidance of an experienced industrial manager. Robinson volunteered to perform that role. By then, the workers had received a £4.2 million loan but had no prospect of paying the £1.25 million in interest, or repaying the capital. To obtain more funds, Robinson pledged to 'fight like hell' to obtain investment from the National Enterprise Board, the successor to the ill-fated IRC, supported by Benn for those projects. Meriden was Robinson's opportunity to prove his professional abilities and political integrity, and emerge from the obscurity impeding all new arrivals in Westminster. A junior ministerial post, he believed, would be soon offered.

Robinson's enthusiasm was not matched by his grasp of realities. James Callaghan, Wilson's successor, destined to become Britain's worst post-war prime minister, was battling to save his party from a coup engineered by Tony Benn, who admitted that 'we were a serious left, and we weren't playing games'. For Labour's right wing, Meriden was a curse which hopefully would wither. Adrift from the mainstream of the party, Robinson was thrashing forlornly as Benn's puppet, searching for non-existent supporters. In desperation, he turned to Harold Lever, a multimillionaire Labour MP for Manchester, who had earned a fortune from gold speculation and ranked among Benn's staunchest critics.

Lever, a benign social democrat inhabiting a palatial house in Eaton Square, enjoyed close relations with Harold Wilson, for whom he had brokered in 1975 a financial package to prevent the American motor company Chrysler closing its operations in Britain with 27,000 redundancies. From his elegant salon, Lever could usually secure the attention of most senior Labour ministers on the telephone. In the company of that rare breed of Labour politician, Robinson witnessed the improbable influence wielded by Labour millionaires. But even Lever, faced by Whitehall's antagonism, obtained only £500,000 for Meriden. 'It's pathetic,' complained Robinson, comparing the Italian government 'pouring money into motorbikes' to Labour's abandonment of the industry.

Robinson made no effort to conceal his disillusion or to ingratiate himself. Standing frequently in the House of Commons' bar, he complained alternately about James Callaghan's failure to appoint him a junior minister and about his marriage. Partly to prove his credentials, he chose in December 1978 to become Meriden's chief executive, rising in the Commons only to protest about the catastrophe enveloping BL and Jaguar. Across that patchwork corporation, bewildered managers were watching militant trade unionists impose anarchy in the production areas. Britain's major car company was veering towards collapse. Robinson's judgement was damning.

The new politician criticised the reorganisation of BL, under the 'disastrous' Ryder plan, into an 'unwieldy monolith' impossible to manage. Since his resignation, one-fifth of the British car market had been lost to foreign imports. Repeatedly in the Commons, as the workers' champion, Robinson castigated his successors for wasteful redundancy programmes and bad sales promotion which, he said, caused more damage 'than all the strikes put together'. The paradox was not evident to him. Donald Ryder, chairman of the National Enterprise Board and architect of Leyland's reorganisation, was a member of the very quango, staffed by nonentities and civil servants and invented by the Labour government, whose help Robinson sought at Meriden. The confusion of the industrial executive posing as an expert, forgetting his own failures at Innocenti and Jaguar, irritated those at BL under attack from his new pulpit.

His former colleagues' suspicion of a vendetta was reinforced by his performance at a meeting at Leyland House in Coventry with three other MPs. Their host was Derek Whittaker, Robinson's former deputy, who occupied the post Robinson had desired. Vociferously, Robinson attacked Whittaker for issuing threats against the repeatedly striking trade unions. 'Give employees understanding and certainty,' the workers' champion urged. 'BL has become an industrial battleground.' Despite Robinson's gratuitous insults, Whittaker remained silent. His visitor's agenda, he believed, was opportunistic.

The collapse of the Labour government in May 1979, and the Tories' election victory under Margaret Thatcher in June amid widespread strikes, chaos and soaring inflation triggered an internecine war within the Labour Party. The selection of Michael Foot, a far-left activist, as Labour's new leader, placed Robinson in a political limbo. He appeared to have attached himself to the left and their trade-union sympathisers, advocating in speeches nurturing 'workers' loyalties', avoiding redundancies and never closing loss-making factories, yet his lifestyle – he drove a Jaguar and lived in comfort in London and Surrey – reflected his desire to accumulate wealth. His piety was cast in doubt, especially after his renewed outbursts against the management of BL.

During the dying days of Callaghan's government, Derek Whittaker had been fired and replaced by Michael Edwardes, a South African industrialist with no sympathies for Labour, the unions or the incumbent managers. Edwardes accepted the task of destroying a lame duck and building a new corporation. Old factories would be closed, incompetent managers dismissed and trade-union wreckers emasculated. Robinson was outraged. He accused Edwardes of 'frightening ignorance of industrial management [which is causing] prolonged uncertainty'. Under Edwardes, he continued, BL was collapsing and the Midlands were becoming 'an industrial disaster area'. In more personal attacks, he condemned the South African's 'manifest failure' while praising his own 'track record' at Jaguar. 'The credibility of Sir Michael and his senior staff,' he asserted, 'is at an all time low.' For Edwardes, the unceasing personal attacks from someone in a privileged position and with a moot past reeked of sanctimony and were an abuse too far.

In spring 1980, Edwardes, accompanied by Arthur Large, BL's company secretary, visited Sir Kit McMahon, the deputy governor of the Bank of England. Large handed over Eric Gregory's report on his investigation of Robinson's activities at Innocenti. It revealed the deposit by Robinson in the early 1970s of thousands of pounds in a Swiss bank, contrary to Britain's laws. To Edwardes's disappointment, despite the compelling evidence,

McMahon declined to undertake an investigation. The new
Conservative government, ignoring the Labour Party's protest,
had abandoned exchange controls and it was deemed inappropriate to pursue Robinson under discarded laws.

Unaware of his escape from embarrassment, Robinson fired one
more shot. Edwardes was manoeuvring towards a showdown with
militant trade unionists formenting strikes in several factories. He
threatened to close one particular factory permanently unless the
strikers returned to work. Robinson and Roy Hattersley met him
to protest about the threat and urged 'mediation'. Edwardes
listened to the familiar language demanding capitulation and
charity for the West Midlands while ignoring the reality of world
markets, and bade the two politicians farewell. In his opinion,
Robinson's poor performance at Jaguar was augmented by the
news from Meriden.

Three hundred workers at Meriden had hailed Robinson as the
workers' champion. He had persuaded the Conservative government to cancel £11 million of debts. Public money had been
wasted, yet the unpaid chief executive wanted more. 'It is like the
Battle of Britain,' he urged. 'We have fought to fight again. We
have a long way to go.' Conservative ministers and their officials
in Whitehall were unimpressed. The co-operative had sabotaged
the creation of a modern motorbike industry in the other Norton-
Triumph factories and, under Robinson, Meriden's administration
was in chaos. Without adequate records, the breakdown of
accounting procedures and no stock control, the company's
auditors had reported, 'We have been unable to obtain all the
information and explanations which we considered necessary for
the purposes of our audit.' As a director, Robinson was also liable
for failing to register the company's accounts, and could be
summoned to appear before Cardiff magistrates. Robinson's non-
chalant disregard for his responsibilities sat oddly alongside his
public protest about Rupert Murdoch's surprise purchase of
Times Newspapers. Loftily, Robinson demanded that Murdoch
should be compelled to 'disclose all financial documents' to ease a
'situation of suspicion' and reassure the public about the deal's

'due propriety and fairness'. His demand for openness and honesty
– a clarion call to the left – was to haunt him later. At that
moment, he was tormented by his own party.

To his surprise, in 1981, despite his support for left-wing
causes, Robinson was deemed politically unreliable by the far-left
activists in his constituency. For the teachers and trade unionists
infiltrating the Labour Party across the country, Robinson was a
soft target who could possibly be replaced by their own candidate
at the next election. On 30 July 1981, the members of the
constituency party met at the Hen Lane club to vote whether
Robinson should be deselected. Robinson was vulnerable. Despite
his record in Westminster and Meriden, and his generous
hospitality to many party workers, he had become notorious as an
absentee MP who had ceased holding regular public meetings and
only occasionally drove up from London in his Jaguar to meet
constituents requesting help. Disagreeably, Will Reese, the left's
candidate, had attracted considerable support.

Among the disillusioned were those who disliked Robinson's
manner. A story had circulated that, during the count of votes at
the 1979 general election (Robinson won, with a majority of 3971
votes), he had joined Pam Davies, an attractive twenty-year-old
Conservative candidate in the local elections, who was standing
with some friends. During a light-hearted conversation with these
strangers, Robinson said to Davies, 'Oh, I thought you'd be
having it all the time.' She interpreted his sexual comment and
other remarks as a proposition for 'teaming up'. Davies flushed
and was 'just a bit amazed'. In the ensuing embarrassed silence,
Bill Hardy, a Labour councillor, hustled Robinson away. Later,
Hardy returned. 'I don't know why he has to do that sort of thing,'
he apologised to Davies.

Rumours of similar unpleasantness had caused disaffection, but
Robinson hoped to count on moderate Labour supporters who
disliked the Marxists and were grateful for his benevolence.
Throughout the protracted count, Robinson's survival remained
in doubt. At the last moment, one branch of the electricians'
union, delegated to vote for Reese, switched to Robinson. By a

whisker, Robinson won. His defeated enemies credited his generosity to the moderates as decisive.

Robinson's 'laziness' was to ignore any lessons from that debacle. 'I never look back,' he said proudly. He revealed himself as an undoubting egoist, disdainful of self-analysis or introspection, dismissive of any events beyond his self-aggrandisement. Having survived, he was contemptuous about the original circumstances. Politics, he concluded, was precarious and disappointing. He would return to earning money.

2

THE PATENTS

Robinson was inhabiting contradictory worlds. The contrast between the Labour Party, whose 1983 draft election manifesto was to be dubbed 'the longest suicide note in history' (it advocated penal rates of taxation and massive state control of industry and the economy), and his encounters with Joska Bourgeois would have disoriented many. She offered a world of unusual luxury, paying the Labour MP for advice which contradicted the politics he espoused in Britain.

In 1979, Robinson had helped Joska Bourgeois negotiate with Tom Hughes of Inchcape the sale for £14.6 million of the International Motor Company, her Belgian company with the franchises to sell Toyota and Daihatsu cars and Bridgestone tyres. Soon afterwards, Bourgeois left Belgium for ever in order to evade paying taxes of £6 million. She settled in Geneva, and bought two adjoining penthouse apartments in Cannes for the summer.

Retirement did not suit her, though she was now sixty-six. Daily, the avid reader of the *Wall Street Journal* devoted time to the management of her fortune. Her concern was not only about the movement of shares but also about the price of gold. Following her sister's death, Joska Bourgeois was the owner of their combined weight in gold in 1939. Worryingly, the metal's price was flat and produced no income. For advice, she turned to Robinson, consummating a relationship based upon mutual dependence.

In London, Bourgeois rented a flat in the Grosvenor House Hotel, in Park Lane, and during her visits invited Robinson to eat with her at the Dorchester and the Belfry. During his brief visits to Cannes, he allowed Bourgeois to entertain him at Mougins, the Roger Vergé restaurant where, with her friends Roland and Véronique Urban, he chose bottles of champagne costing 2000 francs. 'The most expensive,' murmured the Urbans, 'but not the best.'

The enjoyment of that lifestyle, his niggling frustration about politics and his new ambition to become an industrial tycoon propelled Robinson to seek a parallel career. Like Harold Lever and Robert Maxwell, who had just begun his commercial resurrection by taking over Britain's biggest printing corporation, Robinson sought to combine the socialist politics imbued in him during his childhood with capitalist enterprise. The contradictions were effortlessly suppressed by self-interest and self-esteem. Still besotted by the importance of state intervention and his experience since the 1960s at the IRC, he was attracted by the commercial exploitation of scientific expertise nurtured in universities. Ignoring his poor record, he invented himself as the originator of 'bringing scientific research into reality'.

The catalyst was Jack Butterworth, vice-chancellor of Warwick University, which was located in Coventry. Robinson had met Butterworth as a fellow director of Mercia Sound, a local radio company. Robinson, Brenda Price and Peter Davis, a solicitor who had evolved as Robinson's confidant, had befriended Butterworth and, as the local MP, Robinson had been automatically appointed a governor of Warwick University. Like Robert Maxwell, who had created his first fortune by publishing scientific articles at Pergamon Press, Robinson asked Butterworth for ideas produced by the university's scientific academics which might be available for his commercial advantage.

Jack Butterworth's introduction of Professor Kumar Bhattacharyya transformed Robinson's life. The politician won the opportunity to earn great wealth using business methods which followed an established pattern.

Kumar Bhattacharyya, the son of an Indian scientist and owner of substantial tea estates, was a former production engineer at Joseph Lucas and a rising star at Warwick University, supervising the application of academic research in mechanical engineering. During 1980, to Bhattacharyya's surprise and pleasure, Robinson called on him at the university, often accompanied by Brenda Price, twice and occasionally three times every week. In his hunt for an idea, the politician was particularly attracted to one development in Bhattacharyya's department, an electro discharge machine, a machine for the precision cutting, shaping and drilling of metals with an enormous market in the aerospace and motor industries. To Robinson, EDM meant Early Day Motion, a parliamentary procedure, but he understood from Butterworth that Bhattacharyya's version of an EDM, already patented with the government's regulator, was more lucrative than the Westminster variety. Robinson's proposition was tempting. The university, he suggested, should allow him to develop the patents commercially. Some of the profits could be returned to the university to fund further research.

In 1980 values, the patents for that particular development of an EDM were worth at least £1 million, Bhattacharyya estimated, and their ownership was indisputable. Although they were registered in the names of Bhattacharyya and their Egyptian inventor, Fawzi el-Menshawy, any financial reward was owned by the state. The research had been funded by grants supplied by Birmingham University and the National Research Development Council (NRDC), and anyone using the EDM's patents would be required to pay a licence fee and royalties to the state. Robinson understood that legality as he sought to persuade Butterworth to co-operate by creating a new joint company to exploit the inventions. The vice-chancellor was enthusiastic and invited el-Menshawy to meet 'my friend Geoffrey' on 15 January 1981 in the House of Commons.

Fawzi el-Menshawy, a lecturer at Warwick University, was a forty-one-year-old engineering scientist who had specialised in thermo-nuclear fusion. He had developed the EDMs in Bhattacharyya's department at Birmingham University and, after registering jointly with Bhattacharyya seven patents, he was discussing with the NRDC his application for funding further research at Warwick. In Bhattacharyya's opinion, three of el-Menshawy's patented inventions were 'the crème de la crème'. Satisfactorily, officials at the NRDC had recognised el-Menshawy's skills and the genius of his inventions, and were considering his application when el-Menshawy and Bhattacharyya arrived at the NRDC's headquarters in Victoria Street, London, on 15 January. The two scientists were welcomed by Peter Woodrow, the specialist in machine patents. The NRDC, established by Harold Wilson in 1949, was universally condemned as a disastrous bureaucracy, but Woodrow was more commercial than most within it. Anxious to persuade Woodrow to assign their patents to Robinson's putative company, the two scientists suggested that Woodrow should meet the politician at the House of Commons restaurant that same evening for dinner. Woodrow agreed and the three men crossed Parliament Square. Waiting in the restaurant with Robinson were Jack Butterworth and Brenda Price, who had become a devoted employee of the Labour MP.

Over a long meal and many bottles of wine, Robinson presented his ambition to form a company to exploit three patents for EDMs invented by el-Menshawy. 'It's all about technology transfer,' said Robinson. Woodrow was captivated by Robinson's 'character and charisma'. At the end of the evening, it was agreed that three patents – GB1604400, GB2075401 and GB1604398 – would be legally assigned to the putative company after the payment of the appropriate fees.

Days after their return to Warwick, Robinson and Bhattacharyya were sitting in Jack Butterworth's office. Robinson offered both academics a directorship of his company. Initially they were enthusiastic. Butterworth, excited by Robinson's energy and intellect, agreed to become the company's chairman.

Bhattacharyya had also become an admirer. Occasionally sitting in the MP's room at the Post House Hotel, the academic heard him working the telephones. 'A tremendous marketing man,' Bhattacharyya thought. To Robinson's delight, Bhattacharyya also agreed to become a director and accept employment as a consultant.

In a four-page letter to Peter Woodrow on 12 February 1981, Robinson described his ambitious scheme involving a £100,000 investment by Coventry City Council, £50,000 from private sources and a huge investment from a 'third party'. He wanted to start negotiations to licence the three key EDM patents. In the reply, on 6 March, Robinson was told by the NRDC that to obtain a licence he would first have to deposit £3000, which was non-recoverable. From the description of further payments, Robinson discovered that the annual payments to use the EDM patents between 1983 and 1985 would escalate from £5000 to £20,000, and he would be liable to 5 per cent royalties. Over three years, he would be expected to pay at least £50,000. Despite the descriptions of his wealth in his letter to Woodrow, £50,000 was considerably more than Robinson possessed, but he was far from being discouraged. The enthusiasm among the academics could be used, he believed, without payment.

One evening, Robinson and Brenda Price were sitting in Bhattacharyya's office discussing the 'brilliance' of Robinson's idea. The MP spoke eloquently. 'Our project is something Britain really needs. Transferring technology from universities to industries.' 'We should call the company that,' said Bhattacharyya. 'Transfer Technology. That fits exactly what you're proposing, Geoffrey. Transferring technology from the university to the market.' Robinson was thrilled. Bhattacharyya even introduced Robinson to engineers at Rolls-Royce and BL who would be interested in buying EDMs developed from the patented designs.

By April 1981, Bhattacharyya and Butterworth began to doubt joining Robinson's new company. 'Geoffrey wants a hundred per cent of your time and then it becomes very difficult,' complained Bhattacharyya. 'There is a borderline between what we can do in the university and what we do outside.' Conflicts of interest were of little relevance to Robinson, a man in haste, but the 'borderline' was proving awkward for the academics.

Their dilemma was Robinson's reluctance to pay the NRDC for the use of the patents. Bhattacharyya was in no doubt. Developing the EDMs on the basis of the patents would cost Robinson 'megabucks'. The charges would be levied both at the outset, for the purchase of an assignment to develop the patent, and later in royalties based on the company's turnover, not profits.

To avoid the charges, Robinson pleaded poverty and asked, 'How can I pay until the machines have been developed and sold?' Bhattacharyya was uneasy about the discussion and suggested that Robinson consult Michael Shattock, the university's registrar. 'If businessmen can get away with blue murder,' Bhattacharyya said, 'they would.' By then, Bhattacharyya had during their many meetings become aware of Robinson's reputation as a man with 'enormous talents, but he does cut corners and universities are not like that'.

Like most university administrators, Michael Shattock was instinctively cautious, but his reaction to Robinson was encouraging. 'He's a breath of fresh air,' said Shattock. 'He's great, marvellous and fun.'

Robinson's proposition to Shattock was tempting. The university, said the MP, would earn money by his development of the patents, and that money could be used to fund further research in the university. His idea, mentioned Robinson, had been blessed by Jack Butterworth, the vice-chancellor. Initially, Shattock was favourably disposed towards the articulate and powerful local MP. But, like Bhattacharyya, he began to have doubts. 'You have to look carefully at the fine print,' he said about a man who appeared unaware 'how universities work'. He agreed with Bhattacharyya. 'There could be a smell. What if it goes wrong and the university is embarrassed?'

'Geoffrey wants total control and the university isn't going to give him that,' the registrar declared. 'He wants a major share and a major say.' On reflection, Shattock announced, 'He wants the whole cake. We'll be sensible not to go along with it.' He told Robinson, 'I can't see a way forward. Come back with an alternative proposal.' Shattock and Bhattacharyya had unanimously announced: 'We don't want to get involved with Geoffrey.' Robinson was undeterred. Both Butterworth and Bhattacharyya were mentioning unrealistic sums of money for a large organisation, and, he decided, he could progress without them and without a formal agreement with the NRDC. If Fawzi el-Menshawy agreed to join TransTec, he believed, he would not need to apply or pay for the use of the patents. Robinson had given a new meaning to Labour's policy of state intervention.

In May 1981, Robinson substituted consultancy agreements instead of directorships for Butterworth and Bhattacharyya in the proposed £200 company called Transfer Technology Ltd.* The new company would be registered by Robinson solely to exploit el-Menshawy's and Bhattacharyya's inventions and expertise. Since Bhattacharyya did not want to become a director, el-Menshawy's participation in TransTec as a director had become crucial to Robinson's plan.

Fawzi el-Menshawy was a poorly paid foreign academic, who understood the commercial potential of his inventions, yet was hoping that Jack Butterworth would sanction a £65,000 grant for further work. Ever since his dinner at the House of Commons, his first visit to parliament, the Egyptian had been excited by the proposed collaboration between the impressive politician and Warwick University. The death of that idea was disappointing, but Robinson had called with an alternative proposal. El-Menshawy, he suggested, should abandon his university career and join Robinson in a commercial partnership to develop his inventions. Cautiously, el-Menshawy told Robinson at the end of their first meeting, 'I'll think about it. I'll let you know when I return from America.' Eager for a fast and positive reply, Robinson pursued el-Menshawy by hourly telephone calls to his hotel in Los

*Transfer Technology changed names several times. To avoid confusion it will be referred to henceforth as TransTec.

Angeles. 'Resign from the university,' urged Robinson. 'I'm sure that Butterworth won't give you a grant.' El-Menshawy was perplexed. Robinson was lobbying against his friend the vice-chancellor. More peculiarly, Butterworth appeared to be encouraging the Egyptian's resignation. 'Geoffrey,' el-Menshawy later cursed, 'was stirring the pot.' The Egyptian was 'a foreigner who was impressed by Geoffrey,' recalls Michael Shattock. El-Menshawy admits that, anxious to prove the value of his inventions, he was seduced by Robinson and succumbed to the politician's pressure. 'I'll take a consultancy until my resignation is approved,' el-Menshawy agreed, acknowledging Robinson's promise of 25 per cent of the new company's shares after he became a full-time employee. Robinson was triumphant. The business, he was convinced, was at last viable. He turned his attention back to Bhattacharyya and Butterworth, repeatedly urging both to join the new company. Both refused and urged el-Menshawy to reconsider, not least because of Robinson's intention to use the patents without paying the licence or royalty fees.

With el-Menshawy's presence, Robinson believed, TransTec was not obliged to pay for using the patents. The NRDC, Shattock, Bhattacharyya and especially el-Menshawy disagreed. All requested Robinson to pay. 'TransTec should pay royalties for using the patents,' wrote Peter Woodrow from the NRDC. Robinson ignored the letters and began building his company.

He recruited Peter Dickinson, employed as a salesman by a rival company developing EDMs. 'Come as soon as you can,' Robinson told Dickinson on Easter Sunday morning, 'and bring as many drawings of your machines as possible.' Dickinson was overwhelmed by the offer and impressed by Robinson's influence. Anxious that Dickinson should not lose a day's work, the politician arranged for his new salesman to be excused jury service at Bradford's crown court.

Robinson next recruited John McGarth, a former colleague at Jaguar. 'Be my chief executive,' suggested Robinson. Attracted by Robinson's intelligence and charisma, McGarth accepted a few shares and undertook to travel to the United States to meet el-Menshawy. His purpose, at Robinson's request, was to scrutinise whether the technology was commercial. 'It's excellent,' McGarth reported on his return, but he rejected the offer of permanent employment. Robinson's operation was still too uncertain.

Housed in dirty premises in an industrial unit in Aston Brook Street, Coleshill, Birmingham, TransTec and its four employees faced a precarious future. The new company's finances depended upon two sources which did not change for some years: the government and Joska Bourgeois. Robinson could borrow some money, using his home as collateral, but only Bourgeois could provide a substantial sum. Her custom was not to give but to lend. Although Robinson subsequently denied receiving any direct help, a £100,000 loan to the company advanced by Crédit Suisse was supported by her collateral. Her importance to TransTec was never in doubt. After one of her regular visits, Robinson swooned to Diane Shaw, employed as assembly worker, 'She's the twelfth richest woman in the world.' On his dingy office walls, he fixed oil paintings donated by his Paymaster.

Obtaining finance from the government rather than Bourgeois required greater skill, but Robinson had become adept in negotiating money from Whitehall. His experience at the IRC, Jaguar and Meriden had taught him a suitable pitch: 'If I don't get the money, this business will go down.' Ignoring an MP's request was difficult for civil servants. By 1982, Robinson had received £75,000 from the DTI as a 'small business loan' and also a grant of £50,000 from the DTI spread over three years for el-Menshawy to develop a multi-purpose EDM generator. His political interest in state intervention and loans had proved personally profitable.

In January 1982, TransTec received its first order. Nine EDM conversion units based on el-Menshawy's inventions were sold to Rolls-Royce for £18,000; the Egyptian supervised their instal-lation in Derby. In gratitude, Robinson offered el-Menshawy a cheque for £10,000 as a contribution towards the purchase of a new house. 'Treat me as a friend,' insisted Robinson. El-Menshawy preferred to reject the generosity; the Egyptian already

felt disillusioned about Robinson. His despondency matched the
experience of his predecessors at Innocenti and Jaguar. Robinson's
generosity was a cover for his self-centred pursuit of wealth. His
seduction of el-Menshawy with promises of 'bringing scientific
research into reality' was, el-Menshawy was beginning to recognise, a figleaf. Earning money, normally a laudable purpose,
appeared to be Robinson's preoccupation but was oddly inconsistent with the politician's vociferous campaign at election
hustings against other wealth-creators accumulating the rewards
for their work.

In 1983, Fawzi el-Menshawy and Kumar Bhattacharyya were
concerned that Robinson was using their patents without the
NRDC's permission and refusing to pay any fees. Repeatedly, the
Labour MP ignored requests by the university and the NRDC to
apply for licensing agreements and pay the royalties. Repeatedly,
he found reasons to refuse, occasionally pleading that TransTec
was not using the patents, was not earning any money from the
patents, or simply that 'I don't need the patents. I've got Fawzi.'
Recruiting the Egyptian, he believed, had provided the excuse to
avoid paying at least £50,000. Bhattacharyya and Michael
Shattock pondered retaliation. 'He's powerful,' said Bhattacharyya.
'He's an MP and could be a bad enemy. It's not an affair we should
get our fingers into.' In Shattock's opinion, Robinson was
'exploiting' el-Menshawy. Unlike the university, which was 'not
going to sell our souls', the Egyptian was ensnared. 'It's a shame,
but all's fair in love and war,' concluded Shattock.

In Westminster, there was also trepidation about involvement
in Robinson's businesses. Barry Sheerman, a right-wing Labour
MP with industrial connections, bumped into John Butcher,
Conservative MP for Coventry South West.

'Geoffrey Robinson may ask you to get involved with one of his
business deals,' said Butcher. 'Don't touch it with a barge pole.'

'What's it about?' asked Sheerman.

'Engineering,' replied Butcher. 'Stay away from it.'

The juxtaposition in 1983 of Geoffrey Robinson campaigning
for re-election by attacking Margaret Thatcher's cruel capitalism

while refusing to pay for patents and pondering new businesses bequeathed a novel cant to a socialist politician. Thirteen years later he said, 'The whole idea of starting TransTec was to see if we could redress the . . . terrible experience in Coventry where every day another factory went.' Robinson's memory was faulty. None of those approached at Warwick University recalled Robinson suggesting TransTec as a cure for unemployment. Even the masquerade of socialist principles was unmentioned. Rather, while his Labour colleagues were preparing an ideological onslaught in favour of mass nationalisation and controls on business, Robinson was seeking personal wealth. In that quest, he applied to become the British representative of Agie, a Swiss manufacturer of EDM machines.

Robinson's strategy was engaging. The company representing Agie in Britain had collapsed in bankruptcy. Robinson arranged to become the company's new agent and employ its twelve staff – engineers and salesmen – at TransTec's offices in Coleshill. In the first year, he would be paid £17,000, a good salary considering that in 1983 an MP earned £15,308. An added attraction was exploiting el-Menshawy's expertise. By attaching the Egyptian's superior control unit to Agie's spark-erosion machine, the EDM's performance was improved by about one-third. The cost of the improvement was small compared to the high price Robinson charged. 'We can get our money back in one year,' Robinson enthused.

The new plan ruffled el-Menshawy. Robinson had arranged for Agie's administrative expenses to be borne by TransTec without any benefits or additional income for el-Menshawy. The latter was expected to tolerate his reduced income without complaint. Their disagreement was aggravated at Christmas. Robinson registered Agie UK as a company and became the chairman. Under his contract with the Swiss, he was paid £50,000 and received 3 per cent commission on Agie's turnover in Britain. Since the company's sales in 1984 would be about £5 million, his anticipated annual income was about £150,000. Whether the money was deposited in Britain or remained tax-free in Switzerland is unclear, but significantly Robinson did not register his lucrative new appointment as a 'member's interest' at the House of Commons, a requirement for any paid directorship. Subsequently he explained the omission as an 'administrative error'. That 'error' coincided with Robinson's metamorphosis into a raw financial operator. El-Menshawy had only just received the legal assignment of his 25 per cent stake in TransTec. With some reluctance, Robinson had delivered to the Egyptian the promised shares in the company, his fees and a company car. Robinson blamed the delay on 'an oversight', but el-Menshawy was more concerned by Robinson's management of their company. 'You only take money out,' he challenged Robinson. 'You put nothing in.' Using the grants procured from the government, Robinson had refined a method of simple profiteering.

The cost of manufacturing the box that housed the EDM was £500. Robinson's price to customers depended upon their wealth. Americans paid $6000, while British companies were charged £2000, about half the Americans' price. That was good business. Less explicable was the discovery by Peter Dickinson that only £4000 out of the £50,000 grant from the DTI was spent on a prototype EDM until it was abandoned in the corner of the workshop. El-Menshawy expected that the surplus had been deposited in TransTec's bank account, to be enhanced after his return from America before Christmas 1983, with new orders worth $150,000. To his surprise, during the company's Christmas party, Brenda Price told him, 'TransTec's bust'. The company's overdraft had risen to £350,000, including a new loan of £225,000 from Joska Bourgeois, who had also guaranteed the overdraft. El-Menshawy was startled and particularly suspicious after witnessing Robinson generously entertaining Roy Hattersley and Michael Cocks, both fellow Labour MPs representing traditional Labour, at TransTec's expense. The scientist, perplexed by those finances, asked Alan Mackrael, managing director of Needle Industries, an expanding conglomerate, to consider buying TransTec. In the guise of a genuine purchaser, Mackrael's accountants were allowed to examine TransTec's financial records. The auditors wrote two reports. The sanitised version presented to Robinson in May 1984 was uncontroversial. The second version prepared for the Egyptian was damning. El-Menshawy's suspicions were confirmed: Robinson was charging his personal living expenses to the company.

Robinson's attitude towards corporate finances had already been shown as unorthodox. At Innocenti and Jaguar, he had drawn huge expenses to fund his hectic lifestyle. At the nascent TransTec, the accountants discovered, his habits had not altered. In the first two years, according to the investigators, the company had incurred £130,000 in non-trading expenses, notably 'travel and entertaining, the purchase of house furnishings and other personal expenses, [and the] cost of leases on several motor cars which were not used for business and not driven by company personnel'. Most of the costs were incurred for Robinson's private use, including many parties and home improvements. His wife had been paid an annual salary of £20,000, although she provided no services for the company or even visited Birmingham. Fawzi el-Menshawy, described by Mackrael as an 'honest individual' and TransTec's 'main driving force', challenged Robinson. 'You've been using the company's money,' he said. 'It's my back pay,' replied Robinson. In early 1984, Robinson ceased charging most of his controversial expenses to TransTec, but el-Menshawy was estranged from his partner. The great adventure was souring.

In retrospect, the birth of any aspiring tycoon's empire often seems a romantic, dare-devil adventure. Years later, colourful anecdotes are swapped about the risks and rascals encountered while building a fortune from nothing. But no memorable land-marks were passed in the creation of TransTec. Rather, the prototype tycoon, with a warped attitude towards capitalism, appeared to some of his partners a casual small-timer groping for a shortcut on to the inside track.

Combining business with his political obligations was demand-ing, but Robinson worked energetically, commuting at the end of the week from London to Birmingham and working tirelessly to direct his TransTec staff in manufacturing the EDMs, finding customers and organising installations. TransTec's employees were always aware of Robinson's double life, but few Labour MPs in Westminster appreciated, when he was appointed as the party's spokesman on science by Michael Foot in July 1982, that, as he was also an employer and recipient of state aid, there was a possible conflict of interest. In that era, the requirements of disclosure were relaxed, and Robinson's plea in the Commons for industry to exploit scientific discoveries attracted some MPs' sympathy. Others doubted, especially after the collapse of Meriden in August 1982, whether an MP wearing a well-cut suit and talking as a businessman could be a socialist. Activists in his constituency were aggrieved by his apparent disengagement from the plight of the estimated 40 per cent of Coventry's workforce who had been made redundant since 1978. They spoke again about his deselection as the Labour candidate.

The divided opinion appeared to confuse Robinson. The far left could never be placated but his fellow MPs, he grumbled in bewilderment, failed to appreciate his talents. His popularity in Coventry and his skill managing Jaguar, he argued, were ideal qualifications for participation in 'running' the party and ought to guarantee him a senior position in any future government.

Robinson's image of himself was not shared by some of his colleagues. The Labour whips had sought to re-engage Robinson in parliamentary life by his appointment as a whip on the Standing Committee of the Transport Bill. During the long late-night sittings he regularly met Ann Taylor, Barry Sheerman and one Peter Mandelson, a researcher helping the party's two shadow spokesmen on the committee. Together, they lamented the party's decline and, in one fateful discussion, Robinson advised Mandelson to earn money before entering parliament, perhaps by pursuing a television career. At the end of that parliamentary session, Robinson's reputation was not enhanced. His fondness for drinking and his slurred contributions during the committee's discussions demolished his resurrection. He was not reappointed as a whip, and so effectively was dismissed.

Some MPs began to suspect that Robinson was not as

intelligent or perceptive as they had first imagined. Detached and alienated from those devoting their lives entirely to the party's internecine and ideological battle, he was unconcerned about his lack of political skills and thoughtless about the unreconciled conflict between his political and commercial ambitions. His unconventional marriage and the discretion surrounding his family life – even the birth of his son, Alexander, in 1978 was unknown in his constituency – suggested an impassive politician, insensitive to vicissitudes. While moderate Labour MPs were unsettled by their party's drift into the wilderness, Robinson appeared slow to understand the repercussions of Labour's disastrous election defeat in 1983.

Robinson's own solution was to propose Roy Hattersley as party leader. Instead, Hattersley was elected deputy leader under Neil Kinnock. To Robinson's disappointment, neither was sympathetic towards himself. Although he had defeated another Marxist bid in his constituency to deselect him before the election, Hattersley professed to be unaware of any personal relationship with Robinson, while Kinnock instantly sacked him as Labour's spokesman on science. Robinson was shocked. Some thought it was associated with his recent purchase of Orchards, an eight-bedroomed, nineteenth-century house designed by Sir Edwin Lutyens, near Godalming, Surrey. The advertised price was £300,000, although Robinson said he paid less. The contrast between the Surrey mansion and his failure to buy a home in Coventry jarred among the left-wing cadres surrounding Kinnock. Others assumed his dismissal was the penalty for his recklessness as a whip. To his good fortune, the opprobrium was only temporary. A sudden resignation from Kinnock's chosen team gave him an opportunity to recover his position.

Seven weeks after his dismissal, Kinnock appointed Robinson the party's spokesman on regional affairs and industry under Peter Shore, a member of the party's centre left. Again, neither Robinson nor his colleagues seem to have pondered whether their spokesman was tainted by a conflict of interests. Even after John Smith, shadow minister of technology, visited Coleshill to inspect

Robinson's operation, which by then employed about twenty people, the issue of a conflict did not arise. Robinson had become renowned as a wealthy MP and his idiosyncrasies were tolerated by Hattersley, Shore and other Labour leaders whose support had become important to Robinson. But his generosity could not offset his poor attendance record. His 'laziness' was stymieing his ambition to become Labour's first millionaire prime minister. Politically, he remained an unknown minor player.

Financially, Robinson was also not a player. Agie UK, with twenty-four employees, paid its chairman £25,000 in Britain and there was a lack of transparency about the fate of the commissions earned by Agie UK. Strangely, despite the company's high turn-over, Agie's accounts showed constant trading losses. Robinson had clearly agreed with the Swiss to run the company in Britain at a loss to avoid British taxes. TransTec, however, was genuinely floundering. Sales were low and the company's losses in 1983 were £125,225. With accumulated debts of £209,941, the company would have been trading at alarming losses without Joska Bourgeois's bank guarantees and the DTI grants. Another DTI grant of £55,122 had been approved, and an application was submitted for a £100,000 grant to develop a machine to mould plastics. Robinson harboured fears about TransTec's future.

His eccentric commercial record was reflected in his erratic personal behaviour. Journalists employed by the *Coventry Evening Telegraph*, the local newspaper, found him particularly difficult to pin down on any issue. He enjoyed parrying questions to avoid commitment. Like the Royal Family, they agreed, he never explained and rarely complained. Disarmingly, he promised generous help to all his constituents and many benefited, although some were left with the wrong impression.

In particular, Annette Witheridge, an attractive twenty-three-year-old reporter living in Allesley, the location of the Post House Hotel, Robinson's home in Coventry, was 'amazed'. After an interview, Robinson told her, 'You're local. You must come round for a champagne dinner tonight.' Witheridge replied, 'I'm afraid I can't. I'm busy.' Robinson found rejection intolerable: 'Well just come for a glass of champagne at six o'clock.' Again, 'terrified' of the politician, she declined: 'No, I don't think so.' In Witheridge's opinion, Robinson regularly exploited his status to ensnare young women. She knew of other female journalists who had been chased round tables and propositioned with slobbering kisses on their cheeks. One drink with Robinson, she feared, would lead to trouble.

At 6.30 that evening, Witheridge heard a bang on her front door. Peering through the curtains, she saw Robinson on the pavement. She hid. The telephone rang. An operator from the *Coventry Evening Telegraph* announced, 'Mr Robinson, the local MP, is waiting on another line, and wants your telephone number.' 'Don't give it to him,' Witheridge said, watching Robinson put the mobile telephone into his pocket and drive off. On Monday morning, he telephoned her at the newspaper with a reprimand, 'You're a naughty girl. I had champagne on ice for you. Now, when will you come round for a drink?'

Under pressure, Robinson was drinking more heavily than usual. The frontbench spokesman, who boasted about travelling around the country in a Jaguar using the novel mobile telephone, was not impressing the party's leaders. 'He's not cut out for politics,' Denis Healey decided about 'a bland personality with a lack of political ambition who refuses to become a party man. He's got no political status. He'll be happier in business.' Unlike Robert Maxwell, Robinson gave the impression of being politically unambitious. That was mistaken. In truth, Robinson, unlike Maxwell, disdained politics and its obligations.

On 23 December 1984, Robinson was found by police asleep in an unlit Daimler on the hard shoulder of the M6 motorway. Asked by a policeman to explain being drunk and asleep in an unlit car on a motorway, he replied in a slurred voice, 'It's none of your business. I thought it was a lay-by.' For a politician, it was a serious embarrassment, compounded by his refusal to obey the law and take a breath test. In court, Robinson described how he had endured a 'very heavy week' in the Commons and his constituency. Despite the circumstances, he was only fined £420 and did not lose his licence. One year later, he was banned from driving for three months after speeding on the M25. In the House of Commons, some Labour MPs were angry. Robinson's attitude suggested an indifference to the obligation of lawmakers to obey the laws.

A similar indiscipline influenced his commercial life.

In 1985, Robinson earned £50,750 as Agie UK's chairman, more than double the previous year's income. Agie's declared profits were £20,343. TransTec, by contrast, was still in debt. In May 1985, el-Menshawy suffered a heart attack, endangering a potential contract with GKN, then a major industrial conglomerate. Robinson could rely on Sami Ahmed, an Egyptian engineer specialising in underwater acoustics, who had been recruited by el-Menshawy, to deliver the EDMs to aerospace customers in Japan, Spain, Russia and South Africa. Ahmed, judged by Robinson to be less emotional and more commercial than el-Menshawy, had proved a more reliable partner, not least in their endeavours to obtain government grants. In el-Menshawy's absence, Robinson applied for a £380,000 grant to support Professor Joe McGeough of Edinburgh University. McGeough proposed to develop an ECM, a refinement of el-Menshawy's EDM. In December 1985 TransTec was awarded the grant, to be paid over three years.

TransTec had also received a £100,000 grant to develop a machine to mould plastics. According to the application, the development of the machine would cost £50,000. In the event, according to Peter Dickinson, only £10,000 was required, the remaining £40,000 being used to sustain the company's thirty employees. 'I thought,' Dickinson said later, 'that he was an honest guy at first. But then it all changed.' On his return from illness, el-Menshawy was puzzled when visiting DTI inspectors scrutinising the expenditure of the grant 'were presented with old machinery and parts dressed up as new'. Robinson's attitude towards grants also riled Lorraine Upton, the company's book-keeper. Upton could not understand various claims for expenses and asked Robinson for explanations. 'You're too busy for your own good,' he replied. 'And you're a barrel-load of monkeys' was her opinion of a patronising employer whose charm, she noticed, was effortlessly switched on and off. His answers, she decided, were unsatisfactory. In 1986, Upton departed in acrimony and Robinson asked Max Ayriss, who was responsible for TransTec's payroll services, to become the company's bookkeeper.

Robinson had cause for some satisfaction. Over the previous three years, he had used el-Menshawy's EDM patents without either permission or payment, thus saving about £100,000 in licence fees and royalties. The incongruity of a Labour MP acting in this way did not appear to concern Robinson. His disrespect for propriety was matched by his contempt for el-Menshawy, who was still recovering from his illness. Anticipating el-Menshawy's early departure from TransTec, Robinson began to negotiate his final coup.

Robinson was concerned that without the inventor's presence he would be financially and legally vulnerable for TransTec's use of the patents. There were also constant demands from the British Technology Group, the organisation which had replaced the NRDC, for TransTec to pay the fees for the renewal of the patents registration. His solution was a campaign towards Peter Hurd, the registrar of the University of Birmingham, el-Menshawy's original employer, to assign the patent rights to TransTec free of any charge. Mentioning his position as the local MP, Robinson said that the inventor was a TransTec director, so it was only right that the patents should belong to the company. Hurd consulted Warwick University and was told, 'It's nothing to do with us.' Eventually, Hurd succumbed to Robinson's pressure. 'Every university wanted to wash their hands of it,' Bhattacharyya recalled. 'Politely, politely.'

After his recovery, el-Menshawy protested to Hurd, 'You can't do this without my agreement. I'm getting no benefit for my invention.' 'It's too late,' Hurd said. 'They've been transferred to TransTec.' Robinson had, quite lawfully, at last achieved his goal without any cost. 'He's cheated me,' el-Menshawy complained.

Robinson's increasing income from Agie and the rise in

TransTec's sales, encouraged him to apply for more DTI grants. Max Ayriss was instructed how to complete the forms to obtain the 'maximum' amounts. Gradually, Ayriss came to believe that Robinson was directing him to include in the application forms work which did not qualify for grants and to describe false developments on a new electric spark drill. Claims to obtain a DTI grant were being made, Ayriss believed, which were 'not appropriate', not least to disguise cheap production materials as 'research and development materials'; or by false invoicing. In a TransTec memorandum, an employee admitted that an official invoice received from Brighton Machines Inc. of Missouri and shown to the DTI was for $71,500, but the actual payment was $30,000.

Ayriss did not protest to Robinson. During 1986 and 1987, he formally submitted successful claims for more than £400,000 in government grants despite his unease.* In 1986, he recorded the receipt from the DTI of £227,000, an innovation grant for an EDT steel-texturing machine, but noted that the grant had been spent on administration rather than the machine's development.

Peter Dickinson, the sales manager, was also surprised that less than £20,000 was spent to develop a hybrid EDM/ECM machine although the grant had been £133,519. The extra money was spent by TransTec on other work. The deception was possible, Dickinson admitted, because he personally had 'successfully flannelled' the representative of the DTI. Before the representative's visit, the abandoned machine was lifted from the corner of a room and dusted. 'He was told a pack of lies,' TransTec employees subsequently admitted. About £500,000 of the £1.3 million received by TransTec in grants during those years, Ayriss calculated, was being misappropriated.

'He's at it again,' Ayriss told John Harrison, who was responsible for TransTec's purchasing. 'He's trying to get me to

---

*Included £90,000 in late 1987 for research into EDM machinery; £227,000 in 1986 to develop four electro-chemical machining machines and £165,794 for a prototype electro-discharge texturing machine.

falsify claims to the DTI for capital grants and if I ever get found out I'm really going to be in trouble.' Ayriss was particularly upset about one incorrect declaration. Robinson had told Ayriss to book Jeff Bagnall, an installation engineer, 'full-time' on a project, although Bagnall was employed for more than 60 per cent of his time on other work. 'This isn't correct,' protested Ayriss, also unhappy that inappropriate 'hours and materials' were charged 'against the project'. Robinson was adamant: 'This is the way the government helps small companies.'

The atmosphere in TransTec's office in 1986 became tense. On Fridays when the Commons was in session and during the holidays, Ayriss heard Robinson from the neighbouring room on the telephone solving problems, especially slow payments by customers or TransTec's delayed payments to suppliers, by adopting a euphemistic style: 'Hello. I'm the MP for the area. I'm trying to help out this company called TransTec and I'd be grateful if you could assist.' In Ayriss's hearing, Robinson did not mention that he was the company's chairman. Robinson, recalled John Harrison, was 'a silver-tongued charmer when he wants to be, but when he doesn't want to be, he's an absolute swine. A very hard man. A very hard man.'

Juggling his relationships with employees was not easy for the aspiring tycoon. His attempts to increase productivity were resisted by some and, in return, the employees' demand for the Labour MP's recognition of a trade union to negotiate on their behalf was rejected outright. Unashamed, Robinson bade farewell to a handful of key assembly workers and relied upon Diane Shaw, promoted as an electronics supervisor, to assemble the EDMs despite her lack of experience. In gratitude, he invited his long-serving, loyal employee and her cousin to lunch at the House of Commons. For Diane Shaw, the drink on the terrace overlooking the River Thames and his present, a Wedgwood coffee set, was a unique occasion and reinforced her loyalty. His subsequent promise of a staff profit sharing scheme and his gifts of perfume on his return from foreign trips augmented her trust.

Fawzi el-Menshawy was not so fortunate. Robinson was weary

of the Egyptian's complaints, especially about the company's accounts. El-Menshawy was a foreign-born scientist, not a businessman, and TransTec was a vehicle to make Robinson himself, not others, rich. Robinson decided upon a divorce, and his method was raw and ruthless. TransTec was recapitalised from a £200 into a £200,000 company. Unable to provide £50,000 to protect his 25 per cent stake, the Egyptian's original shareholding worth £50 became minuscule. Rather than a principal shareholder, el-Menshawy was an employee. With mutual relief, he resigned in October 1986. By then, Robinson and Sami Ahmed had discovered that their route to wealth was to import many components from the Far East.

In 1985, Robinson had flown with Ahmed to Taiwan to buy part castings, the body of the EDM machines and electronics. With a minimum of work in Coleshill, the Taiwanese product could be completed and sold with a 'Made in Britain' label. The castings were bought in Taiwan for £4000, the additional work in Britain cost about £6000 and the total product was resold for £25,000. 'The quality wasn't very good,' Ahmed conceded, 'but we earned good profits.'

When travelling with Ahmed, Robinson was careful with money, travelling economy and not eating in particularly expensive restaurants. He would spend generously, he had told Ahmed during a serious conversation, only when required to impress people, and then he would 'spend big'. Robinson's negotiation technique in Taiwan was tough but unstructured. Rather than carefully deciding his optimum price in advance, he spontaneously selected the rate and relentlessly negotiated, interrupted only by his request to visit the workers' living accommodation. Despite the embarrassment, he entered the dormitories and saw twelve men living in a single small room. 'I understand people better if I know how they live,' he told Ahmed. 'I can then deal with them.' After his inspection, he continued the negotiations, demanding a lower price.

Profits rather than quality was Robinson's measure, an irony considering his complaint in the Commons in 1982 that British industry failed to exploit scientific discoveries and produce good products. The result was complaints from British Steel about shoddy texturing machines supplied to the steel mills in South Wales, and complaints from Brighton Machines Inc. of Missouri that, during the installation of an EDM machine, TransTec's team had damaged transformers, caused financial loss and, having caused chaos, disappeared. El-Menshawy could not console himself with that disaster. Robinson, he discovered from a British Steel scientist, had registered in his own name two patents of inventions for EDTs – steel-texturing machines – completed by the distraught Egyptian before he left TransTec. The registered owners of Patent Number GB2191435 for 'Apparatus for working electrically conductive material by electric erosion' were Geoffrey Robinson and Sami Ahmed, although Fawzi el-Menshawy had applied for the patent on his invention before his heart attack. Ahmed had slightly adapted el-Menshawy's process for steel-texturing and, with Robinson's agreement, inserted the MP's name on a patent which he barely understood. 'Geoffrey,' as Ahmed admits, 'is not a technical guy.' Robinson's memory on patents is hazy. 'I don't know if we even used patents,' he says.

In 1986 Robinson had reached a Rubicon. Despite the increase in trade, TransTec losses were £46,091 and the accumulated debts were £286,418. The company's survival depended upon government grants, the £250,000 loan from Joska Bourgeois and a further loan of £27,000 from Robinson himself. The income from his businesses was declining. His declared salary that year from Agie was only £17,269 and from TransTec merely £2675, which he did not draw. With time and effort, he believed, he could build TransTec into his dream, a £500 million company, but his sources of finance were limited. A $3 million contract with China Steel in Taiwan to buy castings could not be financed from the cash flow, the banks or Joska Bourgeois. If he was to transform TransTec into an international public company he needed a partner, and the search required his complete attention.

Politics and his attendance in Westminster were a handicap. On any assessment, Robinson's decade in politics had been wasted.

Personally, he had achieved nothing and the Labour Party had no prospect of winning the next election. His offered contribution was ignored. Those who heard his lament – 'I understand business. Labour is still anti-business. Opposition is a waste of time, so I am not going to bother' – were disinclined to respect a man who equated ministers with managing directors. His absence, he knew, would hardly be noticed. The only benefit of his parliamentary seat was using the address to promote his business.

In summer 1986 he resigned from the front bench to devote himself to his wealth. While formally remaining a backbencher, he decided to disappear from Westminster. 'My sister's husband has died,' he told Peter Mandelson. 'I need to earn enough money to support two families.' Others were given another pitch extolling his mission to improve Britain. TransTec, he told inquirers, would adapt academic research and technology from institutes of higher learning into manufacturing and practical engineering. Ten years later, he embellished the circumstances of his resignation. 'I made way for Gordon Brown,' he told Mary Riddell, a journalist. 'Gave the boy a chance. He was immensely grateful and he's never forgotten it. Yes, we had this secret pact.' Brown had become an MP in 1983. By any measure, Robinson's decision was unconventional. Most politicians earn their fortune before entering the Commons. Robinson's decision to become rich while remaining an MP confirmed his disengagement from the rules of the game.

Robinson's disappearance caused little sorrow. His interest in business rather than politics and the lingering embarrassment about the drink–driving conviction had marked him as unreliable. His approach to Robert Maxwell as the catalyst of his new ambitions cast him as unwise.

3

THE PROFITABLE
RELATIONSHIP

Geoffrey Robinson's meeting with Robert Maxwell in autumn
1986 was carefully considered. The proprietor of Mirror Group
Newspapers was hosting a party at the Labour Party conference
in Blackpool, holding court for the party's leaders, who were
anxious to secure and retain his sympathies. That year, Maxwell
dominated the news; he was involved in so many bids in so many
guises that it was quipped, 'Maxwell has more fingers in more pies
than most people have fingers.' In the City, image was as
important as substance, and during those months Maxwell had
projected himself as an irresistible entrepreneur who led an
international corporation with surging profits. Seventeen years
after his downfall for fraud, and the damning judgement by DTI
inspectors that he was not 'a person who can be relied on to
exercise proper stewardship of a publicly quoted company',
Maxwell was rehabilitated in the City and had stood beside the
Queen at the opening of the Commonwealth Games in
Edinburgh. Bold newspaper headlines – 'The Global Player', 'The
Incredible All-performing Robert Maxwell' – confirmed his
position at the centre of the stage.

Just prior to the party conference, Hollis, a small timber
merchant and furniture manufacturer controlled by Maxwell since
1982 but managed by his son Kevin, had bid for a diverse package
of engineering, electronics and crane manufacturers. Maxwell was
treading in Robinson's territory and the Labour MP had good
reason to revive an acquaintanceship forged nineteen years earlier.

Robinson recalled meeting Maxwell for the first time in 1967
as the Czech-born tycoon, elected Labour MP for North
Buckinghamshire in 1964, was boarding a private jet at a London
airport. Robinson was delivering a briefing paper prepared by
Transport House for Maxwell's meeting at the Council of Europe.
During their short conversation, Robinson was 'in some awe' of
Maxwell's personality, of his 'looks, stature, voice, brains, money,
languages – he had the lot,' recalled Robinson; and the young
researcher was especially impressed by his wealth. Private jets in
that era were rare and Robinson could not forget Maxwell's reply
to his query about the expense: 'Money is the only problem I
haven't got.' In 1986, Robinson wanted to taste that heartache. 'I
liked him,' Robinson recalled, admitting the danger of his confession. 'It was hard not to be in some awe. He was an appealing
sort of bloke. I wasn't turned off by him.' But his confession was
disingenuous. Robinson also insists that Maxwell 'didn't have an
impact on me'. The contrary was the truth. Maxwell became a role
model. In 1986, as the owner of the Mirror Group, the only
national newspaper company supporting Labour, Maxwell
enjoyed access to the party's leaders and deluded himself that he
influenced the very powerbrokers whom Robinson had forlornly
served for the past decade. Maxwell's compensation for his
frustrated ambition to become Britain's prime minister – he had
been a Labour MP between 1964 and 1970 – was to employ many
Labour politicians as directors and staff of his companies. 'Bob's
the perfect parent,' Kevin Maxwell said dismissively to a friend
about those Labour Party members seeking employment, 'because
he always pays cash to look after his orphans.' Like many businessmen, financiers and professionals in Britain, Robinson prayed that
Maxwell would cast some crumbs in his direction. Their short

meeting in Blackpool, so unimportant to Maxwell, became critical to Robinson after 3 November 1986.

In his less lucid moments, Robert Maxwell's vanity invariably suppressed his judgement. The billionaire newspaper owner and publisher was selling Europe's biggest printing company to finance his investment in the nascent communications revolution. At that moment of divine prescience, Maxwell succumbed to the sales patter of a smart banker, and became eager to invest in Britain's ailing engineering industry. Maxwell possessed many talents but his knowledge of engineering was barely more than recognising the difference between a nail and a screw.

The banker, Leslie Goodman of Hill Samuel, had persuaded Maxwell to bid for AE, a well-known Rugby-based engineering company. The attraction to Maxwell was the addition of £150 million in turnover to increase the size of his empire. Maxwell's bid was rejected. The rebuff incited him to consider a slew of other industrial companies.

In 1987 Maxwell invited David James, a company doctor hawking Central & Sheerwood (C&S), a stricken industrial conglomerate on the verge of insolvency, into his smoke-filled dining-room in Holborn at the end of an intoxicating lunch. Over the previous three years, James had cared for the conglomerate, which manufactured cranes and packaging machines, and, in particular, for A. L. Dunn, a foundry supplying moulded aluminium parts to Ford, Nissan and Land-Rover. To insiders he admitted that it was 'in dreadful trouble', with 'more problems than God has apples'.

'You may stand there, Mr James,' slurred Maxwell. 'Your company is about to go bust and you will accept my offer which is six pence per share. Take it or leave it.'

'I'll leave it,' replied James crisply, turning to the door.

'Well, if you take that attitude, we'll have to sit down and negotiate,' grumbled Maxwell. Eventually, he bought a 60 per cent stake, intending to sell off some parts and absorb others into Hollis.

Hollis was an aberration for a corporation with ambitions to become a media giant competing with Rupert Murdoch. The folly of Maxwell's ownership of Hollis was not lost on Kevin, his twenty-seven-year-old son. As penance following the reconciliation of a dispute, in 1985 Maxwell had appointed Kevin executive deputy chairman of Hollis. With even less knowledge than his father about engineering, Kevin hired Michael Stoney as his finance director and then sought a manufacturing expert. His solitary candidate was Colin Robinson, a businessman who had departed from Heron International, a property company, without a glowing reputation. Colin Robinson, who was not related to Geoffrey Robinson, had recruited a team and within months transformed Hollis from loss into profit. Kevin began lobbying his father to sell the company to Colin Robinson in a management buyout. 'We've got to get rid of it,' urged Kevin.

Robert Maxwell, usually reluctant to sell, was nearly persuaded. Hollis, enhanced by some parts of C&S, could be sold to the management, while Maxwell would retain a significant shareholding. 'You'll need to appoint a non-executive chairman,' advised Andrew Capitman, his banker, 'to look after your investment.' Maxwell's candidate was Geoffrey Robinson. He had received several calls from the MP since their meeting in Blackpool. In his opinion, Robinson was another ambitious Labour politician who rightly saw the advantage of staying close to the *Mirror*'s proprietor. If Robinson was amenable, Maxwell would agree to the management's purchase. The Labour MP was invited to Maxwell's office in Holborn.

Visitors to Maxwell's imperial office suite underneath his personal helipad could not fail to acknowledge how his affluence extended the tycoon's influence, including too his own football teams, Oxford United and Derby County. 'The Publisher', as he liked to be addressed, was on the verge of launching one of the year's biggest billion-dollar takeover bids in New York. Hollis, by then a conglomerate of thirteen companies, was a distraction. To Geoffrey Robinson, it was a God-sent opportunity for an insignificant businessman to negotiate with the City institutions, in the certainty of introductions to key personalities. Those relationships, Robinson assured himself, would be his passport to serious wealth.

Geoffrey Robinson's appointment as chairman, Maxwell conceded to Kevin, would at worst be 'a valuable letterhead'. Robinson would only be required to attend board meetings. But he was, Maxwell recognised, a man who understood the requirements. Unlike Dickson Mabon, a former Labour MP and a current director of Hollis, who had proved worthless and would be retired, Robinson could be expected to obey instructions without further explanation. For the moment, Maxwell and Robinson agreed, there would be no payment. Since he had abandoned the front benches and concentrated on his business, Robinson's finances had improved. TransTec's gross profits during 1987 had increased by 80 per cent and he turned a £46,091 loss into a £43,490 profit, which was set to increase in 1988 to £277,392. The company's accumulated debts would be purged.

Before the end of 1987, Robert Maxwell was reassured by Robinson's efficient style. He was matter-of-fact, knew what he wanted and moved the agenda smartly towards a conclusion. Socially, he appeared as the jolly man who made people feel good by slapping backs and squeezing arms. Geoffrey Robinson, Maxwell decided, was a kindred spirit. In a mutually flattering and self-interested relationship, both enjoyed money and its consequent power. Unlike himself, Robinson did not desire to rule the world and appeared content to serve Maxwell's interests. 'The Publisher' and his son were not displeased that some regarded Robinson as yet another 'Maxwell gofer', a run-about man with the potential to become, like other Labour exiles, a political fixer. Even if some engineers in Hollis's factories doubted whether Robinson 'knows his arse from his elbow', Kevin was grateful that Robinson, who did know the difference between a nail and a screw, patiently gave advice on the telephone. With that reassurance, Kevin convinced his father finally to sell Hollis to the management. The finance would be provided by loan notes issued by Maxwell and the army of bankers fluttering around the empire begging to lend money. The safeguards of Maxwell's investment

would be Michael Stoney, the company's finance director, and
Geoffrey Robinson as the non-executive chairman.

Geoffrey Robinson was naturally serving his own interests. Two
companies owned by C&S, Apex and Dunn, were profitable
suppliers to the motor industry. If the Maxwells were ever willing
to sell, TransTec would be transformed by their ownership.
Inserting himself into Maxwell's empire was the best tactic to win
that prize. On 29 July 1987, Robinson was appointed a director
of C&S. The chairmanship of Hollis with extra responsibilities
would be a natural progression. Within Maxwell's empire, as
within Westminster, Robinson was an anonymous minnow whose
ambitions were limited by his ability, but he was ambitious. To
enhance his image, he invited Andrew Capitman, the American
banker arranging the finance for the Hollis sale, for lunch at the
House of Commons. Only one memory survived for the American:
'Just another smooth socialist MP acting the ruthless capitalist.'

On 23 May 1988, Hollis was sold to Colin Robinson and his
team for £118.5 million, more than it was worth. To increase the
appearance of his wealth and increase bank loans which he could
pocket, Maxwell had insisted that Hollis's value be inflated to use
the receipt of £56 million in cash from the sale to create Pergamon
AGB, a company specialising in market research. The formal
statement announcing the birth of Hollis Industries emphasised
that 'the buyout [is] led by Mr Geoffrey Robinson MP'.
Robinson's association with the Maxwells was his seedcorn for the
future.

The absentee MP's time was taken up with criss-crossing the
globe searching for contracts for TransTec. His fleeting visits to
Coventry left strange memories, especially for John Chalmers, a
Labour councillor employed at TransTec for fourteen years, who
was also the trade union's representative. Chalmers was annoyed
that Robinson failed to provide good conditions of work, but
Robinson rarely agreed to meet and negotiate improvements. On
one of the few occasions, he was a passenger with his wife in the
back of Robinson's car driving to a Labour Party function. The MP
laughed when his passenger mistakenly assumed that the woman

in the front was Mrs Robinson. The politician, Chalmers realised, was 'a ladies' man', who did not conceal his affairs. 'He was always seen with a different female,' recalls Diana Leslie, a local Conservative activist. 'I've seen his wife in a photograph and I was surprised it was her.' No one could understand the nature of Robinson's relationship with Marie Elena. Despite her threats of divorce and his complaints to fellow MPs of an unhappy marriage, they occasionally lived under the same roof, possibly in the interests of their money, their children or sheer convenience. Since Robinson was an unknown politician, his private conduct attracted no interest, allowing him freely to enjoy an eccentric lifestyle.

Only one woman could be sure of undivided attention: Joska Bourgeois. Daily, regardless of the time, he received telephone calls from the divorcee to discuss investment opportunities mentioned in the *Wall Street Journal*, her concerns about completing an official document, her anger about a leaking tap in the kitchen of one of her three homes, or her demand for his attendance during one of the regular visits by insurance assessors to revalue her furniture.

Even if he was in the middle of a world-wide journey, Robinson responded to the command 'Come immediately' from Bourgeois. 'I have to see him,' Bourgeois told John Morgan, who had retired from Jaguar and now lived in Monte Carlo. Morgan was baffled by Bourgeois's businesses and admired Robinson's obedience. Summoned one afternoon from New York, he flew direct to Nice. At the airport, in the minutes before his arrival, Bourgeois rushed around clucking to Morgan, 'Poor Geoffrey, he'll have no clothes.' Obeying without question, Robinson had rushed to Kennedy airport without a bag. With Morgan in tow, Bourgeois scooped up Yves St Laurent clothes and toiletries for Robinson's brief stay. Twelve hours later, Robinson had departed, content that Bourgeois's loyalty and financial support for TransTec were secure. Inevitably, there was another chore he was asked to undertake.

Robinson had agreed to meet Bourgeois and Saad Boudamagh, her Algerian boyfriend, a few days later in Paris with Sami Ahmed. She was waiting for the two visitors from England in her favourite restaurant near the Champs Elysées. Over dinner it was agreed that Ahmed would travel with Saad to Algeria to supervise Bourgeois's investment of £500,000 in a sweet factory which she had given to her lover. Just as she financed Robinson, she also cared for Saad, but she was concerned that he would waste her money on the wrong equipment. With that business settled, the two returned to Britain.

Reassurance from Joska Bourgeois was vital for a man whose company's finances were gyrating and whose relationships appeared to be unstable. After the visit to the Coleshill industrial unit by Neil Logue, the auditor employed by Coopers & Lybrand, the company declared that in 1990 TransTec had enjoyed a £6.9 million turnover and earned pre-tax profits of £304,426. Soon afterwards, Logue was appointed TransTec's financial director. Logue's audit had not commented on one sensitive issue: TransTec had failed to pay the full amount of the company's contributions to Equitable Life for the employees' pensions.

A dispute had also arisen between Robinson and Professor McGeough about the division of the £380,000 DTI grant, which threatened to become a battle in the court between Robinson and Edinburgh University. 'Don't pass any information to Joe McGeough,' Robinson ordered Peter Dickinson. 'Forget he exists.' At the end of December 1988, the DTI paid the last instalment of the grant. Six weeks later, on 11 February 1989, Robinson fired the professor; his usefulness had expired. He later claimed to be owed £25,000.

Another dispute between Robinson and el-Menshawy had also arisen. After leaving TransTec in October 1986, el-Menshawy had established his own company, Spark Tec, offering substantial improvements on the designs he had completed for Robinson. Their competition to supply texturing machines to British Steel in Shotton ended in victory for el-Menshawy, which Robinson appeared unwilling to tolerate. Their paths crossed again in 1989. Robinson bought Sarclad, a machine manufacturer on the verge of bankruptcy, with over one thousand employees. By coincidence, el-Menshawy was engaged in a ferocious court battle, alleging that Sarclad was using his patents without permission. Kumar Bhattacharyya supported the inventor but refused to testify, especially after Geoffrey Robinson bought the defending company, because he remained fearful of antagonising the MP. Robinson won the court case. For the Egyptian, it was the ultimate humiliation. At each stage, he had been outwitted by Robinson, and he was now practically bankrupt.

El-Menshawy's only consolation was that Robinson's much-lauded contract with the Modern Hard Chrome Corporation of Chicago for an EDM/ECM to produce turbine blades had soured. The Americans had sued Robinson for delivering faulty machines and won a court judgment for new machines and $400,000 compensation for loss of production.

In London, Robert and Kevin Maxwell were unaware of Robinson's shortcomings, while Robinson was similarly unaware that Hollis was sliding into chaos. Nine months after the management buyout, Kevin Maxwell and Hollis's finance director, Michael Stoney, formed the opinion that Colin Robinson, the chief executive, was woefully inadequate. The original plan had been to sell six companies to reduce the debt and form a 'core business' of three companies, but Colin Robinson had master-minded some sales and contracts which had devastated Hollis's finances. Six companies valued nine months earlier at about £80 million had been sold by Colin Robinson for £23 million. Neither the Maxwells nor Geoffrey Robinson, their expert and the company's chairman, had monitored the mismanagement. 'It's a disaster,' pronounced Andrew Capitman, the banker.

Hollis's demise struck at a moment of vulnerability. The Maxwells were juggling a huge mountain of debt while the tycoon himself, constantly dictating a blitz of multimillion pound acquisitions across the globe and seeking to influence the world's political leaders, could barely spare a few minutes to resolve the misadventure at Hollis. Pursuing Colin Robinson would raise questions about the Maxwell empire's stability. No action, he decided, would be taken against the chief executive. 'I've got bigger fish,' Maxwell said to Kevin, nevertheless furious that

Geoffrey Robinson had not supervised his namesake.

Kevin turned to the future: 'Hollis is a waste of time. We've got to save the whole operation. Let's get out of engineering.' His solution was simple: 'Let Hollis go bust.'

'No,' declared the imperial voice with curt dismissal. 'Whatever it costs, buy it all back. My reputation with banks is at stake. I cannot upset the banks.'

'That'll be a nightmare,' sighed Kevin, anticipating the negotiation of loans with twelve banks and teams of lawyers for the resumption of ownership.

Obeying his father, on 23 January 1990, Kevin Maxwell repurchased Hollis and all its debts for a nominal £1, organised the resignation of Colin Robinson and six other directors and incorporated Hollis as a subsidiary of the Pergamon Group. During that process, Robert Maxwell had summoned Geoffrey Robinson to his office in the Mirror building. Minions irritated Maxwell but Robinson possessed three assets. He was a Labour MP, and the party's prospects in the election due by 1992 were good; Robinson knew more about engineering than either of the Maxwells; and Robinson was an intelligent companion for hunting commercial opportunities. He was also, in that era, one of an unusual breed: a driven man, constantly moving from one meeting to the next with no small talk, except constant chatter into his portable dictaphone and his mobile telephone. Robinson, Maxwell calculated, could be trusted to serve the Maxwells' interests loyally and save the remainder of Hollis.

Michael Stoney and Kevin disagreed. Stoney found Robinson a bumbler who understood little about engineering, disliked detail and was vague about finance and accounts. That opinion was confirmed by Alan Swann, Hollis's technical director, who was irritated by Robinson's lack of technical knowledge. Robinson's hyperactivity, they agreed, was a performance concealing ineptitude. Kevin simply suspected that Robinson's interests were not altruistic and there was little to show for his management expertise, but he accepted that Robinson and his father would form an alliance from which he was excluded. Robinson, he assumed, would be given 'operational responsibility' for Hollis.

Before meeting Maxwell, Robinson briefly considered resigning and disappearing but, on balance, concluded that the Maxwells' disaster might be his golden opportunity. Despite the bad publicity that Maxwell had recently attracted about his indebted empire, Robinson perceived value in staying close to the *Mirror*'s proprietor. His strength when they met was to offer a solution. 'What is the publisher of the *Daily Mirror*,' he asked, 'doing in the engineering business?' There was no sane answer, Maxwell acknowledged. 'Let me sort it out for you,' offered Robinson. Maxwell accepted that proposition, ignoring Kevin's protests.

During the first six months of 1990, Robinson worked hard, visiting most of Maxwell's manufacturing plants. Three companies particularly interested him: Lock, a manufacturer of metal-detection equipment for the food industry; Petroleum Seals and Systems Ltd (PSS), a manufacturer of weighing machines and rubber seals; and Dunn, which moulded aluminium parts for the motor industry. There was every reason for Robinson to accurately highlight the deficiencies of his inheritance. 'The management of Lock by Colin Robinson and his cronies,' he wrote to the Maxwells on 24 July 1990, 'should serve as a text-book exercise for business schools on how to ruin a company. It is impossible for me to think of anything the CSR [Colin Robinson] management did that was right. This is unique in my industrial experience.' He sought to blame the 'incompetent' directors who had been 'sacked'. His solution was to reduce employees from 182 to 95; close sales offices and rectify the 'non-existent' control of costs. The companies were prepared for his ownership. TransTec, which was still floundering, would be saved by incorporating Hollis's jewels.

As the management of Hollis and C&S consumed more time, Robinson reconsidered his original stipulation of working without payment. In his meetings with Robert Maxwell, he began requesting a one-off fee. On 29 May 1990, he had written to Stoney suggesting that 'on reflection' an annual salary of £200,000 'is fair'. After the summer holidays, Robinson began complaining, first to Michael Stoney and then to Kevin Maxwell: 'I haven't been paid.' Occasionally, Robert Maxwell agreed to the demand but later ordered Stoney to withhold the payment. At 5.30 p.m. on 7 September 1990, faced in his office by Robinson renewing his demands, Robert Maxwell agreed to a fee of £150,000 for rescuing and successfully managing A. L. Dunn and Coventry Apex, two engineering companies. The money would be paid by C&S, the owner of the companies. Robinson registered that payment under 'members' interests' in the House of Commons in January 1991 but it missed the printer's deadline to appear in the official record. Curiously, Michael Stoney recalled making the payment in December 1990.

Shortly after agreeing that payment with Robert Maxwell in September 1990, Robinson approached Stoney and Kevin asking for an additional fee for his work at Hollis. 'I want £200,000,' he told them. All three realised that Robert Maxwell would protest but Kevin agreed that Robinson should submit an invoice. Dated 24 October 1990, Robinson's invoice to Hollis was submitted on the letterhead of Orchards, his home near Godalming, Surrey. He asked that the cheque should be made payable to TransTec. By any measure, issuing a TransTec invoice on the notepaper of his home was peculiar. Robinson blamed that incongruity on a secretary who used the 'wrong notepaper' but since he himself presented the invoice to Stoney, he had ample opportunity to obtain a properly headed invoice. The notepaper was the first of many oddities about that payment.

The following day, Michael Stoney scribbled 'Approved' on Robinson's invoice. No cheque was issued and Robinson complained. 'I want £200,000,' Robinson said alternately to Kevin and his father. 'OK, we'll pay you,' said Robert Maxwell, but after Robinson left his office Maxwell ignored his promise. 'I'm not paying him,' Maxwell said to Stoney, blaming Robinson for Hollis's failure, but also wanting to protect his dwindling supply of money.

Over the following four weeks, both Maxwells were engrossed in the beginning of their battle for survival. Pension-fund shares were being used to raise loans and the money was being misappropriated for private use. Every five minutes, Kevin was lying to bankers, lawyers and accountants to conceal the developing insolvency of the Maxwell empire, still valued by the benign at £2.1 billion. Geoffrey Robinson's was one of many demands for payment which the Maxwells delayed. But they accepted that Robinson's demands, unlike others, could not be resisted.

On 16 November 1990, Stoney sent an internal memorandum stating that a £200,000 payment to Robinson for 'management fees' should be included in Hollis's 1990 accounts. Ten days later, on 26 November 1990, Stoney sent another memorandum to Kevin: 'I understand from Geoffrey Robinson that at a recent meeting with him you agreed that Hollis Industries would pay Geoffrey a fee for management services of £200k. I enclose herewith a copy of his invoice and would be grateful if you could approve this. Geoffrey has chased me a couple of times on this matter.' In haste, Kevin scribbled on the memorandum, 'B/F RM for approval.' Translated, it was an instruction to Stoney to 'Bring forward to Robert Maxwell for approval.' At 5 p.m. on 13 December 1990, Geoffrey Robinson entered Maxwell's office. He demanded payment of £200,000. Robert Maxwell at last relented.

Soon afterwards, Stoney and Robinson met at the Charterhouse bank. Stoney noted Robinson's banking details for the cheque. Robinson now wanted the cheque payable not to TransTec but to another payee. Subsequently, Robinson telephoned Shirley Caddock, Stoney's secretary, and asked that the cheque be made payable to a company which he named. In neat handwriting, Caddock wrote on Robinson's invoice that the cheque was to be paid to Robinson 'personally', without VAT since he was not registered. That change was a possible explanation for Robinson originally submitting an invoice on Orchards notepaper.

On 21 December 1990, a cheque drawn on Pergamon AGB for £200,000, was cashed. Stoney wrote 'Paid' on Robinson's invoice and noted that the money, while paid by 'PAGB', should be 'recharged to H. Industries', namely Hollis. In PAGB's cash book, the payment was entered under the name 'Orchards'. The

£200,000 fee to Robinson was entered in Hollis's final accounts, completed by the auditors, which Robinson eventually signed. Two hundred thousand pounds had been transferred to Geoffrey Robinson. Eight years later, Robinson was to deny in Westminster requesting or receiving that payment.

The Hollis accounts for the eighteen-month period between January 1989 and June 1990 were completed in early January 1991 and revealed chaos. The auditors, Coopers & Lybrand, included a dividend payment of £1.2 million in June 1989 by Hollis to Pergamon AGB, Maxwell's company. Robinson, the chairman, approved that payment although Hollis appeared to be technically insolvent. The company had only survived after Maxwell explained that the Headington Group, his holding company, was providing £6 million financial help to Hollis. In January 1991, Headington was itself technically insolvent. Hollis's payment of £1.2 million was window-dressing from 'money' which had been juggled around the Maxwell empire. During Geoffrey Robinson's chairmanship, the company had become a catastrophe. Hollis's accumulated losses were £71.6 million; the company, which had originally been worth £155 million, was valued at minus £26 million and even those figures were estimates. Proper accounting records, including those of the pension fund, were missing. The auditors were denied the necessary information and explanations to complete their task. The unsubstantiated support by Headington was one of many reasons why Coopers & Lybrand qualified their annual audit, recording, 'we are unable to form an opinion whether the profit and loss account . . . give a true and fair view'.

Without evident protest, as the company chairman, Geoffrey Robinson signed those accounts. Either he signed in ignorance or he was aware of Maxwell's plight and avoided any diligent verification of the company's finances. Both explanations served Maxwell's interests but exposed Robinson to an accusation of culpability and close association with a tycoon lying to save his empire. Robinson knew that Hollis's finances were precarious, yet he approved accounts which allocated a £200,000 payment to himself and a further £1.6 million in other directors' fees.

In normal circumstances, Geoffrey Robinson would have been embarrassed. Hollis could be added to his association with previous business troubles at Innocenti, Jaguar, Meriden and TransTec, although he later piously asserted that his chairmanship required nothing more than his appearance at the infrequent board meetings and, subsequently, his attempts to save the company. But by then Robinson's financial affairs were, especially for a Labour politician, stigmatised by unorthodoxy.

In 1988, Robinson's two brothers had agreed a plan to minimise taxation on the sale of Crafthour, the family furniture business founded by their father. In 1988, Crafthour was dissolved and the surplus value worth £7 million was transferred to Latchuser Ltd, a company with 38,000 shares owned by five Robinson family trusts based in Bermuda. In 1990, Latchuser was revalued and declared to be worth £12 million. The company's property portfolio had been revalued and the extra profit was safely stored in Bermuda, beyond the grasp of the British Inland Revenue. Consequently, about £3 million in potential taxes had been avoided. Robinson denied any personal interest in the family trusts and the tax-avoidance scheme, since his shares in Latchuser were owned by himself in Britain. In public, his opinion of tax avoidance was caustic. During 1988, he had vociferously condemned a legitimate tax-avoidance scheme favoured by many media stars investing in forestry, demanded a 'crackdown on loopholes', and urged the chancellor to 'use his budget to close down these major tax dodges which do nothing for the efficiency of our economy'. In a particularly incensed interview Robinson damned 'tax avoidance by the rich, which has become a big industry'. His own family's efforts to minimise taxation avoided his criticism.

In April 1991, on the last day of the tax year, and just before the government restricted the benefits of offshore tax havens for British residents, Robinson sold his 2445 shares in Latchuser, worth £380,000, to the International Trust Company in Bermuda. He later said he had sold his shares to his brothers Noel and Peter for £262,523 and, at their suggestion, the sale was to the off-shore family trusts. Geoffrey Robinson indignantly denied the damaging allegation that he was transferring money offshore. There was no evidence of his interest in the Bermudan trusts, but the transfer of the family's fortune to Bermuda was consistent with his own banking arrangements in Switzerland, another tax haven, during his management of Innocenti, but Latchuser's books were never opened to explain Robinson's innocence.

Latchuser's history thereafter became incomprehensible. In 1991, the company's fortunes rapidly declined. By 1993, it had lost £4.3 million, and by 1997 it was worth only £2.5 million. The loss of £10 million either was planned or else suggested that Robinson's brothers were, like their famous sibling, unsuccessful businessmen. Haplessness as an explanation seems unlikely. Robinson's brothers developed LeatherTrend, a successful manufacturer of furniture in San Diego using Mexican labour, and lived in great style.

Robinson's unconventional attitude towards financial laws also affected his employees in Coleshill. In December 1990, Diane Shaw, his longest-serving and most loyal employee, had noticed on her pay slip that TransTec had failed to pay her pension contributions over the previous three years. Her inquiries were rebuffed by Robinson's spokesman who blamed Equitable Life, the insurance company. That excuse collapsed after Equitable Life revealed Robinson's failure to pay the required amount. The deception was remarkable and was compounded by Robinson's behaviour. After paying £30,000 to the insurance company to complete the company's pension contributions, Robinson declared Shaw redundant on grounds of 'restructuring'. Her abrupt dismissal after ten years' service provoked a bitter eleven-month battle for compensation. On the eve of the tribunal hearing, Robinson agreed to pay Shaw £13,000, a substantial amount in 1991.

The payment avoided an embarrassment for the Labour MP, although his political profile had practically disappeared. During 1988 and 1989, he never spoke in the Commons or participated in any political activity. His appearances at Westminster were so rare that most MPs forgot his face, while the few who recognised the Coventry North West MP commented on his increasing girth. Robinson's constituents heard even less from their Surrey-based representative. One of the few clues of his continued existence was the news in spring 1991 that his shotgun had been accidentally fired, wounding the foot of Alexander, his twelve-year-old son. Consistent with Robinson's disregard for rules, he did not possess a shotgun licence. His embarrassment was compounded by the visit of a neighbour bringing flowers to commiserate over his son's injury. Guy Gammell, aged sixty-four, was attacked by the Robinsons' two Great Danes. 'All I could feel was teeth tearing into my flesh,' moaned Gammell, displaying his injured arm, chest and neck. 'The beasts came at me like bullets. I was covered in blood from head to toe.' Robinson was in Guildford hospital visiting his son when his wife delivered Gammell to the same hospital's casualty department. Strangely, Geoffrey Robinson denied liability and his neighbour threatened to sue to recover lost income after four days in hospital.

Money was Robinson's palliative for resentments. His generosity had lubricated his relationships in his constituency and there was no reason to doubt its efficacy in Westminster. He donated about £200,000 to the Political Economy Unit managed by John Smith, the shadow chancellor, for tax research, investigating how traditional Labour could penalise the rich. The obvious contradictions do not appear to have concerned Robinson. Nor did his absence completely dull his political antennae. During his regular conversations with Kevin Maxwell, he mentioned that Gordon Brown and Tony Blair were Labour's rising hopes, praising Gordon Brown's policies to control capitalism and Tony Blair's political moderation. But those were casual asides by a man preoccupied with his personal wealth.

During early 1991, the recession of Britain's economy compounded Robert Maxwell's financial plight. Land prices were collapsing and he abandoned a plan involving Robinson to pool and exploit all his property in Britain through C&S. His engineering factories were another liability.

'Let Hollis go bankrupt,' Kevin again repeated.

'No,' replied Maxwell angrily.

'Geoffrey keeps saying he wants to buy the engineering factories,' countered Kevin. 'Why not accept Geoffrey's offer? It'll get rid of a problem.'

His father paused. 'All right. Get him up here. We'll see what Mr Robinson has to say.'

Robinson was summoned to Robert Maxwell's office. Maxwell was sick and suffering delusions. Darting around the world at a frenetic pace, he was brokering the fate of Soviet Jews between the leaders of Russia and Israel, negotiating to sell supplies of Soviet human blood to the West, and reporting his political observations to the British prime minister, the German chancellor and the presidents of France and America. In between, he was struggling to reassure irate bankers that his massive debts would be repaid, while instructing Kevin both to lie and to misappropriate more shares belonging to public companies and the pension funds. In his frenzy of telephone calls and meetings across the globe, Geoffrey Robinson, a maverick backbencher, remained classified as a reliable ally.

Other directors on the same boards of Maxwell's companies as Robinson observed his attraction to the tycoon. 'Geoffrey is fly,' quipped Richard Baker, the finance director of Maxwell Communications Corporation, in the corridor. Other gossips were harsher after seeing the cosiness of his relationship with Maxwell. He had proved to be a businessman prepared to cut corners and resist the rigorous diligence that others might apply to a company's accounts. 'He's not absolutely straightforward,' said a fellow Labour politician and director of other Maxwell companies.

Those qualities appealed to Maxwell. During one of his flying visits to Israel, he dispatched a helicopter to bring Gwyn Morgan, formerly a Transport House official but who had now risen to become a senior official for the European Union, to his hotel in Jerusalem. Maxwell hoped to hire Morgan for his new newspaper, the *European*. Maxwell's pitch struck Morgan as ill-considered: 'You should join us because Geoffrey Robinson is working close to me. He's the sort of man to follow.' Morgan could only recall how he had despised Robinson in Transport House twenty-five years earlier and he had not changed his opinion. 'What qualities does Robinson have?' he asked. 'He's sharp financially and delivers deals,' replied Maxwell. Money, Morgan concluded, cemented the relationship between the two men.

Robinson could not disagree with that judgement. His proximity to the proprietor of the Mirror Group was as financially invaluable as politically instructive. Maxwell's easy access to Neil Kinnock and Roy Hattersley, the leaders of the Labour Party, and their gratitude for his financial contributions, reminded Robinson how many other Labour politicians and former party officials were still linked to the tycoon, as employees and directors of his companies. There was good reason to emulate Maxwell by also contributing money to Kinnock's office, paying for Labour Party opinion polls. But, more than others, Robinson also wanted to replicate Maxwell's fortune and the wide span of his activities.

During his months managing the rump of Maxwell's engineering companies – Lock, PSS and Dunn – Robinson appreciated their significance to himself and their meaninglessness to Maxwell. TransTec was again languishing. Under the Conservative government, wasteful grants were no longer available and finding finance had become difficult. In the truncated accounts for 1991, his company's turnover had collapsed and its profits had turned into a £1 million loss. His relationship with Maxwell offered salvation.

His goal was to organise TransTec's takeover of Hollis's three profitable companies. Once that was achieved, he could at last become a player in the City. The offer to Maxwell, he calculated, would be enticing. Maxwell would be rid of engineering and would receive more money than he anticipated.

Robinson's scheme was to become the major shareholder of Central & Sheerwood (C&S), which at that time was a publicly quoted company owned principally by Robert Maxwell. Under Robinson's proposal, first, C&S would buy Lock and PSS from Hollis to add to its ownership of Dunn; second, C&S would buy TransTec from Robinson; finally, Central & Sheerwood would be renamed TransTec plc and the shareholding would be readjusted to give Robinson control. Robert Maxwell would own 27 per cent of the new TransTec, while Robinson would own 28 per cent of the shares in the company. In that scheme, Robinson avoided the expense and hazards of a formal flotation to convert TransTec into a public company and overnight he would become the major shareholder in TransTec, a public company with a turnover of £38 million, with the possibility of raising money from other shareholders.

Although Maxwell enjoyed a reputation as a hard dealer, who by nature would never do a favour in business for anyone, among the sharpest dealers in London he was by then known as a sucker with expensive self-delusions, especially that he could dominate the stock market. During 1991, bankers Goldman Sachs were earning £400 million in profits from Maxwell. The bank was buying, at Maxwell's request, shares in Maxwell Communications and selling, on their own account, the same shares short, driving the price down, to earn twice on the deal. Unaware of his folly, Maxwell clung to the assumption that he remained king of the market rather than a player past his prime. Among the several beneficiaries of Maxwell's follies was Geoffrey Robinson. Maxwell did not resent granting the Labour MP an opportunity. The proposed deal solved a problem and if Robinson succeeded Maxwell would also rescue some money. However, since the prospectus admitted that they were acting in concert, they were open to the charge of profiteering against the interests of the other shareholders.

Between 1988 and 1991, Lock and PSS, the two companies Central & Sheerwood was buying to include in the new TransTec, had been valued in the accounts at £38.4 million. The transactions before their ownership passed to Robinson dramatically reduced that value. On 23 April 1991, Hollis, the original owner of Lock and PSS, sold them to Headington Investments, a Maxwell company, for £2.974 million. On the same day, Headington resold the same two companies to C&S for £4.053 million. Headington had kept £1.153 million of PSS's cash. That stark variation in price – over £1 million – was as inexplicable as Hollis's loss of its only valuable assets, which were worth £38.4 million. To compound the loss to Hollis's shareholders, Hollis was still responsible for Lock and PSS's debts, which were worth £2.946 million. In effect, Maxwell and Robinson had taken Hollis's assets for their own benefit within the new TransTec at the expense of Hollis, which had no money to pay either creditors or, subsequently, the pensions of its former employees.

The endgame during those days in April 1991 was C&S's purchase of TransTec for £6.25 million, of which £1 million was in cash. Even that transaction aroused doubts. C&S's shareholders, the public, were misinformed by Maxwell about the value of TransTec. The company, they were told, was worth £6 million but Maxwell's prospectus did not mention an £800,000 inter-company debt owed to TransTec by Roll Center, an unprofitable company which Robinson partly owned in Indiana. Robinson was to excuse himself by blaming an oversight but similar mistakes appeared to recur. The independent shareholders were aggrieved that Maxwell, Robinson and the institutions were allowed to buy shares at 3 pence while the stock market price was 4½ pence. No member of the public could buy shares at the lower price. Maxwell and Robinson, it appeared to their critics, were profiting at the public's expense.

The financial benefit to Maxwell, Robinson and the public shareholders was soon apparent. In June 1991, TransTec's shares rose within one week from 4½ pence to 25 pence. That sharp increase suggested that Lock and PSS were worth between £20 million and £40 million, rather than £2.9 million paid by Robinson. Quietly, Maxwell took his profit. Without Robinson's knowledge, he sold his 27 per cent stake for £8.24 million. Laing & Cruickshank, the brokers, bought the shares from Maxwell before lunch and resold them in the afternoon, earning over £400,000 profit. Many earned profits from the disintegration of the Maxwell empire.

In summer 1991, Robinson was hugely satisfied. His new company had become a specialist engineering group with 1900 employees, serving the international motor, aerospace, oil, food and pharmaceutical industries. Shareholders were reassured that Westminster would not interfere with Robinson's management duties. 'Save for the time necessary to fulfil his obligations as an MP,' they were told, 'Mr Robinson will devote substantially the whole of his time to the affairs of C&S.'

In the aftermath, Kevin Maxwell and Michael Stoney were nevertheless surprised by Robinson's reaction. 'I'm not happy,' Robinson complained. 'I haven't got enough.' He wanted more. 'Geoffrey Robinson's got a bargain,' snapped Kevin. 'For a bargain-basement amount.'

4

FULFILMENT

The aftermath of Robert Maxwell's unexpected death on 5 November 1991 endangered Robinson's ambitions. As the frauds were revealed, the legacy from his collaboration with Maxwell during the previous four years was potentially devastating.

On 9 December 1991, soon after the Maxwell empire was declared to be bankrupt, policemen attached to the Serious Fraud Office entered Kevin Maxwell's offices in Holborn. The chief executive was feeding papers into a shredding-machine. 'Please stop that,' said one officer. Kevin ignored the request. 'Please stop that,' repeated the officer glancing at sacks of papers on the floor marked 'shred'. Kevin continued feeding the documents into the whirring machine. After two more demands, the officer pulled the machine's plug from the socket. Kevin smiled. The cover-up was not complete but Kevin's attitude was, he would proudly maintain, 'robust'.

The roll-call of those who had accepted Maxwell's hospitality and employment embarrassed many famous personalities but Geoffrey Robinson's name rarely featured on any list. None who had loyally served the Maxwell family needed to fear incrimination by Kevin. Robinson's added good fortune was Robert Maxwell's quiet sale of his TransTec shares, saving him from the threat of destabilisation. Robinson appeared to be rid of the 'Max factor' and blessed by the support of institutional shareholders in the City. The residue of the relationship was his directorships of two main Maxwell companies which were both bankrupt – Hollis had debts of £44.5 million and Pergamon AGB International's debts were £200 million – and his directorships of several property companies.

Robinson did not sever his links with Maxwell's associates. He remained a director of two property companies; he entertained Michael Stoney, the finance director unemployed since the collapse of Maxwell's empire, and his wife for lunch at the House of Commons; and he employed Ron Codrington, a company secretary for Maxwell who had signed the Hollis accounts, to perform the same duties for his own companies, which by then numbered nearly thirty. To all, Robinson appeared ebullient. His decision five years earlier to withdraw from the Commons and earn his fortune had proved lucrative. Subsequently, he said he was only on the 'periphery of Maxwell's businesses', which was accurate; but Maxwell had been at the heart of Robinson's business and, unlike others, Robinson had emerged as a winner.

The proof was Robinson's sale, soon after Maxwell's death, of 350,000 TransTec shares for £1 million. The ease of that transaction confirmed that his company was not contaminated by any Maxwell connection. The sale also confirmed that his fortune, including his remaining TransTec shares, thanks to Maxwell, had increased by £30 million.

Flush with money for the first time, Robinson spoke in Maxwellian echoes about transforming TransTec into 'a company of European scale' with sales of £500 million and annual profits of £50 million. Spouting vocabulary which connoisseurs instantly recognised, he optimistically touted the company's dash for growth: 'Our profits were £1 million in 1988, they'll be £9.5 million in 1992 and £13 million next year.' Characteristically, he ignored the fact that Maxwell's downfall had been precipitated by a reckless bid for expansion at any price. He revelled in the image of a millionaire politician, working from mobile headquarters, winning the plaudits of unsceptical journalists, who described Robinson as the leader of a 'highly successful company': 'I live in my Jag with three telephones – one for myself, one for the driver and one for Neil Logue, the finance director.' Seducing those who could further his ambitions made him an attractive partner, especially in the grim world of engineering and technology, where his generous character made him exceptionally interesting for those targeted in his buying spree partly financed by issuing new shares worth £1.26 million. The cost of that ambition soon manifested itself.

Within months, Robinson's businesses were afflicted by a shortage of cash. Unpaid suppliers refused to deliver parts. To survive, he arranged for Agie, the Swiss company, to order supplies which were diverted to TransTec. Now that he ran a public company, Robinson's business style was for the first time subject to scrutiny. No one called his attitude 'lazy' but to a handful of seasoned City observers his indifference to detail and his carelessness raised questions about his stability and sureness. Sceptics were puzzled by TransTec's new accounts. Robinson had paid £11 million for four new businesses, but their value was shown in the accounts as £6 million. Robinson's finances were unorthodox. The more curious wondered why Agie had for the fourth year registered losses. Looking through the records, the sceptics discovered that in the eight years since Robinson had become chairman, Agie had registered losses of £396,236 and profits of only £52,374. Yet Robinson had collected over £300,000 in salary. There were inconsistencies which, especially in the wake of Maxwell's collapse, were puzzling to a few. For the majority, Robinson's ebullience soothed suspicions into amusement about an eccentric.

Local journalists in Coventry noted that in the latest list of the twenty worst attenders in the Commons, Robinson ranked nineteenth, just one above Tony Blair. They reported with surprise Robinson's vocal support for stricter laws against drink-driving,

his support for a ban on handguns, and his acceptance of a
hospitality trip from the Philip Morris tobacco company although
he criticised smoking. All three gestures, contradicting his own
behaviour, suggested hypocrisy. And, despite his protestations
that he was not a Tory because 'I owe everything to Labour', he
lived like a tycoon. The fair-minded described Robinson as a
riddle; the more sceptical mentioned smokescreens. His behaviour
baffled many, especially before the general election in April 1992.

Paul Dale, a local journalist, and the editor of the *Coventry Evening
Telegraph* were anticipating a stimulating lunch after accepting
Robinson's invitation to meet at Lino's, Robinson's favourite
restaurant in Coventry. The MP was always delighted by the
warm, regal welcome from the Portuguese owners. 'My car will
pick you up and take you to Lino's,' insisted Robinson with a
characteristic flourish. 'I'll drive myself in my other car.' During
the journalists' journey, Robinson telephoned his chauffeur. 'I've
left TransTec for Lino's,' said the local MP, 'and I'm lost.' 'Where
are you?' he was asked. 'I don't know,' he replied. 'The sign says
"Birmingham".' 'But we're in Coventry,' he was told. One hour
later, after the journalists had consumed two expensive bottles of
wine, Robinson arrived. Their host had little to offer about
Coventry and memorably predicted that Neil Kinnock would win
the election. Robinson seemed to his guests disengaged not only
from politics but from reality.

The politician had protected himself from the latest threat of
deselection as the Labour candidate by nurturing loyalty among
the local party officials. His proffered kindnesses and bonhomie
cemented relationships with key party activists. The dissidents
were isolated and he was readopted to fight the April 1992
election. Robinson's anticipation of Labour's victory evaporated.
John Smith's promise of higher taxes and Neil Kinnock's
unappealing performance sapped Labour's advantage, although
Robinson retained his own seat with 51 per cent of the vote and a
convincing majority of 16,432. Once his political critics were
silenced, he successfully disarmed his detractors in the City. In

May 1992, TransTec raised £24 million in a rights issue to fund more acquisitions and his increasingly luxurious lifestyle.

His celebration was the purchase in July 1992 of Castello Mucchio, a small but potentially stunning ten-acre estate with a dilapidated three-storey neoclassical villa in San Gimignano, Tuscany, for £250,000. Located at the end of a long private drive through cypresses, oaks and pines, with its own church and cottages, the property's potential was enviable. Robinson's ownership was registered in a company, whose shares were divided between himself (19.8 million shares) and Véronique, his twenty-two-year-old daughter (200 shares). Those close to Joska Bourgeois insisted that the Belgian had provided some of the money.

The intensity of Robinson's relationship with Bourgeois had not altered. Now seventy-nine, she still telephoned daily for advice, and occasionally he flew to Geneva, showing some disdain for her continuing relationship with Saad Boudamagh, her Algerian companion, and her affection for Roland Urban. To them, Robinson appeared irritated by the possible access of anyone else to Bourgeois's wealth. Roland Urban, the amusing film stuntman, when he himself was summoned to Geneva, regularly accompanied Joska Bourgeois to her bank vault to view her collection of jewels. They were, she repeated, worth 'millions of dollars'. Before leaving the vault she invariably told Urban, 'I'll leave something for you when I go.' She regularly made such promises to everyone whose attention she desired.

Loneliness was her greatest fear and on New Year's Eve 1992, she insisted that the Urbans, John Morgan and the whole Robinson family should attend a dinner party in the roof restaurant of the Park Lane Hilton, London. The strained atmosphere was aggravated by Robinson's late arrival. At the end of a torrid evening, Robinson announced, 'I'll pay.' As usual, Joska Bourgeois slipped her credit card to her adopted son under the table. Robinson, those disgruntled by the 'awful meal' noticed, smiled.

The new year, 1993, promised glory. At fifty-four, Robinson

had good reason to believe that his pact with Maxwell had delivered his dream. TransTec's cash problems had been resolved and the share price rose from 160 pence in 1991 towards 545 pence in mid-1993. His company was valued at £104 million and that year's profits were projected to be £13 million. As a reward, Robinson arranged for his salary to be increased by 48 per cent to £396,000, part of a £600,000 income from TransTec, including pension contributions and dividends.

To the few who expressed curiosity about the champagne socialist profiting from Thatcherism, he curtly denied any debt to the scourge of Labour. Rather, he presented himself as 'a lone industrialist' offering his company as an example of why 'we need to make manufacturing the priority and to create the conditions in which it can thrive'. Citing his own achievements, he attacked British culture for failing to support technical innovation and industry. His triumph, he emphasised, was 'unique' in the House of Commons.

George Bartholomew, a physics graduate who had become a marketing director, certainly found the MP unusual. Bartholomew had been invited to lunch at the Commons to be interviewed for a job. Robinson spoke enthusiastically of his ambition to control a billion-pound hi-tech company and his need for qualified staff. 'How much do you want?' asked Robinson, staring obsessively at a young waitress in a particularly unEnglish and definitely politically incorrect manner. Bartholomew thought of his probable worth and recklessly added 10 per cent. 'Fine,' replied Robinson. Bartholomew was startled. His new employer, he realised, was a talented businessman but impulsive and complex. His unquantifiable instability, disguised by his charm, could be interpreted as recklessness. How else could his quick collapse into drunkenness in the box at Ascot later that summer be explained? Yet Bartholomew was grateful to Robinson for the opportunity to improve his career and create his personal fortune.

Towards the end of 1993, the halo of a 'highly successful company' began to slip. The sunshine and goodwill were souring. The projected profits of the company that year were no longer

£13 million but £7 million, substantially less than the previous year. In the City, analysts were questioning even that estimate, because TransTec was trading at a loss. The assets of the four companies which he had bought in 1992 for £11 million and revalued at £6 million had been revalued again to £2.6 million. That unusual but legal manoeuvre, justified by Robinson for 'tax reasons', had artificially boosted TransTec's profits but the accounts revealed other peculiarities. TransTec had bought Roll Center Inc., a privately owned company in Indiana, for $100,000, although Roll Center only existed because of a personal $1.5 million loan from Robinson and a guarantee for further loans of $2 million. Robinson appeared to have transferred to the shareholders of the public company the responsibility for repaying his personal loans owed to him by Rolls Center.

Inter-company deals between private and publicly owned companies had characterised Robert Maxwell's operation and the revived memories of Robinson's association with him reduced the City's confidence, already strained by TransTec's dismissal within one year of its auditor, stockbroker and PR adviser. For Scottish Amicable, an investment trust, TransTec's future had become too uncertain. The trust sold its 3 per cent stake. On 5 November 1993, the second anniversary of Maxwell's death, the company's shares fell to 83 pence and Robinson admitted that profits would be 'below market expectations'. Other City investors began pressing Robinson to appoint a professional, full-time chief executive.

At the Christmas party for his staff at Robinson's Surrey home, there was no sense of depression. Robinson's exuberance and hospitality guaranteed a fizzy atmosphere. The focus of attention was Joska Bourgeois, whom Robinson introduced to his grateful guests as 'the cleverest woman in the world'. Bourgeois was in Britain not only for Christmas but also to finalise her purchase for £630,000 of Marsh Court, a Lutyens house in Stockbridge, Hampshire, with forty-seven acres and a glorious view over the River Test. The building, converted into a school, was in appalling condition. Asbestos partitions divided the rooms and sheds were strewn across the overgrown gardens. Like all Belgians, who reputedly have 'a brick in their stomachs' symbolising their love of property, Joska Bourgeois anticipated the excitement of Marsh Court's renovation into a stunning residence with the twenty bedrooms, a huge ballroom, cottages, swimming-pool and stables. She could rely on Robinson to supervise the work and allowed him to pose as the house's owner. Soon after the purchase was completed in early February 1994, Robinson was asked why he had bought the house. After all, he owned a Lutyens house in Surrey and a second mansion seemed extravagant. 'This is a private matter,' he replied, 'and we want to keep it that way if you don't mind.' Thereafter, he was content to allow himself to be described as a collector of Lutyens houses, not least because the Grosvenor House Hotel was also designed by Lutyens. Eight months later, on 9 October 1994, Joska Bourgeois died in Cannes and he inherited Marsh Court.

Joska Bourgeois's death heralded for Robinson unprecedented wealth to finance his hedonistic lifestyle and buy himself influence. Thanks to her, he was the occupier of three more homes – the penthouse in Cannes, the Lutyens mansion in Hampshire and a rented flat at the Grosvenor House. The annual maintenance of five homes would cost at least £200,000 but his inheritance from Bourgeois would, if carefully managed, effortlessly finance that expense. His financial planning, however, depended upon discretion and subterfuge.

Joska Bourgeois had protected her wealth by crude tax evasion; she had simply transferred her wealth from Belgium to Switzerland and fled from her native country, permanently beyond the reach of the government. In her endless discussions with Robinson about the management of her money, including its fate after her death, she naturally speculated on how to prevent his inheritance being confiscated by the British Inland Revenue. Switzerland, with its discreet bankers and anonymous numbered accounts, would be a natural repository for Robinson's money, but its management would always expose him to accusations of hypocrisy and even illegality. Under British law, a British citizen is obliged to declare the deposit of foreign income in foreign bank accounts to the Inland Revenue. For a Labour politician, that potential exposure was too dangerous. Robinson also anticipated using the inheritance for his business activities in Britain. A secret bank deposit in Switzerland precluded that option.

The safe legal solution was an anonymous discretionary trust beyond the authority of the Inland Revenue in the Channel Islands. Under British law, it would be quite legal for Robinson and his family to receive income from the trust without paying any taxes if the trust was funded from abroad by someone not resident in Britain. The anonymous trustees were obliged only to declare that any money remitted to Robinson was income from the interest or dividends from shares, and not from the outright sale of an asset. Similarly, it would be quite legal for the trustees to use the money for Robinson's benefit without incurring the risk of taxation. Robinson, as Bourgeois's executor, decided that the destination of his inheritance was the Orion Trust in Guernsey. Having decided to transfer the money to the Channel Islands, he began directing the Swiss lawyers to liquidate her assets into cash. The process took eighteen months.

Although Robinson later insisted, 'I didn't have any say in how the bequest was arranged. That was arranged by the lady, the benefactress', he provided no evidence to support that assertion. His emphasis that the money 'did not go from here to there' – from England to the Channel Islands – avoided the issue.

A Treasury statement on 29 November 1997 stated that Orion was created by Joska Bourgeois. That statement was contradicted by Robinson. On 14 December 1997, he told the *Observer* that the trust had been established in 1996, about eighteen months after Joska Bourgeois's death, by her 'Swiss advisers'. A principal adviser and an executor of Bourgeois's estate was Robinson himself. The selection of Orion was peculiar for a woman with no connections in the Channel Islands.

The Orion Trust was managed by Richmond Corporate Services, who enjoyed a working relationship with Wilder Coe, Robinson's personal accountants. Richmond Corporate Services was associated with Alan Chick, a resident of Guernsey. RCS also acted for Orion Nominees, a company established in 1988 and managed by Chick. Although there was no known legal relationship between Orion Trust and Orion Nominees, Alan Chick was a common factor. In 1994, Chick was criticised by DTI inspectors for failing to co-operate during an inquiry into insider dealing shortly before a takeover bid for Consolidated Gold Fields, a South African mining company. The DTI inspectors reported that Orion Nominees, a British Virgin Island company, had bought the company's shares in September 1988, earning a tenfold profit. The BVI's regulations protected the identity of those breaking British laws.

Only one more bequest – concerning her jewellery – hindered the final settlement of Joska Bourgeois's fortune. She had bequeathed her jewels to the Pasteur Institute in Paris. To obtain the best price, they were included in a Christie's auction in Geneva in May 1995. But to the surprise of her friends, especially Roland Urban, who had seen the collection in the bank vault, and Véronique Urban, who had accompanied Bourgeois wearing her finest pieces to parties, the sale catalogue did not contain some of the most valuable items. Instead of raising $10 million, as anticipated by Bourgeois herself, the Institute received only 5 million French francs, about $750,000. Robinson later explained that much of Bourgeois's jewellery were copies or 'fake'. His explanation suggested that her behaviour had been bizarre: paying huge insurance premiums and bank charges, and engaging in the charade of inspecting her 'fake' jewels in a bank vault.

Geoffrey Robinson's huge inheritance and its dispersal were unknown in Britain in 1994. The anonymous politician whose name prompted the query 'Geoffrey Who?' was protected from embarrassing inquiries. Astutely, he had compartmentalised his affairs. Only two people, Brenda Price, his assistant, and Peter Davis, a solicitor, were privy to the secrets of his trusts and corporate activities. In the Commons register, he had belatedly declared his directorships of Agie and TransTec, but he had failed to register his directorships of the Maxwell companies and several minor companies. Some suspected deliberate secrecy, others excused him as careless of detail or inattentive to rules. Any explanation called into question his judgement as a member of parliament.

Robinson's political colleagues were unaware of his private and commercial life although he had, after the 1992 election, re-engaged in Westminster life. John Smith, the new party leader, understood the antagonism Labour had provoked among the middle classes and wealth-creators but was unsure of the solution. One remedy was to persuade Labour's traditional enemies that the party would be economically competent and not hostile to the private sector. His ambassador in 1994 was Geoffrey Robinson, with a seemingly ideal background to ameliorate the disaster of Labour's 1992 campaign in the City and industry. That endorsement coincided with the exposure of Robinson's weaknesses as an industrialist.

Deal-making delighted Robinson. After tough negotiations, he loved declaring, 'We'll buy that.' The previous year, he had bought a succession of companies involved in digital print, industrial lasers, metal-machining and metrology, but the tight management and attention to detail required to micro-manage expensive precision machinery and parts were not among Robinson's strengths. His strategy of creating a hi-tech conglomerate was faltering.

Robinson had been guilty of a sin of which he accused others. Although he was a popular employer, under his management the factories supplying the automobile industry with oil adapters, gearbox housings, exhaust chambers and mouldings had not invested in new machinery or buildings. Several of his dilapidated and dirty factories – especially the sheds in Coleshill, with their unlevel floors and faulty sewers – were producing ancient designs on old machines at uncompetitive prices. His expansion had been undermined by tough competition, a failure to invest and the end of the Cold War, which had reduced military spending. He planned to raise more money by issuing new shares to finance more purchases.

Robinson was oblivious of the criticism of his management. His credibility as a custodian of a publicly quoted company was not enhanced by the fall in eighteen months in TransTec's share price from 125 pence to 45 pence, a collapse of profits to £4 million in a recovering economy, while his salary was £396,000. Scrutiny of his accounts again revealed legitimate but unorthodox techniques which flattered profits and quoted optimistic values of unfinished projects. For ten years, Robinson had conducted his business uncriticised in the shadows. Objective judgement cast doubts on his commercial conduct. Ignominiously, he was compelled to abandon his plan to raise money for a second time by issuing more shares and formally warn shareholders that the company's losses would be £12.4 million. TransTec shares were described as a 'disaster stock' and City investors demanded Robinson's resignation as chief executive.

On 3 November 1994, Robinson resigned and became the company's non-executive chairman. To the list of Innocenti, Jaguar and Meriden, the debunked minority shareholder added TransTec as another blot on his record. To avoid public humiliation, he denied the truth. 'There's been no pressure from investors at all,' he said. 'I volunteered to split the roles.' He welcomed Richard Carr, a forty-three-year-old accountant, as his successor. Carr had just received a £10 million bonus from Tomkins, a conglomerate owned by Greg Hutchings, another extravagant deal-maker. Among Carr's questionable coups had been the purchase of the gunmakers Smith & Wesson, which prompted a fall in the price of Tomkins shares just before Carr's appointment to TransTec.

Like Robinson's, Carr's strategy was aggressive expansion. TransTec would manufacture high volumes at low prices for Ford, Rolls-Royce, Epson, Sony, Hotpoint, Hoover, Dyson and other customers in the motor and aerospace industries. Soon after Carr's appointment, Robinson bought 1.9 million shares, increasing his stake to 18.4 per cent. (His original 28 per cent stake had been reduced by sales and the 1992 rights issue.) His investment appeared shrewd. By 1995, TransTec's shares had risen to 98 pence. In one final bit of tidying up, Robinson resigned his directorship of Agie after two more years of combined losses of £164,257. The following year, 1995, and thereafter, Agie earned substantial profits, in surprising contrast to its financial accounts in the previous decade.

Robinson's commercial retreat was fortuitous. His intention in 1986 to earn his fortune had been fulfilled. Financially, there was no reason to prolong those neglectful years away from parliament and coincidentally, after eighteen forlorn years in the Commons, his political value had unexpectedly improved. John Smith had died in 1994 and Tony Blair, his successor, advocated the adoption of Thatcher's revolution.

The architects of New Labour, Tony Blair and Peter Mandelson, sought a partnership with business; and Gordon Brown, the shadow chancellor, while adhering to Labour's old tax-and-spend policies, echoed those sentiments. Labour's re-election, they agreed, depended upon abandoning socialist dogma and embracing the free market.

Unlike previous Labour leaders, the forty-one-year-old Blair, a lawyer by training, had never enjoyed friendly relations with businessmen, yet he harboured a natural deference to their skills. That cordiality carried a risk. Past Labour leaders had been mired by relationships with entrepreneurs. In particular, Harold Wilson had regularly entertained businessmen at Downing Street; some had later been declared bankrupt, had been imprisoned for fraud or had even committed suicide to avoid public shame. The history of the sleaze that plagued the last Labour government, unprecedented in post-war history, was unknown to Blair. During his rise to the party's leadership, he had never read authoritative books describing the unscrupulousness among Wilson's entourage. In his ignorance, Blair adopted no yardstick to gauge the honesty or motives of those dedicated to maximising their wealth while seeking a relationship with politicians. Nor was he more than dimly aware of the grievous record of most businessmen switching careers to politics. Even had he been more enlightened, Geoffrey Robinson would have been presented as the exception.

The champion of science and manufacturing had arrived after his re-introduction to Gordon Brown, offering the same services as he had provided to John Smith: as backroom ambassador, adviser and fixer.

Both Blair and Brown were isolated from the leaders of Britain's financial and commercial community. That handicap was compounded by the wealth-creators' ingrained suspicion of Labour. The party's constitution still demanded the nationalisation of Britain's major industries and the party still favoured high taxation. Gordon Brown sought credible ambassadors to carry the message that those policies would be abandoned.

In early 1995, Robinson presented himself as a success at Innocenti, the hero of Jaguar, the champion of Meriden and the ethical industrialist. He was 'the genius at business', offering the expertise and credibility to potential supporters which Blair and Brown required. His apparent commercial success was matched by political purity. Unlike others with nearly twenty years' membership of the Commons, Robinson, because of his disconnection from Labour's internecine wars, was uncontaminated. He could advantageously speak as a man with front-line political experience, popular among the party faithful in Coventry, and posing no threat to the younger leaders. Those leaders were even flattered by his approval. Top brass, it appeared, was patting the duo on the head as being competent and worthy of his financial support. 'In many ways,' Robinson said shortly afterwards, 'I was New Labour before anyone thought of it. I used to say to management and the unions that you cannot have rights without responsibilities.'

Robinson's re-entry into politics during 1995 was as unusual as his exit nine years earlier. Both were characterised by money. In 1986, he had departed to earn money, and on his return he offered money to compensate for those absent years. In particular to Gordon Brown.

There was much for Geoffrey Robinson to admire about Gordon Brown. The Scotsman possessed an original mind, was obsessed by politics and was committed to the metamorphosis of

Labour into a socialist party appealing to capitalists. In the 1994 leadership election, Robinson had supported the shadow chancellor, who one year later offered him the fulfilment of his thirty-year dream: to wield influence on the inside track. In the scheme of Robinson's life, his relationship with Brown followed an established pattern of self-advancement through an association with the wealthy or powerful; first Harold Wilson followed by Lord Stokes, Joska Bourgeois and Robert Maxwell. In varying degrees, Robinson attached himself to his heroes, but the bond to Brown became akin to that of a limpet.

Brown encouraged the increasingly emotional but rational relationship. The brooding Scotsman enjoyed Robinson's bonhomie, efficient practicality and his money. Brown had no independent source of income and was not generous. (When he married in 2000, he chose the cheapest wine for his reception, economy air fares across the Atlantic for his honeymoon and a low-cost hotel in America for his wedding night.) On that personal level, Robinson was invaluable. In the summer holidays before Brown's wedding, Robinson gleefully accepted Brown's invitation to join his holiday party in Cape Cod, generously paying many of Brown's personal bills. Money was the passport to fulfil his ambition of ministerial office.

Politically, Robinson's value to Brown was his commercial experience. Among the ranks of the parliamentary Labour Party, only the self-made millionaire industrialist could authoritatively approach personalities in the City and industry, naturally using the vocabulary and customs of the chief executives whom New Labour sought to attract. As he mastered his ambassadorial brief around London, Robinson flattered himself that, during the encounters between equals, he could persuade the sceptics to trust him and the rejuvenated party. Certainly there were good reasons to doubt Robinson's credentials as a tycoon meeting fellow chief executives on equal terms, but politeness and self-interest stifled awkward comment. The Labour Party's dominant lead in the opinion polls and the disarray in the Conservative government bestowed considerable authority on Brown's ambassador.

Robinson was excited that his appointment brought him into proximity to an untainted team of Labour evangelists. He especially admired Ed Balls, an outstanding twenty-six-year-old economist who was producing the comprehensive blueprint to implement Brown's strategy. Within a short period, Robinson grew to adore Balls, the type of son he never had and even the young man Robinson might have liked to have been. As their bond developed, Robinson began to ponder the chance of the ministerial office he had yearned for in 1976. The likelihood would increase if he offered a 'concrete proposal' born from an advantage over his younger patrons. Unlike the new generation, who barely understood the cause of Labour's fiascos in the 1960s and 1970s, Robinson had been an eyewitness of Labour's abject failure to deliver on optimistic promises. Thirty years later, he could draw from his experience. In preparing for government, he suggested, Brown should recruit London's best accountants and bankers to produce workable schemes to be presented to civil servants after the election for immediate implementation on behalf of a Labour government. Robinson volunteered to finance the research for new policies of taxation and private investment in the public services. That sensible idea cemented Robinson's relationship with Brown's Treasury group.

The first sign of Robinson's emergence as a serious politician was the praise he attracted in the *Observer* in October 1995. Michael Gillard, a scourge of financial chicanery, described Robinson as 'that extreme rarity, a successful businessman and Labour MP'. Even his salary of over £600,000 in 1994, commented Gillard, was beyond criticism because his earnings 'as the chairman of a public company' were 'transparent'. Robinson had won a convert, especially by his condemnation of MPs' excessive secrecy about their earnings outside parliament. 'What we earn while we are MPs,' Robinson said with a display of thumping sincerity, 'should be fully disclosed.' Gillard's praise of Robinson for that honesty assured the MP that his commercial history and secret income were safe from scrutiny. Even his association with Robert Maxwell was carefully obscured. The ambiguous MP had not been asked by the media to reflect on Maxwell's life in the days after his death; he had carefully omitted any mention of his Maxwell directorships in *Who's Who*; and had not registered his directorship and income from Hollis or Central & Sheerwood in the Commons. Neatly, he also side-stepped one potential embarrassment by withdrawing his undertaking to testify in Kevin Maxwell's favour at the criminal trial in autumn 1995.

The paradox was a well-kept secret. Gillard's praise and Robinson's research on Labour's behalf to increase taxation in Britain coincided with the beginning of Robinson's expansive spending spree using his tax-free money deposited in the Channel Islands trust. Like most self-made men, at the end of his commercial toil, Robinson sought the benefits of his fortune. He desired enjoyment and applause.

In November 1995, Robinson invited Bryan Richardson, the chairman of Coventry City football club, to lunch at the Grosvenor House. With money to spend, Robinson offered to lend the financially beleaguered premier division club £10 million in two halves to buy new players. The first £5 million would be interest-free for the first year, the equivalent of a gift of £500,000, and the remainder of the loan was available at low interest. The security for the money would be the players themselves, a risky venture.

Richardson was perplexed. 'I wonder what he wants?' he later asked Derek Higgs, a respected City banker who, like his father, had close connections to the club. 'He says that he wants to help.' Neither had ever seen Robinson at the club or ever heard him mention any interest in football. But both understood the reasons for his interest. The first flotations of football clubs on the stock market, propelled by the high fees paid by television companies for the transmission rights of matches, had excited potential investors. To Higgs, a banker whose activities at Warburg and the Prudential had introduced him to most of Britain's City players, Robinson was nevertheless a puzzle. The politician was risking £10 million in cash without any certainty of its return. Higgs might have recommended rejecting the offer if a respected City scion had not advised reassuringly: 'He's fantastic on a good day on the right subject.' The source of Robinson's money was assumed to be his profits from TransTec. In reality, the money was to be drawn from the Orion Trust. At the very outset, Higgs was not aware about the offshore trust.

'I stressed to him,' Robinson wrote subsequently about his conversation with Bryan Richardson, 'that the decision [to invest] would not be mine but the trustees of my family trust.' Robinson explained that he had discussed the investment with Orion's two trustees before meeting Richardson: 'One trustee hated football. The other was fortunately a long-standing Spurs fan.' That was a curious admission. Two years later he insisted that he knew the identity of only one trustee; the second, he said, was unknown to him. Contradictions were not uncommon in Robinson's explanations of his financial history.

Robinson was seriously spending his inheritance from Joska Bourgeois and, in his boastful manner, was unable to adhere to the fiction about his legal inability to determine the fate of the trust. At his behest, the trustees had risked £10 million to satisfy his wishes, although he later suggested that Orion was a family trust with seven other beneficiaries, all members of his family. If true, the trustees in Guernsey were also charged with caring for the interests of those seven, yet they were apparently acting in Robinson's sole interest.

The lifestyle of a football potentate suited Robinson. On Friday evenings, he was driven up from London to perform his duties as a Coventry MP, meeting constituents, according to local legend, in the back of his Jaguar. At midday on Saturday, he joined fifty others in Coventry City's directors' suite for a buffet lunch. By kick-off, Robinson had often lived up to his reputation for 'drinking like the tide'. During those afternoons, Robinson spoke energetically about the management of the team. An investment of £10 million, he assumed, gave him the power of influence. Despite his recent introduction to football, Robinson even claimed some sway in the removal of Ron Atkinson, the manager. If true, his leverage would be curtailed by Derek Higgs who would be sold sufficient shares to hold the balance of power. At the end of Saturday, the politician was driven to Surrey. 'I spend Sundays with my wife,' he was fond of saying. Marie Elena had not been seen in Coventry since her husband's first election victory, and for the MP to even spend one day a week with his wife was unusual.

Robinson's relationship with Bryan Richardson inspired another opportunity for investment. Nineteen per cent of Coventry City had been owned for nearly forty years by Derrick Robbins, a former chairman of the club. In the mid-1970s, Robbins had abandoned his wife and settled with his secretary in South Africa. Few at the football club lamented his departure, especially Bryan Richardson. A feud between the two had thwarted an attempt by Richardson to buy Robbins's shares. Always pleased to help, Geoffrey Robinson proposed to resolve the problem by offering to purchase the shares.

With his customary amiability, Robinson telephoned Robbins and presented himself as an independent agent who also disliked Richardson. 'The shares,' he told Robbins, 'are for myself.' To confirm his offer he used House of Commons notepaper, clearly breaching parliamentary rules forbidding the use of the House for private business. But, as intended, the letter on crisp, cream Commons notepaper reassured the exile of the sender's sincerity. On that basis, Robbins agreed to the sale of 10,619 shares for £350,000. After Robinson's stratagem over his illwill towards Richardson was exposed, Robbins's protest was brushed aside. 'I do not feel bad about the way the purchase was transacted,' wrote Geoffrey Robinson. 'No one seemed to bother much.' His avuncular tone concealed a harsh contempt towards those worsted in any professional relationship.

The normal arrangement for the transaction would have been for a British-registered company, using funds in a British bank, to purchase the shares. But Robinson chose a scheme to avoid future tax liabilities. He decided to 'ask' Orion's trustees to invest more money in Coventry City. They agreed. The lawful deal was executed by Alan Chick, the merchant banker who managed

Richmond Corporate Services in Guernsey. He and Robinson agreed to purchase the shares through Craigavon Ltd, a company owned by the Orion Trust. Craigavon was registered in the British Virgin Isles, where the law did not require shareholders to reveal their identity. In the local Coventry newspaper, Robinson spoke like a man who had decided to invest his own money: 'The money will be invested in the club. None of it will be taken out,' he announced. With emphasis on himself, he added later, 'I have never sought to make any money out of support for my local team.' In the newspaper reports and his own letters about the purchase, he said and wrote that 'my role has been as an investor'. The involvement of the family trust was concealed. Although Robinson later said, 'I seem to remember it being referred to in the newspapers', there was no mention anywhere of the involvement of Robinson's offshore trust. Orion's trustees allowed Robinson remarkable discretion to pursue his own agenda, contradicting his posture of merely 'suggesting' an investment to his trustees.

Once the purchase was completed in 1997, Robinson transferred to Richardson 2,525 shares at no cost and promised, in self-denial, to sell a balancing stake to Derek Higgs to prevent any further attempts by himself to influence the club's management. In theory, Orion had lost about £168,000 to conclude the deal. That would have been irrelevant if Robinson had remained an anonymous backbencher in a provincial outpost but his insignificance was a curse which Robinson was resolved to cure. Ever since his service at Transport House, he had been intent on becoming a political star, wielding influence and power. Money had bought friends and admirers in Coventry. He wanted the same in London.

The opportunity was offered in early 1996. The *New Statesman*, the left-wing weekly journal founded in 1913, had been placed into administration. Bereft of money and good editors, the magazine's circulation had slid from 90,000 in the post-war years to less than 20,000. Only a multimillionaire eager to lose money and win fame would desire the ownership of a bankrupt and dying magazine, not least because the idea was encouraged by Blair and Brown. Robinson was told that the two leaders were predisposed to secure a trusted candidate's control over a newspaper with influence among their supporters. Robinson was viewed as the ideal purchaser. With the encouragement of Ed Balls, he bought the magazine in February 1996 for about £375,000. There was no modesty in his dream: 'I hope that the *New Statesman* will become a key element in the evolution of Labour Party thinking.' There was equally no self-deception in Robinson's acknowledgement that his appointment of Ian Hargreaves, a former editor of the *Independent*, as the new editor, required the approval of Blair and Brown. After his appointment, Hargreaves described his new employer, from whom he was receiving over £100,000 per annum, as 'a distinguished businessman', reflecting the opinion of Blair and Brown.

One comparison was arguably evident to Robinson. In 1996, he was a part-owner of a football club and the owner of a small magazine. Five years earlier, on a grander scale, Robert Maxwell had also owned newspapers and football clubs. Both used their ownership as a magnet to invite powerbrokers to their parties. Maxwell had hosted gargantuan celebrations at Headington Hill Hall, a Victorian mansion steeped in history, outside Oxford. Robinson's more modest receptions were held in his two-bedroom suite on the eighth floor of the Grosvenor House. Despite its uninspired décor and lack of space, the location and the view over Hyde Park suggested to visitors a celebrity of enormous wealth.

Those invited to champagne receptions on the expensive advice of Hobsbawm Macaulay, the new public relations company co-owned by Gordon Brown's future wife, Sarah Macaulay, were encouraged to appreciate their presence at a hub of history-in-the-making. The home of Geoffrey Robinson, the socialist and self-made millionaire, became renowned as the headquarters of the 'Hotel Group', the handful of confidants advising Gordon Brown about the next government's economic policy. Several evenings every week, Brown, Ed Balls and their researchers met in Robinson's suite to discuss strategy and decide policies in a jolly atmosphere lubricated by Robinson's order of pasta and wine from the hotel or, laughing as he threw £50 notes on to the table, 'Pizzas for everyone, and get some beer as well.' At the heart of their party was Charlie Whelan, the laddish representative of Old Labour's alliance with the trade unions, selected by Brown as his spokesman. Robinson was blind to the menace of Whelan, a man who admitted on television his readiness to lie in the Treasury, but that mistake was shared by everyone attached to Brown. The promise of future glory in the opinion polls blinded many to vulnerabilities among the power-seekers, including Robinson's.

Those were halcyon months for Robinson, proud to be crowned as the man who would 'virtually do anything that Gordon asked him to do'. For years he had belonged to that old Westminster tradition of an expert outsider whose skills were never used. The resentment of his past isolation was brushed aside as he welcomed his new friends into his many homes. As an integral member of the Treasury team, performing as the experienced but jaded politician devoid of personal ambition, he selflessly provided his services whenever required. New Labour offered the opportunity to reconcile and complete his long journey since the turbulence at British Leyland. He could devote his money to Labour's dream of financial competence and social values. Gladly, he donated about £200,000 to finance Brown's research; he was honoured to invite John Prescott to his suite to meet Brown for peace talks; and with thrills, he invited his new, inseparable friends to watch Coventry City from the directors' box or obtained tickets at Wembley for international matches and the cup final. Hospitality had worked at Jaguar and in his constituency. Westminster, he assumed, would be similarly susceptible. Proffering the luxuries of a tycoon's lifestyle, he ingratiated himself into Labour's citadel.

Money was no longer a sin for New Labour and Tony Blair. Thanks to Michael Levy, a man of limited wealth but a persuasive personality, Blair had met and raised funds from many British entrepreneurs. Gala dinners costing £1000 a head were organised to welcome and collect millions which had formerly been donated to the Conservatives, replacing Labour's exclusive relationship with the trade unions. The new union of magnates, the 'tycoons for Labour', expected only honours, jobs or access to ministers in return for their money. Matthew Harding, a businessman, pledged £1 million; the publisher Paul Hamlyn and Chris Haskins of Northern Food only slightly less; printer Bob Gavron promised £500,000 in the hope of a peerage; film producer David Puttnam wanted the same honour for his money; and the media aristocrats Waheed Ali, Melvyn Bragg, Gerry Robinson and Clive Hollick all promised thousands of pounds with a hope of a place in the House of Lords. Their money was pocketed and their dreams were soon fulfilled. Dispensing honours caused no qualms in Blair, nor did the acceptance of money from those who wanted more. Bernie Ecclestone, owner of Formula One racing, had previously supported the Conservatives but he donated £1 million to Labour in the expectation of access to Blair in Downing Street.

At the top of the pile was Geoffrey Robinson, delighted that the 'Geoffrey who?' factor had disappeared. At last the newspapers' references to him omitted his conviction for drunken driving and the shooting accident which had injured his son. Instead, he was praised as a member of the government-in-waiting. Even Peter Mandelson, on leaving his Park Lane suite after a party, reminded Robinson 'that he [Mandelson] knew me when I had nothing and was no one'.

Mandelson's typical barb was also a salutation. Robinson's money had bought potency. His suite at the Grosvenor House Hotel was his stage on which to perform as the helpful adviser. Yet, as a measure of opulence in London, his rented home was unimpressive. Nearby, tens of thousands lived in considerably better style. But none was a New Labour insider. For the architects of New Labour invited to the functional lodgings, the natural suspicion of wealth dissipated when drinking his champagne. Robinson's hospitality was alluring to those excited by the prospect of political office, who welcomed the opportunity to discuss their future in comfort. In his own excitement, Robinson was untroubled by the limitations of his political instincts and culture. Although participating in Labour's rebirth, his focus on economics and his chance of ministerial office suppressed any engagement in moral or constitutional agendas. With a dulled sense of propriety, he deployed his money without conscience to obtain influence. Among those whom he particularly embraced were the other members of the self-styled 'Gang of Four'.

Roughly every three months, Anji Hunter, Sue Nye and Fraser Kemp were guests for dinner in the suite. Hunter was Tony Blair's personal assistant; Nye was Gordon Brown's political secretary; and Kemp was the party's national general election co-ordinator at Millbank and the prospective MP for Houghton. The two women's presence attested to Robinson's new importance. His relationship with Kemp was more deep-rooted. Over the years, as the West Midlands organiser for the Labour Party, Kemp had been a particularly useful ally and had recently become an asset to Robinson, whose age precluded friendships with any of the party's young strategists. Kemp was also loyal, describing Robinson as 'a genuine, decent individual. There is never any side to him.' Like so many in the party, he spoke of Robinson's period at Jaguar as a 'huge success story'. Kemp's arrival for dinner with the two other intimates in early May 1996 seemed another opportunity to celebrate Labour's certainty of an election victory.

The dinners were usually light-hearted exchanges of political gossip and friendly teasing, but on that occasion the mood became sombre. Anji Hunter began speaking of 'a bitter, vicious, internecine civil war between Gordon [Brown] and Peter [Mandelson]'. Sue Nye agreed, mentioning her shock about the 'immature, petulant and dishonest' methods the protagonists were adopting against each other. 'Even in their worst moments, my own children would not do what they're doing,' agreed Kemp. Robinson's three guests, all at the heart of New Labour, feared that the abuse and recriminations were so uncontrollable that the party might be on the verge of returning to the old factionalism. Not about ideology, but between personalities. In the jargon New Labour favoured, they spoke not about ideological splits but of 'conflicting lines of management' threatening the strategy for the general election. 'This has got to be resolved,' said Hunter. 'It can't go on.'

Like many middle-aged Labour loyalists, Robinson had been scarred by the lunacies of the left during the 1980s and the residue of despair after the 1992 election defeat. Known as 'Brown-family' and 'Blair-friendly', he lacked the political sophistication to understand the war but he spotted an opportunity to augment his influence. The role of deal-maker, broker, backstage fixer, was overwhelmingly attractive to a man recently re-admitted from the wilderness and would more than justify his £1 million losses that year at the *New Statesman*. 'Well, should I go and see Peter?' he asked. The suggestion was not absurd. Robinson was not labelled as a member of any camp and he was instinctively emollient. Unlike the spiteful and stubborn personalities tussling for advantage, Robinson was polite and even tolerant. 'Yes. That's a good idea,' replied Hunter, assuming it was another example of her host's generosity. 'That would be great,' added Fraser Kemp. 'I'll invite Peter here for dinner,' said Robinson, convinced of the remedial qualities of his hospitality.

Over the years Robinson had displayed many merits, but his ability to act as a broker was unproven. His notion that an older, absentee politician lacking noted political achievements or a Westminster constituency could mediate between two prima donnas estranged by an unexplained hatred confirmed his fantasies about the power of generosity.

In Robinson's commercial world, the prevailing criterion for judging a man was 'How much is he worth?' In Robinson's political world, the prevailing criterion was 'Who knows him?' On the first question, Mandelson was worthless; on the second, he was invaluable. Robinson's business and political antennae were always seeking vulnerabilities. Mandelson's could be effortlessly identified.

Greeting Mandelson for dinner at the hotel on 23 May 1996, Robinson did not want to admit how much the two men had in common. The host was the son of a furniture salesman and his guest, fifteen years younger, was the son of the advertising director of the *Jewish Chronicle*. Both were outsiders, unburdened by political philosophy, seeking personal power and the prize of fame.

Both were uncertain about their future, but, unlike Robinson, Mandelson had wholly devoted himself to politics and New Labour. While Robinson, after all those years in the shadows, was initially satisfied with a junior role in the Treasury team, Mandelson sought and expected the highest office. Like Ed Balls, Mandelson possessed the profile within the party that Robinson had craved twenty years earlier. An understanding with another of New Labour's architects would not be damaging to a man who had recently become a grandfather.

Although they had met occasionally in the early 1980s, there was little personal reason for Mandelson to accept Robinson's unexpected invitation. Curiosity and politeness were barely justification, although Mandelson was easily lured by wealth. Political reason, however, justified his acceptance. The offer of a meal from the owner of the *New Statesman*, a man whose large financial donations to the party leaders had elevated a nobody into an aspirant, could not be ignored, especially since the pretext was the resolution of the dispute between Blair and Brown. 'It's important to prevent an irreparable split between Tony and Gordon,' said Robinson. There was never any chance that Robinson's expensive dinner could resolve the history of Mandelson 'knifing Gordon in the back' after the death of John Smith, so inevitably, their conversation drifted into an area chosen by Robinson, Mandelson's vulnerabilities.

Mandelson was unpopular with many Labour MPs. The benefits of his engaging intelligence and unusual abilities were neutralised by a prickly hauteur, sly ambition and social adventurism. His lack of candour encouraged ridicule in the media and at Westminster. His greatest sensitivities were his homosexuality, concealed with some effort, and his comparative poverty. At the age of forty-three, he lacked a home life and even, in his opinion, a proper home. His commitment to politics had destroyed the chance of accumulating any wealth. Foolishly, he had become seduced by the glitter of social life among London's millionaires and society hostesses, who competed to include Mandelson at their dinner table. He had become a social catch, anxious to be caught. His regular return to reality was miserable. Many nights, after enjoying sumptuous hospitality in the designer houses of London's grandees and powerbrokers, he returned to a small flat in Clerkenwell. Depressed by that soulless area, he sought the chance of a stylish home amid the glitterati.

For a seasoned commercial negotiator like Robinson, finding that vulnerability was not difficult. In Gordon Brown's interests, it was valuable to know the enemy, and to an outsider the inner turmoil of a powerbroker was always intriguing. In Robinson's version, Mandelson recounted his plight with the cry 'and there is no one to help me'. The truth of what followed will probably never be conclusively established, but even Robinson concedes that Mandelson, an acquaintance with whom he had barely spoken for more than ten years, could not have arrived in Robinson's flat with the intention of seeking Robinson's financial help for a new home. Yet, in the course of their conversation about Mandelson's life and his misery about not possessing 'a decent flat where he could relax', Robinson concluded that Mandelson was 'looking for a loan'. His judgement was questionable. Robinson could not explain how a friendly conversation between relative strangers became a plea for a loan, whereas Mandelson offered a persuasive scenario. As Mandelson described his domestic plight, Robinson, the businessman, encouraged his guest to consider his future income. The value of his eventual memoirs, said Robinson, would repay any debt. At his age, continued Robinson, men borrow now with the prospect of repayment later. Each fed from the other as Robinson encouraged Mandelson to borrow, while Mandelson replied that he required more money than any building society would offer. The climax was confusing. At the end of the meal, Robinson, who had invited Mandelson for dinner without contemplating the offer of a loan, had willingly manoeuvred himself into a position to display his customary generosity: 'Let me help you. I can make life much easier for you.' Robinson's new friends said that his woolly manner, and the impression of diffidence, 'belies a very sharp mind'. Others suggest that his confused appearance accurately reflects his disposition.

That evening, Robinson did not estimate the size of the loan. He merely made an offer. Such generosity is unusual even between good friends, but between acquaintances suggests a purpose to win favour and create a dependency. For his part, Mandelson encouraged Robinson's belief that an anticipated loan from his mother would mean the repayment of Robinson's money in the near future.

At nine the following morning, Mandelson telephoned Robinson. Overnight, he had clearly considered whether Robinson's offer was genuine and the possibilities his money provided. Robinson gave the reassurance that the offer was genuine: 'Of course, if that's what you want.' Mandelson's next request was decidedly odd. He asked for Robinson's help to search for his new home, and Robinson agreed, because 'with eight or so properties in Britain and Europe I might well be placed to do so'. Robinson is known to own four properties and rent the one in the Grosvenor House Hotel. The additional four remain mysteries.

By any reckoning, the scenario was bizarre. Two men, who had little in common and enjoyed utterly different lifestyles, embarked on a house-hunting expedition. Flats, stipulated Robinson, were unsuitable. Mandelson should consider a small house. Over several days, the two MPs were chauffeured around west London in Robinson's Jaguar until they found Mandelson's dream home in Northumberland Place, Notting Hill Gate. The scenario added authority to Ken Follett's splenetic outburst in July 2000 attacking Mandelson as one of the 'rent boys of politics'.

The size of the loan surprised Robinson. He had anticipated lending £100,000; instead he was committed to £373,000 without any plan for its repayment. 'I had no immediate requirement for the money,' he explained and, after signing the cheque, 'I gave no more thought to the loan.' The conditions of the loan between two acquaintances were remarkable. The interest rate was the Midland Bank's base rate; the loan was not secured on the property; and there was no agreed timetable for repayment. As a business proposition, Robinson could recognise a lousy deal. The loss of interest alone was £5,000 per annum; and if Mandelson died Robinson might have difficulties to immediately recover his money. Treating that sum as small change with no prospect of repayment for the foreseeable future, suggests the very motive Robinson denied. Namely, that Robinson was 'buying influence, power or even office'. He later insisted, 'I am simply not like that and do not operate like that in practice.' There are many rich men in London, much richer than Robinson, but, despite their association with politicians, none was known to be offering large sums in Robinson's style. Mandelson's gratitude for the loan was not displayed to the world. Robinson 'felt a bit miffed' that he was not invited to Mandelson's house-warming party. All he had to show for his generosity were handwritten letters from Mandelson expressing his urgency to understand the details of the loan's transfer. The letters were carefully filed. The original purpose of the dinner had not been achieved. The feud between Mandelson and Brown blazed until the imminence of the election. But the consequence of Robinson's spending was the kudos he desired.

In summer 1996, the offer and acceptance of the loan was not an isolated instance of Robinson's generosity. Gordon Brown had accepted his invitation to stay, with his brother, in his seaside flat in Cannes; and Tony Blair had accepted his invitation to stay with his family in San Gimignano, Tuscany. The publicity about the 'golden young lion of democratic socialism' as Robinson's guest flattered the host's self-importance. Without his money, those associations would not have existed. Blair, Brown and Mandelson were all indebted to him. Money, he consoled himself, was not the only reason. At his summer party at the Orchards in Surrey, swarming with New Labour's stars, he repeated to a friend that his rank was assured after a famous guest had confided, 'You're the only one with a brain.' Gordon Brown might have been more wary of his host in Cannes had he known that Robinson repeatedly received writs from the agency representing the neighbours' apartments in France for failing to pay bills and for failing to protect the neighbouring properties from damage to their homes. There was a high-handedness in Robinson's relationships which was unknown to his new friends.

Robinson's proximity to Blair and Brown encouraged the complementary speculation in the newspapers that he would be rewarded with a 'front-line role' in the new government. The unpleasant consequence was a briefing by Blair's spokesmen that a 'fat cat' like Robinson would not be appointed to the cabinet, and even the suggestion of a lesser post was classified as a 'complete fabrication' and 'malevolent'. That violent reaction confirmed Robinson's dilemma: he remained unknown and untrusted. The sentiment, prompted by suspicion of rich socialists, was not misplaced. During those months, Gordon Brown mentioned to Robinson his intention to penalise those who used offshore tax havens. Robinson nodded his agreement. But neither Brown nor Ed Balls was aware that Robinson, at that very moment, had completed a secret manoeuvre to benefit from the very loophole they sought to remove. From the same suite of rooms in the Grosvenor House Hotel where Brown spoke about the curse of tax havens, Robinson was negotiating with Orion's trustees an investment in TransTec to avoid British taxes.

Under Richard Carr, TransTec was planning another bout of expansion. In June 1996, the company published a prospectus offering new shares to raise £57.6 million to finance the purchases. Carr's strategy of 'limiting risk' by producing huge volumes of low-cost products in mature, low-tech industries seemed sensible. He had transformed the company's £12 million losses into profits of £6 million after securing new contracts to supply steel-texturing machines to Japan, Spain, Russia and South Africa, and he had built a £14 million factory in Northern Ireland with a £6.9 million government grant to supply cylinder heads for the engine of Ford's new Explorer. The annual value of Ford's contract was £26 million. Unfortunately, deliveries to Ford had been delayed and that was causing, Robinson knew, 'big problems' when the prospectus was issued. Although he denied any knowledge of Ford's demand for $100 million in damages, Robinson did not query the omission of a detailed description of the dispute from the prospectus. On the contrary, he decided to invest more money in the company and buy his allocation of 9.8 million shares.

The arrangements were unusual. Instead of buying the shares outright, Robinson 'persuaded' Orion's trustees to invest. First, Robinson sold his 'rights' to the shares to Stenbell, a private British company he owned, for £1.75 million, earning a profit of £882,000. Stenbell was the company that had loaned £1 million to the *New Statesman* as working capital and paid the journalists' salaries. Robinson's directorship of Stenbell was not registered as required in the Commons.

Second, in August 1996, Stenbell paid £10.1 million for the TransTec shares. Finally, on 3 September 1996, Stenbell resold the shares to Orion for about £11.75 million. Thereafter, Robinson could receive all the annual dividends of the TransTec shares in Britain from Orion without paying income tax.

To comply with Companies Act 1985, Robinson should have disclosed both stages of the deal – first, his sale to Stenbell, and second, Stenbell's sale to Orion. Instead, he disclosed only one stage. But more serious suspicion arose about the identity of Stenbell's source of money to buy the shares. Robinson refused to identify who had advanced the money to Stenbell. If Orion's trustees had guaranteed a loan, it would confirm that the trust was operated at Robinson's behest as an effective device to avoid British taxes. Robinson's decision to limit his disclosure in the Commons register raised an issue whether there had been any concealment. He revealed that he had acquired an interest in the shares but did not disclose his £882,000 profit. The convoluted transactions and the secrecy undermined Robinson's subsequent insistence that all the dealings were 'at arm's length', beyond his control.

One paradox perhaps escaped his attention. The transactions coincided with Sir Gordon Downey's investigation of the failure by Neil Hamilton and Tim Smith, both Conservative MPs, to register in the Commons payments to them by Mohamed Fayed. Tory sleaze had become Labour's vote-winner. Insensitive to that contradiction, Robinson had nevertheless concealed a financial transaction.

The TransTec deal terminated Robinson's spending spree of

over £23 million. He had contributed £10 million to TransTec's expansion; he had promised £10 million to Coventry City; he had committed £2 million to the *New Statesman*; he had spent £1 million on improving his Italian estate and committed a substantial sum to the restoration of Marsh Court in Hampshire; he had lent £373,000 to Mandelson; and his annual personal living costs were at least £300,000. Not one of those investments was the insightful result of a shrewd investor; rather, they were those of a man whose spending was dictated by vanity and self-interest. Against that expenditure, there were doubts about the declared sources of all his income.

Officially, Robinson's salary from TransTec and the Commons provided £288,000; and his dividends from TransTec a further £2.78 million since 1991. But that could not explain £23 million of profligacy during 1996 by a man who disclosed his total fortune as £30 million, including, on his estimate, variously £9 million or £12 million inherited from Joska Bourgeois. Robinson's accounts of his wealth could not be reconciled. Either he had raised considerable loans using the TransTec shares as collateral or more had been deposited in the Orion Trust than he disclosed. In 1996, no one queried the source of his money. Robinson, everyone assumed, was rich and the trusts, the tax havens and the detail of the transactions about the backbencher were unknown. As the Labour Party prepared for the 1997 general election, Robinson did not pause to contemplate the consequences if his financial affairs were revealed once his ambition of ministerial office was realised. The recriminations would be levelled at a short-sighted politician for either 'laziness' or recklessness. On either judgement, Robinson had been cavalier.

By early 1997, Robinson had good reason to believe he would shortly be employed in the Treasury. Robinson had become an important and loyal ally to effect Gordon Brown's ambitions. The security safe in his suite contained the Hotel Group's most sensitive policy documents. The Scotsman was excited by business and entrepreneurship, but inveterately suspicious of their practitioners. Uniquely, Robinson, the socialist politician, had proven himself a trustworthy guide, perfecting an honest balance between mammon and socialism, who aroused no suspicions. To the increasing number of visitors invited to meet the Treasury-in-waiting, Robinson was the honest millionaire, pacifying anxious capitalists. The few sceptical visitors sensed that New Labour's broker revealed only one-tenth of himself. They were uncertain about a man with an obscure commercial track record but speculated about Robinson's apparent deal with Brown of financial support in return for a ministerial post. In that opinion, they were partially mistaken. Robinson's use of money was not crude. While he believed that some people could be bought, he was sufficiently smart to acknowledge that the price for some was too high. His generosity appealed to the susceptible, and Brown was among those who unquestioningly accepted his host's generosity because Robinson's energy was producing results.

Robinson's proposal to arrive in government with carefully argued and costed programmes was a masterstroke. He had volunteered to finance with his own money the research on the proposed windfall tax and the privatisation of the London Underground. Negotiating a cut-price deal with London's top accountancy partnerships, whose fees were normally astronomical, would be his pleasure. He would, he proposed, exact 'a good price' from the professionals, who he expected to work for free to win favour with the new government. His choice of accountants was felt by many to be significant.

Coopers & Lybrand had been TransTec's auditors but their reputation was mired by several allegations of negligent audits, including those of Maxwell's empire. His choice for the Labour Party's research was Arthur Andersen, excluded by the Conservative government from all the lucrative privatisation work in retribution for the partnership's performance in the late 1970s relating to a disastrous motor car development by John DeLorean in Northern Ireland. Andersen's were desperate to return to the gravy train of government commissions. Coincidentally, Andersen's had been appointed the administrator in 1991 of Robert Maxwell's private companies, which included Hollis and Pergamon.

A clutch of Andersen's senior partners had agreed with Robinson to produce for no fee a scheme to levy a one-off windfall tax on the privatised utilities that had been sold to the public, in Labour's opinion, too cheaply. To avoid the civil service raising obstacles, Andersen's completed work was submitted to senior lawyers for approval and to parliamentary draftsmen to prepare a draft Bill. That 'watertight' package to raise £5 billion, Robinson's feat, was placed in the Grosvenor House safe, not in Brown's office in the Commons.

Robinson's influence was still not quite appreciated when he arrived at Warburg merchant bankers in April 1997. 'I'm on a commission from Tony Blair and Gordon Brown,' he began, 'and we'd like you to prepare a plan for privatisation of the London Underground.' In his normal manner, he offered his audience a deal. 'If you do the work cheap,' he suggested, 'I'll make sure that you get the commission from the Treasury when we're in government.' Cautiously, the bankers, who were employed normally by governments, not opposition parties, inquired about Robinson's credentials. Among the City's principal bankers, Robinson was an uncertain figure. Recently, as a representative of Labour's New Business Committee, he had been the guest of honour at a dinner to promote the new philosophy. In his unexpectedly brief speech to five hundred guests, his manner was disjointed. 'A Labour government,' he commenced, 'is going to be friendly to industry. It really is.' Pause. 'We are going to have a Labour government. I think I'm sure.' Pause. 'One of the biggest problems I have is getting money.' And, finally, 'I've got to vote in the House.' With that, the guest of honour abruptly departed. The gossip was humorous and did not tarnish the replies to Warburg from Westminster confirming the truth of Robinson's representations. He spoke on the future chancellor's behalf and was the liaison with Steve Robson, a senior official at the Treasury famous as the architect of rail privatisation.

Three senior people, Robinson was told by Warburg, would be assigned to the project for three weeks. Although the normal cost would have been £100,000, the bank agreed to charge a peppercorn – just £10,000 – in return for his promise of a favourable recommendation for the government's commission. Before the end of the month, Warburg delivered a detailed proposal to Grosvenor House. The plan reduced the Tube's wage bill and financed the reconstruction of its infrastructure. The result delighted Robinson's patron. Once again, Robinson had proved himself an ideal counsel. Old Labour joined in praising Robinson. Former chancellor Denis Healey revised his opinion and hailed Robinson as a man who was 'going to be the biggest influence on Labour's industrial policy'.

In the last days before the general election on 1 May, Robinson sought to cocoon his private finances to avoid future embarrassment. On 25 April 1997, as chairman of TransTec, he signed the company's 1996 accounts. The company reported losses but did not fully describe the threat to the company's existence from Ford. Throughout the first six months of 1996, while Robinson was chairman, Ford had been pressing for compensation for the delayed supplies. In summer 1996, Richard Carr, the chief executive, had agreed to pay £11.2 million ($18 million) in compensation, although TransTec's finances would be imperilled. Carr allegedly did not fully disclose the repayments by allegedly arranging, on all future orders, for the damages to be listed as a credit to the customer. Ford would not pay for those supplies and TransTec's loss of the income could not be easily understood from the company's central accounts.

Though he was not told by Carr about the proposed concealment of the payments to Ford, Robinson was aware that Ford threatened to reduce future orders and that the continuing losses at the foundry in Derry were a disaster for TransTec, endangering his own 17.65 million shares, which were worth about £30 million. Repeating the same carelessness which characterised his conduct towards the contract for the paint-shop at Jaguar, he signed the annual report, with its euphemisms of 'production difficulties', losses of £2.6 million and the chairman's optimism about the future. The losses in 1997 would be £6 million and the total debts were rising towards £70 million. Unwittingly,

Robinson was once again chairman of a company veering towards bankruptcy. He planned to resign his chairmanship immediately after Labour's victory and entrust his shareholding to a blind trust. At best, his conduct reflected a bad manager and a businessman who was inattentive to important detail. With remarkable gullibility, he had entrusted practically his entire fortune in one company.

On 30 April, the very day before the election, 2.95 million TransTec shares were transferred to Robinson's Orion Trust, bringing the trust's total ownership to 12,755,550 shares. The shares' ownership was not disclosed. The peculiarity of that final transfer to Orion was later compounded by Robinson's protestations of ignorance. 'Honestly,' he said, 'these are just total coincidences.' The timing of the transaction exposed him to the suspicion that he had secretly accumulated 2.95 million shares, wanted to avoid their disclosure and intended to receive the dividends tax-free. Robinson denied all those suggestions but the substance and chronology of his activities were to expose him to damaging criticism.

The following day, 1 May 1997, Robinson drove around his constituency in his Jaguar, content that he would not only be re-elected but would also realise his dream to become a minister. In his Grosvenor House safe was a draft letter to the governor of the Bank of England written by Ed Balls declaring the bank's independence. In the spare bedroom, Anji Hunter had left some clothes after her occasional use of his suite during the frenzied campaign – another important New Labour personality who had become indebted to the paymaster. During his last appearance in the Commons, Robinson had stopped to regale one of his friends with a self-revelatory insight. 'The most important relationship in government is between the prime minister and the chancellor,' he intoned in an unusually confident tone, emphasising his assumption that as an insider he would act as a broker between the warring factions. Despite the hint of pomposity and his unimpressive record over the previous twenty-one years, there was goodwill towards Robinson. Only a few older MPs resented his elevation. Their own loyalty during the wilderness years, they felt, deserved to be rewarded; instead, they had to put up with Robinson buying his way to the top.

Robinson was unaware of that sentiment; just as he was unbothered that among his party's election pledges was a proposal to terminate offshore trusts, which were used by 'the rich . . . principally for tax avoidance'.

5

'PURER THAN PURE'

The sun shone over Britain on 2 May 1997. Labour's thundering election victory was welcomed as a glorious dawn by the majority of Britons. Even many Conservatives felt relief at the departure of the sleaze-ridden, ineffectual government of John Major. Sleaze had been highlighted by Peter Mandelson as the issue to destroy the Tory government, and Tony Blair's promise, televised as he drove in a regal procession from Islington to Downing Street, to lead a government that would be 'purer than pure' was hailed as a redemption from evil.

Geoffrey Robinson, like dozens of other hopeful Labour politicians, waited by the telephone for the summons. He was content to be on the verge of finally becoming a star, albeit a small star. He was simply infused by a ferocious desire to compensate for the wasted years and join the first flush of Blair's honeymoon. Unlike other hopefuls waiting for the new prime minister's call, Robinson had been assured of his appointment as paymaster-general, the fifth-ranking minister in the Treasury. Nevertheless, there could be a hitch. Although Blair sought to oblige the requests of his senior ministers, all nominations were subject to scrutiny by civil servants, identifying potential embarrassments. One insuperable hurdle would be those under investigation by two DTI inspectors still examining the stock exchange flotation of Robert Maxwell's Mirror Group in 1991.

Over one dozen active and ambitious Labour politicians had been associated with Robert Maxwell including Charles Williams, Bernard Donoughue, Helen Liddell and Geoffrey Robinson. Even Alastair Campbell, the prime minister's press spokesman, had as a journalist become close to Maxwell after a trip to Ethiopia and had been visibly emotional after Maxwell's death.

At the request of Jack Cunningham, the new minister of agriculture and the son of a corrupt councillor jailed for dishonesty, Blair approved the appointment of Lord Donoughue as spokesman for agriculture in the House of Lords. Before the election, Blair had been given substantiated facts about Donoughue's role as the executive vice-chairman of a Maxwell private investment company involved in the misuse of the pension funds. Principally, in February 1990, twenty months before Maxwell's death, Donoughue had noted in a memorandum to Kevin Maxwell that the Maxwells' misuse of the pension funds was possibly criminal. But after that protest Donoughue had remained silent and tolerated abuses of trust by Maxwell's senior executives, subordinates of Donoughue himself, who were perpetuating the misuse of the pension funds. On his resignation from Maxwell's employment, just four weeks before the tycoon's death, Donoughue had accepted an additional £50,000 payment to remain silent about his knowledge of Maxwell's activities. Nevertheless, Blair agreed to Donoughue's appointment as a government minister.

Helen Liddell had been Maxwell's director of personnel and public affairs at the Mirror Group in Scotland and later negotiated commercial contracts in Bulgaria on his behalf. Since Maxwell's death, she had unconvincingly related a story of an unexpected approach by the tycoon, inviting her to join his organisation, but in a letter dated 26 October 1987, she had directly asked Maxwell for employment, described by her as 'a major career advance'. Liddell remained tainted by loyally serving the notorious businessman. Her excuse of innocence echoed the previous leadership of the Labour Party. Neil Kinnock and Roy Hattersley, his deputy, had accepted Maxwell's money on the party's behalf and had also enjoyed his hospitality. Before his death, neither had ever publicly protested about Maxwell's past. After his death, they preferred to remain silent about the party's intimate relationship with the party's benefactor.

Inquiries and recrimination about Labour's relationship with Maxwell were best avoided. Six years later, the pact between Labour and Maxwell was near forgotten. The appointments of Donoughue and Liddell were approved; and although there was good reason for Whitehall to query Robinson's appointment as paymaster-general, neither Gordon Brown nor Blair was aware of the details of Robinson's relationship with Maxwell or that he might be included among those Britons criticised by Blair in 1994 as touched by the 'scandal' that, 'just by hiding money in the right places, [these people] can avoid paying tax altogether'. On the contrary, like Donoughue and Liddell, Robinson was counted among the 'purer than pure'.

As Blair composed his government – figuratively on the back of an envelope – he commended Robinson's appointment as a signal of the government's commitment to business. The simultaneous agreement of David Simon to resign as chairman of British Petroleum and become a junior minister in the DTI, and David Sainsbury's recruitment as a minister of science, reflected Blair's enthusiasm for entrepreneurs. Robinson was another image of that wisdom: the son of a furniture salesman, he had become the brilliant saviour of Jaguar and the creator of an engineering empire, and his champagne lifestyle in his five homes was beyond criticism. The prime minister could scarcely ignore or condemn Robinson. He had already accepted another invitation to the dream house in Tuscany for the coming summer; and he was grateful for Robinson's generous contributions to the party's election fund and to his office, negotiated in a private meeting by

Jonathan Powell, his chief of staff. Blair's knowledge of Robinson's substantial contribution to his office through the party was officially denied, as was Powell's involvement in raising funds, but denials of the truth were untroubling to a government with an overwhelming majority in the Commons, facing a discredited opposition.

Victorious revolutionaries never care about the sentiments of the vanquished and on 2 May Gordon Brown marched into the Treasury to impose his image on the citadel. Those following Brown lusted for the blood of the inhabitants. Few had greater contempt for the Treasury's culture and past performance than Geoffrey Robinson and none was more willing to display his sentiments. Robinson introduced himself as the architect of Labour's industrial policy with the task of keeping 'the Treasury in the real world'. His experience in manufacturing, he declaimed, would enhance the government's new troubleshooter against the Treasury's blinkered officials bound by arcane and worthless traditions. Insensitively, he reprimanded officials for 'what had gone wrong in the recent past'. He took it upon himself to force-feed humble pie upon an institution responsible, he believed, for 'a series of unforced errors'. Disregarding the comedy of his own record, he damned 'the Treasury's tendency towards optimism . . . and monetary laxity'. The cure, he urged, was providing his civil servants with 'clear and firm direction'. Winning hearts and minds was Robinson's strength, but the cream of the Treasury's intellectuals were unlikely to be attracted by the same backscratching as party workers, trade unionists and factory employees. Robinson made no allowance for that distinction.

Robinson's arrival with Charlie Whelan in Great George Street was, some Treasury mandarins muttered, 'a sad day. We've never previously allowed spivs to set a foot inside this building.' By the end of his third day in office, those mandarins were uttering another complaint: 'I've never been so cuddled in my life.' Robinson and Whelan were 'touchy feely', constantly putting their arms around shoulders and squeezing arms. Robinson's bid to win friends had cast a shadow over his credibility.

One person not squeezed was fifty-three-year-old Terry Burns, permanent secretary to the Treasury since 1980. In the months before the election, Burns had energetically prepared for a Labour government. Indefatigably, he had negotiated with Brown and his team to effect a smooth transition. His pains were worthless. Gordon Brown and Ed Balls unjustly considered him an untrustworthy Thatcherite responsible for major blunders. After 2 May, Burns was automatically excluded from the Hotel Group's intimate discussions, often conducted, as before the election, in the evenings at the Grosvenor House Hotel over pasta and champagne. That immediate ostracism influenced Burns's delicate task during Robinson's first month in Whitehall.

Under the British system of government, the permanent secretary was obliged to instruct Robinson on the proprieties expected of a minister. The procedures had been developed over a century to secure accountability and honesty in public office. In particular, Robinson was expected to relinquish his control over those personal financial investments which might compromise the government or suggest a conflict of interest. Resolving that issue depended upon Robinson's complete co-operation and honest declaration as required according to a Whitehall document called 'Guidance for Ministers'. His completed schedule would be handed to Burns, a man whom he had in advance condemned as a professional failure, not least for his ambitious scheme to refurbish the Treasury building using private finance.

Burns had noted Robinson's demeanour during the first hours after his arrival. Brashly, the paymaster-general had strutted through the dilapidated building boasting that orthodoxy was banished. The gossip about one 'secret' had already spread: Robinson had rejected a salary and forsaken his beloved Jaguar for the official Mondeo. Self-deprivation, he expected, would win favour, although he eventually lamented, 'I had to give up my Jag, which I didn't like at all.' The self-sacrifice was hardly endearing to Burns, a puritan, renowned as subtle, clever but occasionally too thoughtful. Burns's judgement of Robinson had not been kept secret among his senior colleagues. 'He's a disaster waiting to happen,' suggested Burns to his confidants. 'A minister who's chased for his job.' The permanent secretary, who continued to enjoy a good relationship with many Conservative and Labour politicians, was puzzled why Gordon Brown, whom he admired, should trust Robinson. 'I can't understand their relationship,' he said to his colleagues. Burns's antagonism, however, was disguised. Robinson clearly enjoyed a relationship of friendship and confidence with the new chancellor, whom, despite the rebuffs, Burns was anxious to please.

Burns's suspicions hardened just fourteen days after the election. The permanent secretary told his colleagues about an invitation by Robinson for dinner at the Grosvenor House Hotel on Friday 16 May 1997. Robinson's original invitation had suggested an opportunity to 'get to know each other' but it soon became apparent that the paymaster-general's agenda specifically concerned the complete renovation of the Treasury building in Whitehall. Among Burns's outstanding chores from the previous government had been to negotiate a contract with private developers to finance the renovation which was due to commence shortly. Burns had found alternative accommodation for the whole Treasury near Vauxhall Bridge. The prospect of departing from Whitehall, the centre of government, possibly for years, terrified Gordon Brown. Robinson, the chancellor's hit man, explained to Burns his boss's fears: 'Gordon feels it necessary to be close to Tony Blair.' Decamping from the proximity of his political rival's power base, explained Robinson, was unacceptable to Brown. The move, suggested Robinson, should be abandoned despite the considerable costs already incurred. Robinson's smiles did not conceal his determination and agenda. Finding a solution to satisfy Brown posed a loyalty test for Burns. Failure to pass the test would damage the permanent secretary's prospects under the new government, suggested Robinson, whose flattery barely masked what appeared to be a threat. During his years in Whitehall, Burns had never participated in a similar conversation. Concealing his surprise, the permanent secretary agreed to 'look into it'. He would, he told the paymaster-general, consider searching for alternative premises closer to Whitehall. The conversation changed. Robinson was asking for details about Burns's private life, probing, it seemed, for personal intimacies. Serving Labour required 100 per cent commitment and Robinson was not certain that Burns was prepared to make that pledge.

The following Monday morning, the paymaster-general tested the civil servant's loyalty. Robinson's private secretary telephoned for confirmation that 'It was agreed that the paymaster-general can tell Gordon that the move is off?' Burns was perplexed. Crudely, and for the first time during his Whitehall career, he was being bounced into a decision. 'No,' replied Burns's assistant. 'The permanent secretary only said he would look into it.' Eventually, Burns was ordered to abandon the plan.

Over the following week, Robinson's methods became established. Like Brown, Balls and Whelan, the paymaster-general was a plotter, critical of anyone sharing information with the Blairites. In his telephone conversations, he demanded dependency and reminded outsiders, 'we're here for a long time so why don't you get on with me and do it our way'.

Three weeks after the election, the atmosphere for most senior civil servants in the Treasury had become awkward. On the afternoon of 21 May, Robinson's private secretary asked Burns to come to the paymaster-general's office. Burns arrived in the middle of a meeting discussing the requirement for Robinson to deposit all his assets in a 'blind trust' to avoid any conflicts of interest.

Two weeks earlier, on 7 May, with the help of Titmuss Sainer Dechert, solicitors introduced to him by Robert Maxwell, Robinson had begun to discuss formally establishing a 'blind trust' for the TransTec shares and his other investments registered in Britain. His independent trustees, required under the rules, were Brenda Price, his long-serving secretary, who had become a director of the *New Statesman* and Coventry City, and Peter Davis, his friend and solicitor in Coventry.

The civil servant discovered the three working their way through the official document, 'Guidance for Ministers'. They had reached a stalemate. Robinson hoped Burns could provide further advice about his proposed trust.

The advice given to Robinson by Burns on 21 May depended entirely on the information the paymaster-general volunteered: the burden of disclosure was on the politician. His most sensitive interest was the Orion Trust in Guernsey, which had not been listed in the 'blind trust'. After careful consideration, Robinson said to Burns, 'Some of my money is already in a family trust, so does it have to go into a blind trust or can it stay in the discretionary trust?' To the permanent secretary, a 'family trust' was irrelevant. His only concern was to protect the minister from a conflict of interest. Effortlessly, Burns accepted the paymaster-general's word, not least to assuage the frisson that flared between the two men, and answered his query: 'The whole issue is one of control. You've got to make sure that your assets are beyond your control.' Robinson remained uncertain whether he could still direct any sale of shares. Again the answer was unexceptional. Robinson, said the official, would be expected to exercise no control over any of his assets. To protect his money, he would be expected to draw up instructions to guide the trustees for any eventuality and thereafter do no more. In the course of their hour-long discussion, Robinson again mentioned his 'family trust' and during the meeting Burns scribbled in his small notebook a summary of the discussion including the phrase, 'family trust'. In Burns's clear recollection, the paymaster-general did not mention the trust's domicile in an offshore tax haven. For that reason, Burns did not probe the details which could present a conflict of interest or imagine the recent transactions between Orion and Stenbell which would cause embarrassment when Brown announced policies to curtail tax avoidance through offshore trusts.

Soon after the meeting, Burns received from Robinson a legal document describing the proposed 'blind trust'. No mention was included by Robinson of an 'offshore trust'. Burns and the Treasury's senior solicitor scrutinised the document before returning it with some comments.

The declaration of his assets did not lessen Robinson's disdain for Burns's advice. 'You must accept my judgement on this,' Burns had said. On certain issues, Burns remonstrated, there could be no compromise. After establishing the 'blind trust', Robinson knew that he would be breaking the rules if he initiated or influenced any transaction affecting his personal finances.

Thirteen days later, on 3 June 1997, Craigavon, the company registered in St Peter Port, Guernsey, through which Robinson had bought his shares in Coventry City football club, sold 5,568 Coventry City shares to Derek Higgs at £66.70. Robinson had originally paid Derrick Robbins £32.96 for the same shares. Craigavon's profit, remitted to the Orion Trust, was £187,864. As Orion was offshore, the profit accruing to Robinson's trust would be untaxed. Later that year, Robinson protested, 'I have never sought to make any money out of my support for my local team.' But, as previously, he stoutly refused to publicise the details of his financial investment in Coventry City. The sale and his silence passed unnoticed. Amid the excitement of the new government, Robinson appeared to have sidelined his business interests. Treasury officials were more preoccupied with implementing his policies, which, he said, 'will deliver value for money'.

Robinson had arrived with briefs for several new taxes including the windfall tax, a programme for the reform of the Private Finance Initiative (PFI), a scheme for the privatisation of the London Underground and a policy to replace the PEPs and TESSAs by ISAs. Rather than raising the expected objections, the civil servants enthusiastically greeted the impressive agenda. 'We'll plan an inter-departmental meeting to discuss this,' volunteered one senior official. 'When for?' asked Robinson. 'In two to three weeks.' 'Well, why don't we have it this afternoon?' asked Robinson. 'Get everyone to change their diaries.' The civil servant's expression delighted Robinson. 'Gobsmacked' was the word used by Robinson's colleagues as they recounted the businessman's 'refreshing, informal approach'. Newspapers were urged to believe that Robinson's eventual appearance on the front bench was not 'if' but 'when'. His promotion would be the reward for his percipient contribution of money and proficiency to produce the policy blueprints before the election. There was no longer any repetition of those pre-election stories describing Robinson, unlike the younger ministers, as a selfless backstage operator forsaking all love of power. His ambition was conspicuous.

As the man assigned to solve problems, Robinson relished his power to raise new taxes on income, pensions and corporations. Attacking the 'fat cats' of the privatised utilities was a badge of courage. Arranging the windfall tax, his proud contribution to New Labour's ideology, confiscated £5 billion from those who had obtained 'such easy money'. Visitors were assured by the minister, 'No one will ever get such easy money again under Labour.'

With the same delight he announced the reform of the PFI, a Conservative policy launched in 1992 to attract private money to finance public hospitals, schools and roads with the intention of introducing efficiencies into the public sector. Under the Conservatives, many schemes had been submitted but ministers and their cautious civil servants feared the consequences. PFI, they realised, was an accounting ruse of 'buy now and pay later', concealing huge expenditure off the balance sheet which would burden taxpayers thirty years later. Robinson was damning of their misgivings and dismissive of their prudence. Their distrust of the private sector, complained the self-styled Master of Industry, had stymied the award of any contracts. In his topsy-turvy ideology, the opportunistic socialist was planning greater risks than the capitalists dared. As in his personal business career, he was shortsighted about the consequences.

Thirty-two years after leaving the ill-fated IRC, Robinson resurrected the discredited notion of government intervention in private industry. Without the customary civilities, four weeks after the election he curtly dismissed Alastair Ross Goobey, the respected chairman of the PFI panel. Revelling in the patronage he would enjoy among lawyers, bankers and accountants in the City, he cast around for admiring recruits and encouraged new applications for PFI contracts.

'Now who can fix this?' asked the wheeler-dealer picking up a telephone and racing through his list of contacts to identify

someone who might be persuaded to grant a favour. 'This is
Geoffrey Robinson,' he smooched, convinced that he could find
someone keen for a deal. In pursuit of solving a problem, he was
insensitive that informality could raise issues of impropriety. The
procedures honed by Whitehall over the previous century to prevent compromising the government were ignored in the cause of
Robinson's crusade. 'He keeps having these private conversations
on the telephone,' complained Terry Burns. 'No one's listening in.
No minutes are kept. We don't know who he's talking to and what
deals he's making. There's no audit trail.' In particular, several
officials feared Robinson uttering similar phrases as they had
heard in committee meetings implying, 'hitch your wagon to us
because we're going to be here for a long time'. On Gordon
Brown's behalf, Robinson was demanding 100 per cent loyalty
from everyone – inside and outside the government. The danger
of censure never occurred to a man whose barter – 'You do this for
me and I'll fix a ticket for the cup final' – tripped naturally off his
tongue. One victim was already complaining.

Robinson had promised Warburg support for their bid to
mastermind the privatisation of the London Underground in
return for their providing a blueprint worth £100,000 at a tenth
of the cost. 'If you do the work,' Robinson had implied, 'I'll make
sure that you get the commission from the Treasury.' After John
Prescott's 'beauty parade', the bankers were appalled. 'Robinson
hasn't lifted a finger to help us,' one complained when Warburg's
bid was ignored and the contract was awarded to Price Waterhouse, whose proposed privatisation plan was not much dissimilar
to Warburg's. On the privatisation of the Post Office, Robinson
had the same object. 'We'll look for free advice,' he insisted.
'That's not possible,' protested a civil servant. 'It could lead to a
conflict of interest.' Robinson was undeterred. He wanted everything fast and cheap. He was thrilled to be the toast of many City
practitioners and oblivious of those few voicing complaints.

The popularity of Robinson's proposed changes for the PFI-
contracts among the majority of bidders and merchant bankers
was unsurprising. The private sector under Robinson's regime

would be allowed to earn profits without bearing any risks. The new terms of PFI contracts approved by Robinson lacked clauses allowing the government to recoup windfall profits earned by the contractors and anticipated that the public would pay more for hospitals and schools than if the funds were wholly provided by the state. Examples of such profligacy were numerous. A PFI-funded hospital in Carlisle would cost at least £200 million more than a state-funded project; the estimated cost for the new Edinburgh Infirmary at the end of thirty years was £900 million, compared to £180 million if built by the state; and the reconstruction under a PFI contract of the GCHQ headquarters in Cheltenham, the top-secret monitoring station, would be triple the original estimate. Consistent with his managerial record over the previous thirty years, Robinson was unconcerned by those forecasts. By offering overtly more generous terms to contractors than his predecessors, he could boast that projects worth £14 billion would be signed by the end of 1999. Just as at Innocenti and Jaguar where Robinson had pursued 'record production', he sought a supreme statistic of new PFI contracts. 'I guess my reputation is going to depend in no small part on making this work,' he admitted. Within the Treasury, his critics suspected that other matters would determine his reputation, not least his unconventional methods. 'His morals and standards are off the edge,' complained one. But Terry Burns was powerless to warn Gordon Brown. The Hotel Group were impervious to his caution. The foursome – Brown, Robinson, Ed Balls and Charlie Whelan – were constantly together and even flew to Rome to watch a qualifying match for the World Cup with tickets arranged by Robinson. The chancellor, grateful for the continuing hospitality, trusted Robinson to contribute to his ultimate goal. 'You don't understand,' a senior official had been rebuked by Robinson after criticising a policy. 'This is all to do with Gordon succeeding Tony.' The paymaster-general appeared puzzled that a civil servant should remain aloof from that contest. He was also impervious to unpalatable advice, especially concerning another 'real world', that of the middle class and their savings.

Gordon Brown's dislike of 'fat cats' included the middle classes. The success of PEPs and TESSAs in attracting savings deposits of over £100 billion offended Brown's socialist principles. The wealthy, in his opinion, were receiving tax relief on savings merely to increase their fortunes. The social benefits and the stimulus to investment through shares bought from those savings were cast as irrelevant by the self-appointed 'prudent chancellor'. On his insistence, Labour's election manifesto had included the pledge to 'introduce a new Individual Savings Account', ISAs.

Labour's proposal did not clarify whether the unlimited accumulation of tax relief as permitted for PEPs and TESSAs would be continued. Before the election, no changes had been envisaged. Alistair Darling, a member of Gordon Brown's team, had written in the *Investors Chronicle* in 1996 that any notion of Labour terminating PEPs 'is not true', and added that he was 'not actively looking at' a limit of £50,000 on PEPs. Shortly afterwards, Tony Blair had told an ITN interviewer, 'The idea that the Labour Party would take action against [PEPs] is absurd'. Labour, the prime minister had insisted, wanted to extend PEPs. Both those pledges were untrue.

Soon after the election, Robinson was told by Brown to terminate the tax-free PEP and TESSA accounts. The new ISAs, as initially conceived, would limit tax relief to £50,000, despite the disincentive to long-term saving by the middle class. Although ignorant about the complex subject, Robinson was proud of the accolade that he would 'virtually do anything that Gordon asked him to do'. Punishing the middle class was consistent with the Brownites' agenda to redistribute their wealth to the poor. Pleasantly, Robinson discovered that Treasury officials supported any policy which limited tax relief, yet most were puzzled by Brown's and Robinson's plan to limit the attraction of savings. Robinson explained the intention: 'We want to encourage the saving habit among the less wealthy.' 'Oh! To the hoi polloi, you mean,' responded an Inland Revenue official, to Robinson's mirth. His more serious advisers warned of a more simple reason why his proposal aroused ridicule: 'The poor don't buy PEPs, Paymaster-

General, because they've got no money. People without money don't save. And for the same reason, they won't buy your ISAs at a Tesco checkout.' The paymaster-general disliked contradiction. He was Gordon's facilitator, his problem-solver, not his hired dissenter. Although he had no understanding of or interest in savings, Robinson simply obeyed Gordon. In a government where Cabinet meetings had been reduced by the prime minister to twenty minutes of announcements and mutual congratulation, Robinson had no inclination to break a long-term habit and consider contradictions. Nor would he take home at night the Treasury red box containing the detailed explanations of savings policies. 'I was determined not to be snowed under by the thing,' he boasted about Whitehall's files. 'So many ministers have said it ruined their normal life.'

Throughout his career, Robinson had failed to understand sophisticated nuances. He confused his own accumulation of wealth and corner-cutting with sagacity. His limited political antennae did not warn him of the dangers of a millionaire limiting the middle class's savings or of the tactlessness of a tycoon advising the poor on how to save. With an assumption of infallibility, he told his officials that PEPs were to be replaced by ISAs regardless of the consequences.

As he worked the telephones summoning favours from City experts to realise a new savings plan curtailing the tax benefits for millions of responsible Britons, Robinson gave little thought to his hypocrisy. In his July 1997 budget, the chancellor had promised the 'vigorous pursuit of tax avoidance and evasion, so that businesses and individuals pay what they should and when they should'. At the post-budget party Robinson hosted at Grosvenor House, offering lobsters and champagne, he believed that Brown's homily – 'The tax burden avoided by the few falls on the many' – did not refer to himself. Rather, his Treasury advisers, unaware of the Orion Trust and his Swiss bank account in the 1970s, were stirred by the minister's determination to terminate the savers' privileges. 'Anything to beat the taxman,' Robinson scoffed with unconscious irony.

That summer, Tony Blair enjoyed a second free holiday in Tuscany. His indebtedness to his host had disarmed any scepticism about the source of Robinson's wealth. Three years earlier, Blair had pronounced his ambition to 'clean up politics', attacking the 'scandal' of those 'who, just by hiding in the right places, can avoid paying tax altogether'. To those Tories who mischievously asked why Robinson had not, in the Commons, registered his income from olive groves as 'income from peasant labour', Blair retorted that Robinson 'has not avoided tax.'

Some blamed Blair for naivety. The prime minister had failed to question how the declared income of his paymaster-general, a British taxpayer, could have financed the purchase and maintenance of four homes and a flat in Park Lane, and an ostentatious lifestyle. Others suspected calculated apathy. The malicious speculated that Blair simply lacked moral judgement. The evidence quickly materialised.

Shortly after his return to London, Blair agreed with his chancellor a pre-budget statement including the government's commitment to reduce tax avoidance: 'There is a limit to what can be regarded as acceptable behaviour in minimising tax bills.' Days later, on 16 October 1997, Bernie Ecclestone, whose Formula One motor-racing business was registered in Guernsey, the same tax haven as Robinson's trust, was welcomed in Downing Street. The billionaire had offered another £1 million to the Labour Party and sought changes in the law of sponsorship. In particular, he wanted Formula One exempted from the proposed law banning the tobacco industry's sponsorship of sport.

Tony Blair agreed to meet Ecclestone and accept his demands beyond the gaze of any civil servants. Ensconced inside the premier's office in Downing Street, Ecclestone's presence dispelled any suggestion of a politician's naivety and confirmed the contrived innocence of an actor concealing his wilfulness. Although a lawyer, Blair displayed no instinctive understanding of his questionable morality in acceding to Ecclestone's request. His folly was to believe that Ecclestone's donation could remain secret. Two weeks later, on 5 November 1997, the change of policy was revealed to newspapers.

Soon afterwards, a journalist asked Downing Street whether Bernie Ecclestone had made a donation to the Labour Party. Blair and Mandelson were horrified. The relationship had been leaked and the implications were obvious. To forestall accusations of sleaze and corruption, Blair decided to keep the offer of the second donation secret. To confuse and conceal the link between the donation and the change of policy, the Labour Party announced that it would 'consult' Lord Neill, chairman of the Committee on Standards in Public Life, whether a further donation was proper; significantly, Blair had not asked about the propriety of accepting Ecclestone's first donation. Disingenuously, Blair's spokesmen and Peter Mandelson suggested that Blair's inquiry to Lord Neill had been dispatched before the first inquiry by a journalist. In truth, Blair's request to Neill was a direct reaction to that inquiry.

The government was beset by public uproar. The man who had promised to be 'purer than pure' compounded his disingenuous presentation. Calculatedly, Tony Blair told a television inter-viewer that he had rejected the second donation from Ecclestone. That was untrue. After all, Ecclestone had just visited Blair in Downing Street and the exemption of Formula One from the law on sponsorship by tobacco companies had been announced. 'I think that most people who have dealt with me think I'm a pretty straight sort of guy,' Blair pouted, 'and I am.'

Labour's promise of integrity and its campaign against sleaze had been a bedrock of its landslide victory at the general election. Peter Mandelson had been an architect of that campaign, yet six months after the victory he confused the public about Blair's dishonesty. The lesson from the affair, Mandelson told the prime minister, was that the public had cast doubts not on the govern-ment's integrity but on its competence. Blair was pleased by that reassurance. In the last week of November, Mandelson sought to reinforce the distraction. In a lecture entitled 'Effective Communication by the Public Sector', he addressed the lessons to be drawn from the Ecclestone scandal. 'Honesty is the first principle of good communications . . . and the purpose of com-munications is not to stall or to hide but to put in context and to explain.' Mandelson, it was assumed, was suggesting that Tony Blair's explanations had been unequivocally honest.

Despite traditional Labour's loathing of Mandelson and their humiliating preference for Ken Livingstone in the 1997 elections to the party's national executive, Blair hailed Mandelson on 1 October 1997 as 'a great guy with a great future', adding, 'in my view, he is one of the most extraordinary and talented people in British politics. It is not just the Labour Party that is lucky to have him. The country is lucky to have him and he will make a huge contribution in the years ahead.' The mutual congratulation confirmed sleaze as a Tory disease. The Ecclestone affair was deemed to be buried. No one anticipated the hydra of sleaze reappearing under another guise.

Just before Christmas, Geoffrey Robinson, enlisted by Blair and Brown as Labour's ambassador to the City, heard troubling news. 'Until I was sixty,' he later reflected, 'I had nothing but good luck. I'd never had a single illness, never saw a doctor and I'd never had a morning off for a hangover. Then, perhaps in the course of life, things stack up against you and catch you out.'

Starting with his unauthorised use of patents, there were several skeletons in Robinson's cupboard. He never anticipated that out of all those vulnerabilities, Orion would be the first to threaten his reputation and test the sincerity of Tony Blair's protestations against sleaze.

6

EARTHQUAKE

Shortly after the uproar about Bernie Ecclestone's donation sub-sided, Chris Blackhurst, a respected journalist on the *Independent on Sunday*, telephoned Charlie Whelan, the chancellor's official spokesman at the Treasury. Blackhurst, an astute financial investigator, had read the latest TransTec accounts and noticed, in a single line in small print, mention that some of Geoffrey Robinson's shares were held by 'trustees of a family trust'. Although the note did not say the trust was offshore, Blackhurst suspected the minister's vulnerability, because Orion, based in Guernsey, was listed as a substantial shareholder. Blackhurst had traced Orion's purchase of the TransTec shares from Stenbell, Robinson's company registered in Britain.

Charlie Whelan's instant reaction was revealing. 'All his shares are in the blind trust,' he scoffed.

'I'm not talking about the blind trust,' said Blackhurst. 'This is different. It's an offshore trust in a tax haven.'

'He hasn't got one of those,' insisted Whelan. 'All the shares are in a blind trust.' Clearly, Whelan had not been told about Orion.

Robinson had already heard of Blackhurst's interest from his

accountants two days earlier, on 27 November. 'It came,' he wrote
later, 'as a bolt out of the blue', but 'At first I could see no real
cause for alarm' because the Orion Trust was 'widely known'. At
the time, he said that 'It is well known locally that the family trust
has shares in Coventry FC.' Both assertions were inaccurate.
Gordon Brown did not admit his awareness of the trust's existence
in a tax haven until its exposure by the journalist; and no one in
Coventry could have discovered from newspapers that Robinson's
offshore trust had bought shares in the football team. Blackhurst's
inquiry came 'as a bolt out of the blue' because Robinson,
handicapped by a low opinion of all journalists, believed himself
impregnable to exposure.

According to Robinson's scenario, after Blackhurst's inquiry he
consulted Gordon Brown. The chancellor had every reason to be
furious. At the 1996 Labour Party conference, he had pledged
ruthless measures against Britain's rich who used foreign tax havens.
'A Labour chancellor,' he had said earlier in 1997, 'will not permit
tax relief to millionaires in offshore tax havens.' Brown was only
echoing Tony Blair's assertion that 'we should not make our tax rules
a playground for revenue-avoiders and tax-abusers who pay little or
nothing, while others pay more than their fair share'. Robinson had
been insensitive to the Labour leaders' pledges. He at first perceived
'no real cause for alarm'. On the contrary, Robinson professed, he was
unashamed of his tax-free trust. No reasonable person, including
politicians, he asserted, 'would have taken the steps necessary to
untangle perfectly legal arrangements to incur tax'. Verbal
gymnastics, Robinson hoped, would placate the sceptics and his
friends, including the chancellor and the prime minister.

Both leaders had good reason to accept his explanation of being
the helpless victim of a trust established without his knowledge;
both had enjoyed copious hospitality from him and were unwilling
to engage in an eyeball-to-eyeball demand for unvarnished honesty
from their benefactor; and both, having lied about the Ecclestone
donation, were terrified of another scandal. Neither demanded an
independent inquiry by the cabinet secretary. Instead, a senior civil
servant was expected to endorse Robinson's fiction.

Frantically that Friday night, Robinson was searching for Terry Burns. The permanent secretary could provide the necessary alibi by publicly agreeing that the paymaster-general had declared his offshore trust during their meeting on 21 May 1997.

Dressed in black tie, Burns's rehearsal of his lines for a witty after dinner speech he was about to make to the Royal Mid-Surrey Golf Club was interrupted by his mobile telephone ringing. Robinson's message was doom laden. 'The *Independent on Sunday*,' he said, 'have a story about my offshore trust. You remember, the one I told you about in May.' Burns was puzzled: 'Hang on, I don't remember you mentioning an offshore trust.' Robinson became slightly agitated. 'Surely you remember? I told you about it.' Burns appeared to fellow guests to be in pain. The ultra-honest mandarin was perplexed. 'No, I don't,' he said. 'I'll call you back.' His speech suffered as he anticipated returning home. That night, Burns searched for his small notebook and turned to the page recording his conversation with Robinson in May. Indisputably he had written 'family trust'. The thought that the Treasury's permanent secretary could confuse an uncontroversial trust with a secret offshore fund was laughable.

At 10.30 on Saturday morning, Robinson telephoned Burns at his home in Ealing, West London. 'I've got a press statement I want to read to you,' said the paymaster-general. Robinson was determined to recruit Burns to resolve his problem. In his Treasury office during the previous night, Gordon Brown had been typing the statement based upon Robinson's explanation. In that task, Brown had been helped by Charlie Whelan. While Robinson sat in his Treasury office drinking champagne, Brown's task had been eased by Whelan's reports received from a friendly journalist on the *Independent on Sunday* disclosing the anticipated details of Chris Blackhurst's allegations in Sunday's newspaper.

Robinson's proposed statement typed by the chancellor and read on the telephone to Burns included the phrase, 'I also told the permanent secretary about the family offshore trust and he told me it would not be necessary to include that in the blind trust.' The completed release endorsed by Gordon Brown implied that in

May 1997 Burns had 'approved' Robinson's blind trust which explicitly included Orion. Having completed reading the text to Burns, Robinson said, 'We just need your agreement for its release.'

'I've got two problems with that statement,' replied Burns emphatically. 'It was never my job – nor is now – to approve your offshore trust; and I have no recollection of you mentioning it.' Robinson sounded agitated, as was Burns. The civil servant was late for his train to Wolverhampton. His beloved Queens Park Rangers were playing away. He had already spoken to Sir Robin Butler, the cabinet secretary. The two senior civil servants reconfirmed the convention. The regulations concerning a minister's disclosures required officials, if consulted, only to give advice. They did not 'approve' any politician's financial arrangements. 'It's not your problem,' agreed Butler. The telephone conversation with Robinson was terminated. At least Robinson of all people would understand the priority of arriving on time at a football match.

Just ten minutes after the kick-off, at 3.10 p.m., the football fan's mobile telephone rang in the directors' box at Wolverhampton. Retreating to a lounge to watch the game on television, Burns listened to Robinson's request for his approval of a new press release again approved by Gordon Brown: 'Mr Robinson is quite clear that he has acted correctly in the performance of his ministerial duties and in registering his interests, and the permanent secretary is as well.'

Instantly, Burns protested. 'I'm not going to be associated with that release. That's impossible.'

'You must say that you approved my arrangements,' urged Robinson.

'I can't,' replied Burns. 'Because to the best of my knowledge you didn't say anything about an offshore trust.'

Robinson was persistent. 'What have you got against me? Why won't you do this?'

Sorrowfully, Burns would later say to friends, 'I wasn't being asked to outrightly lie but I was being asked to say something which I didn't believe to be true.'

Harold Wilson invited Geoffrey Robinson to work at Transport House (*Syndication International*)

Lord Stokes promoted Robinson as a protégé at Jaguar (*PA News*)

Geoffrey Robinson's business empire and future expanded thanks to his association with Robert Maxwell (*Syndication International*)

Geoffrey Robinson (second from right) at Jaguar, 1974 (*Coventry Evening Telegraph*)

Geoffrey Robinson toasts the success of Meriden Motorcycles, 1978, which later collapsed in debts and acrimony (*Coventry Evening Telegraph*)

Coventry Evening Telegraph
Lunch

No 26,314   FRIDAY MARCH 5 1976   6p

LABOUR DOWN A GUINNESS

IAMPAGNE flowed until dawn today
a party to celebrate the election of Mr
offrey Robinson as Coventry's newest
P.

The Labour candidate was whisked to a
hotel in a Jaguar XJ6 after his party's
jority vote had been halved in the crucial
entry North-West by-election.

HOW THEY VOTED

G. Robinson
J. Guinness (
A. Leighton
A. Fountaine
J Kingsley Re

A triumphant Mr Geoff
Robinson pushes his w
through a crowd of s
porters outside the Pol
Assembly Hall, Covent

(Above) Geoffrey Robinson on the
campaign trail, 1983 (*Coventry Evening
Telegraph*)

(Left) A triumphant Geoffrey Robinson
pushes his way through a crowd of
supporters after winning the Coventry
North-West by-election, 1976 (*Coventry
Evening Telegraph*)

(Below) Labour Chief Whip Bob
Melish welcomes Geoffrey Robinson
and his wife to Westminster in 1976
(*Coventry Evening Telegraph*)

(Above)
Geoffrey Robinson and his wife, Marie Elena, attend the wedding of MP Yvette Cooper to Ed Balls (*PA News*)

(Left)
Italian actress Annabella Incontrera described a tempestuous relationship with Robinson over many years (*Hulton Getty*)

(Above right to left)
Joska Bourgeois, whose fortune supported Robinson's ambition, with her companion, Saad Boudamagh, in Cannes with Roland Urban, John Morgan and Veronique Urban

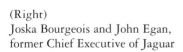

(Above)
Saad Boudamagh and Joska Bourgeois

(Right)
Joska Bourgeois and John Egan, former Chief Executive of Jaguar

Geoffrey Robinson, Paymaster General, posing at the Treasury when Tony Blair wanted his dismissal (*Syndication International*)

(Left to right) Stephen Byers, Patricia Hewitt, Gordon Brown, Dawn Primaralo and Geoffrey Robinson posing on the balcony at Number 11 Downing Street during the ministerial reshuffle, July 1998, when Robinson's fate was in doubt (*PA News*)

Gordon Brown relied on Geoffrey Robinson for financial support and an opportunity to enjoy a match between Coventry City and Arsenal at Highfield Road, 1997 (*PA News*)

Tony Blair and Alastair Campbell at the Labour Conference in Brighton, 1997 (*PA News*)

Kevin Maxwell, right, relied on Robinson to manage Maxwell's engineering interests and was sympathetic to the politician's demands for large fees (*Syndication International*)

Former Hollis Finance Director Michael Stoney who received Robinson's invoice for £200,000 (*PA News*)

Peter Mandelson outside his house in Notting Hill Gate bought with Robinson's loan (*Syndication International*)

Shadow Secretary of State for Trade and Industry David Heathcoat-Amory was prevented by successive Labour ministers from discovering the truth (*PA News*)

In December 1998, Robinson's lifelong political ambitions were terminated (*Syndication International*)

By the time Burns returned to Euston station, the press release, originally typed by Gordon Brown, had been issued without the phrase referring to his approval. His mobile rang as he was driving towards West London. At 8.15 p.m., Robinson was still fighting hard for his political reputation and believed that Burns owed him a duty of support. 'Why are you being so difficult?' asked a man unused to refusal and irritated that he lacked any lever against the stubborn official. Normally, the paymaster-general accumulated some debt which could be cashed in at the required moment but Burns's account was empty. 'Call me in ten minutes when I get home,' said Burns.

The telephone was ringing as the official opened his door. Robinson was presenting a new proposal. 'I'm going to write to you and ask you to confirm that you were happy with the handling of my financial interests and my performance as paymaster-general.'

'That's unbelievably silly,' scoffed Burns. The official was puzzled. As his colleagues later explained, Burns had never been asked such questions before and was perplexed to understand 'Geoffrey's game'. Surely Robinson realised that Tony Blair, not Terry Burns, decided whether a politician was a suitable minister? Despite twenty years in parliament, Robinson appeared unable to grasp the constitutional truism that permanent secretaries were not policemen to give 'approval' to ministers' financial arrangements or pass official judgement on politicians. Nor could Robinson understand that if Burns were to lie, the advantage to the paymaster-general would be short-lived. The official's inconsistencies would be exposed and the embarrassment would reflect on Robinson.

'I'm not writing any letter,' said Burns.

'Are you saying that I am not fit to be a minister?' Robinson asked in desperation.

Burns repeated the reasons for his refusal. Their conversation ended amid mutual suspicion.

The statement Robinson offered to the media on Saturday, 29 November 1997, suggested that he was a discretionary beneficiary of a trust established without his knowledge. 'Madame Bourgeois was a Belgian national, resident in Switzerland. Therefore there was no UK tax avoidance. Moreover, at no time have I transferred capital or other assets into the Orion Trust for tax or any other purposes.' Robinson knew that the whole purpose of offshore trusts was to prevent outsiders disproving his statement. He refused to ask the trustees to present themselves for questioning.

On Monday morning, the balance of opinion in Westminster was firmly sympathetic towards Robinson. Labour MPs crowding the bars in the House of Commons were unconcerned by the offshore trust. Universally, his story of lack of knowledge was accepted: a non-British subject had legally established a trust and Robinson happened to be the beneficiary. Led by the endorsement of Gordon Brown, the MPs voiced the general opinion: 'Lucky bloke. If he inherited millions by shagging a rich old woman, he was cleverer than most.' Tory cries of 'Hypocrisy!' aroused their contempt. Still exalted by their election victory, Robinson's colleagues were unconcerned about protests by the cash-for-questions party.

Nor were they concerned by the two questions Robinson refused to answer. With a chuckle, he refused to deny having an affair with a woman twenty-five years older than himself. 'I don't want to go into that,' he replied, adding, 'but I know a man who did.' And when asked the reason for the bequest, he replied, 'I have no idea. Do you want me to dig her up and ask her?' As a gratuitous aside he added, 'She left me £9 million.' That was subsequently changed by Robinson to £12 million.

Those jocular asides were self-destructive. By then, Orion had spent over £20 million, or $32 million, on Robinson's investments. The discrepancy between the admission of £9 million (or £12 million) income and $32 million (or £20 million) expenditure suggested either that Robinson had not told the truth about the size of his inheritance or that he had deposited other money into Orion. In the flush of the sensation, that discrepancy passed unnoticed. Rather, the focus was on a hitherto unknown politician dubbed 'possibly the richest Labour MP ever', who had 'money coming out of his ears', who never counted his millions, handed out £50 notes and 'bought houses like other millionaires buy paintings', houses he had no time to use. Like the Great Gatsby, Robinson was portrayed to the public as a man of mysterious wealth, offering exotic holidays in Tuscany and the South of France, hosting champagne parties in picturesque Lutyens mansions and issuing valuable invitations to football matches.

During those first hours, few grasped the importance of Robinson's admission concerning the sale in 1996 of his 'rights' to buy TransTec's shares. He had sold those rights to Stenbell, who had resold the shares to Orion. Robinson explained that the transaction was 'on an arm's-length basis', unaffected by his influence over Orion's trustees. The man who defined his job as 'keeping the Treasury in the real world' apparently hoped that no one understood the real world of offshore trusts.

Robinson had good reason to be flustered two days later, on 2 December 1997. He arrived at the Queen Elizabeth II Conference Centre on Parliament Square to present the government's proposals to abolish PEPs and introduce ISAs with a low, £50,000 limit. Under any circumstances, his task was difficult. Not only had the pre-election pledges by Alistair Darling and Tony Blair been broken, but savings policies, a complicated subject, was unsuitable for someone averse to concentrating upon intricate detail. Robinson had failed to master his brief.

Robinson had not wanted to rebut publicly the accusations of hypocrisy and dishonesty, but Gordon Brown and others resisted his plea to withdraw from the presentation to journalists. No one realised that Orion was merely the tip of an iceberg of concealment. Nor did Blair and Brown order a probe to discover the truth. Robinson's new friends were willingly convinced by his performance.

Like a fugitive, Robinson was smuggled into the conference centre, an unhappy, wounded man who feared the worst; he pleaded to Peter Mandelson, 'I'm just an ordinary guy. Why should anyone take an interest in me?' He was too rich to be subjected to doubts. Explanations were irksome for someone who

had always resisted apologies and was notorious for parrying
questions with bursts of contemptuous temper to avoid being
'pinned down'. Playing those games had shielded him from
embarrassment by young journalists in Coventry, but his
adversaries in London were less likely to accept incomplete
explanations. Tetchily he faced his small audience; he was
protected only by Charlie Whelan's assertion that 'Geoffrey is a
rich man who has got nothing to hide. He has done nothing
wrong. He offered to stand aside but we were determined not to
be blown off course. Geoffrey is a serious player . . . He is an asset
for the government.' With that endorsement, Robinson's fate
scarcely depended upon his performance.

The first questioner asked how the ISAs would affect holders of
PEPs and TESSAs. 'I don't want to talk about these people,'
snapped Robinson. 'I want to talk about the new savers.' Another
asked him to reconcile the disadvantages to mortgage holders of
abolishing PEPs. 'I don't want to discuss this issue,' he growled.
'You might not want to,' retorted his questioner, 'but we do.'
Under pressure, Robinson habitually displays confusion. His
customary charm becomes aggressive impatience with those
daring to disbelieve his word. His fluency often conceals his
limitations, but on this occasion he was ignorant about ISAs and
terrified about his plight. Asked about the effect of his proposals
on old established savers, Robinson imploded. 'Right, that's it,'
announced Robinson's escort. The performance was declared over
and Robinson rushed from the building. The 'press conference
itself,' Robinson wrote in his memoirs three years later, 'passed
without hostile questioning'.

The Hotel Group was unfazed. Although the champagne,
lobsters and pizzas provided by their host had been bought with
tax-free money, they assumed that the history of every self-made
fortune was mired by a cut corner. None volunteered to recall
publicly the imprecision of Robinson's repeated assertion, 'I made
no secret of the existence of the trust.' Equally, none contradicted
their benefactor. Four weeks after the Ecclestone earthquake, Blair
and Brown wanted to bury the controversy before any scandal

erupted. No businessman, both knew, was involved with offshore trusts except to avoid taxes, but Robinson's resignation would reflect badly on the government.

'Are you sure there's nothing more?' the paymaster-general was asked. Readily, he gave the reassurance. The reputation of Sir Gordon Downey, the parliamentary commissioner for standards, was invoked to justify Robinson's conduct. Downey's past record on the forensic investigation had not been universally applauded. To reinforce that approval, on Friday, 5 December, Gordon Brown, who was visiting New York, telephoned Burns. The chancellor did not hide his irritation. 'What's he done wrong?' Brown asked, apparently not considering the allegations against the paymaster-general to be serious. 'What more could he have done?' The politician appeared to be angry about a difficult official who had failed to satisfy the paymaster-general's request and approve a statement which he knew not to be true. 'I refuse to be involved,' replied Burns. Strangely, although the chancellor had good reason to suspect that Robinson was lying about his declaration, he directed his anger at an honest civil servant rather than Robinson. Even though Brown admitted that he himself had not been told about Orion – and it was only Robinson's word that Joska Bourgeois had deposited millions of pounds in Orion – he expected Burns to publicly declare that Robinson had confided a sensitive secret to an official whom he patently did not trust. 'It's crazy,' Burns told friends. That Friday, Brown did not order an inquiry by the Treasury or any government agency to establish whether Robinson's explanation of Orion's pedigree was true. If he had asked to see the official document submitted by Robinson after the meeting on 21 May, Brown would have instantly noticed the omission of an offshore trust. Either his close personal association to Robinson or New Labour's determination not to provide any political advantage to the Conservatives by a resignation paralysed the chancellor's moral obligation.

Practical problems about the paymaster-general's predicament, however, required Brown's attention. During that week, Burns and Sir Robin Butler had discussed how the replies to the parliamentary questions about Robinson could be limited to protect the government; how the draft reply to a letter from Peter Lilley, the Conservative shadow chancellor, should be as brief as possible; and what areas of work should be removed from Robinson to avoid a conflict of interest. Preparations for the new Capital Gains Tax, they agreed, should be withdrawn from the paymaster-general.

Gordon Brown's response to that list of problems outlined by Burns was frosty. He opposed limiting Robinson's authority in the Treasury and personally directed how all the parliamentary questions should be answered. Whether he approved Charlie Whelan's entire spin that weekend to newspapers reporting Burns's advice to Robinson that there was no need to register Orion in the Commons is unknown. But Brown did authorise a Treasury spokesman to state: 'All that Geoffrey Robinson was supposed to reveal has been approved. Mr Robinson has reaffirmed that he has revealed everything.' Robinson was heartened by Brown's endorsement. On Whelan's advice, at the end of a torrid week, he defiantly resisted further explanations beyond the cursory admission, typed by the chancellor, that 'I made a full statement last Saturday. I have nothing further to add.' The Hotel Group persuaded themselves that the worst was over.

The Sunday newspapers, on 7 December 1997, dislodged their complacency. The *Sunday Times* exposed Robinson's sale of his Latchuser shares to the family trust in Bermuda, implying that he might possess an interest in the offshore trust. The *Observer* revealed that he had brokered the sale of 2.95 million TransTec shares to Orion, suggesting that he had influenced the trustees to avoid income tax on dividends. The image of a benign beneficiary of an anonymous trust was tarnished. Suddenly the possibility arose that Robinson might rank alongside two other recently scandal-tarnished Labour MPs. Mohammad Sarwar, the member for Glasgow Govan, had been charged with election fraud (and later acquitted); and Robert Wareing, MP for Liverpool West Derby, had been suspended from the Commons for one week for failing to register a directorship, a shareholding and a £6000 retainer. Following the Ecclestone scandal, contemporaneous criticism of Robin Cook for amorality and protests that Lord Simon had retained BP shares worth £2 million while appointed as a minister, Robinson risked being labelled as a politician damaged by sleaze.

On Monday morning, Robinson blustered his innocence and raged for revenge against the Sunday newspapers. At risk was ministerial office, the prize he had attained after twenty-one years in politics. His anger led him into a trap of his own making, a sharp contrast to the testimony of Dr Liz Hasthorpe, his personal assistant over the previous fourteen years: 'He's pretty thick-skinned. Nothing much fazes him. He's a pretty tough character.' Robinson summoned to his office at the Treasury Bernard O'Sullivan, his solicitor at Titmuss Sainer, the firm of solicitors that had advised Robert Maxwell to avoid disclosure of his bankruptcy.

In their own self-interest, lawyers rarely deter rich clients from spending money, and only the most astute probe sufficiently to grasp their client's vulnerability. O'Sullivan was disadvantaged in the advice that he gave concerning his client's relationship with Orion and his trade in Coventry City shares by the information which he had received. He could either draft a defiant statement of innocence or advise silence. Robinson's fury, demanding retribution to assuage the concern of Blair and Brown, allowed no choice. For two hours, Robinson and O'Sullivan studied the previous day's newspapers, convinced that threatening a writ for defamation was the best tactic. Ten years earlier, Robert Maxwell's similar threats had often succeeded. By the time Ian Pearson, MP for Dudley South and Robinson's parliamentary private secretary, arrived, the threat to the newspapers' editors and a menacing press statement had been completed. Pearson was appalled. 'Why don't you just telephone the *Sunday Times* editor and get an amicable settlement?' asked Pearson, unaccustomed to the sight of Robinson's rage. 'No way,' snapped Robinson, revealing his lack of political sophistication. Even Charlie Whelan's advice to 'Keep quiet' had been rejected. 'Gordon agrees,' said Whelan. 'It's in your best interests.' Robinson was dismissive. He revealed himself as an unreconstructed Old Labour politician, full of a 1970's-style hatred of 'the Tory press' and seduced by the power of a threatened writ. On Monday evening, instead of making a statement to the Commons, he demanded an apology from the two newspapers for publishing 'ill-informed and defamatory statements', and threatened to issue a writ if they did not comply. That evening, Robinson believed he would humble his critics.

Charlie Whelan had decided that Robinson could not cope with a Jeremy Paxman interview on *Newsnight* or an interview with John Humphrys, the following morning on *Today*. Instead, a blitz of endorsements was arranged. The Downing Street press office offered a helpful statement: 'Geoffrey Robinson has the full confidence of the prime minister . . . [and] the rules have been carried out.' The Treasury spokesman supportively confirmed that the paymaster-general 'has not broken any ministerial code'. Gordon Brown generously described his friend as 'a highly successful businessman', proved by his confession to have paid £1.5 million in income tax over the previous five years. In personal interviews, the prime minister reinforced his support for a 'high-calibre' businessman and 'an extremely good minister'. There was no equivocation in Blair's pronouncement: 'Geoffrey Robinson is an exceptionally able minister.' Neither politician considered requesting a discreet probe of Robinson's activities. The prime minister's endorsement was even supported by the left-wing MP Ken Livingstone, who said Robinson had been the victim of 'sanctimonious hypocrisy' and rightly sought to minimise his taxes. At that time, no one realised that Livingstone had failed to register in the Commons his own considerable freelance earnings from speeches at private functions and that his private company had delayed submitting its accounts to the registrar of companies. By the end of a turbulent day, even Blair preferred the safety of a cryptic reservation: it was not 'remotely clear,' he observed, that Robinson had avoided tax.

Semantics could not trivialise the allegations. Blair had committed his ministers to being 'purer than pure'. Only Robinson's full disclosure could remove the suspicions, even about his fortune, and he was unprepared for that. He acknowledged his worth – 'I don't know, £30 million, something like that' – including his inheritance of £12.75 million from Bourgeois did not bear scrutiny. No one could compel his disclosure of the truth, but his sophistry and his reliance upon writs for defamation did not encourage any belief in his candour.

Few at first seem to have appreciated what the consequences would be if Robinson's demand for an apology for 'a most serious libel' failed. After issuing a writ for defamation, he would be required to resign automatically from the government and eventually appear in court for cross-examination about his finances and his relationship with Orion's trustees. By mid-week, he understood his mistake. The newspapers refused to apologise and he did not dare to issue a writ. Robinson risked ridicule and he began retreating, withdrawing first from public meetings and then from the launch of the Social Exclusion Unit. The solution, it was agreed, was for him to offer interviews on Saturday, 13 December 1997, to the Sunday newspapers, and Ed Balls would speak to the newspapers' editors before the encounters. Robinson agreed, expecting that all would obey the requirements stipulated by Balls.

Ed Balls was attached to Robinson in a friendly relationship, grateful for his indulgent hospitality, but no one could recall his admission of personal knowledge about Orion. Nor when he telephoned Will Hutton, the editor of the *Observer*, did he assert that Robinson's claim 'I made no secret of the existence of the trust' was true. But Balls did not hide his anger with the left-wing editor. In the interests of the Labour government, Balls believed, Hutton should 'trim and back off'. The interview, demanded Balls, should not embarrass the paymaster-general. The Treasury's favoured treatment of Hutton, Ball threatened, would be terminated if the editor did not join in Robinson's defence. Hutton refused to be cowed. The Treasury team, he grasped, were desperate to draw the sting and had bought Robinson's defence for their political survival. Loyalty after many evenings in the

Grosvenor House Hotel had compromised their judgement. Hutton agreed, nevertheless, to review the evidence and Robinson's answers during the interview carefully.

The first accusation concerned the circumstances of Robinson's purchase of the rights to TransTec's shares in 1996. Stenbell, his company, had bought the rights from him and resold them to Orion. The possible collusion between Robinson and the 'independent' trustees to avoid British taxes on future dividends seemed credible. Robinson's explanation to Will Hutton was stilted: 'The TransTec board asked me whether I could take up my rights and I said, no, I did not have the £10 million. The board were rather keen for my 17 per cent to be taken up, so I suggested to the trust, "Are you interested in looking at this? It would be helpful to the family." It would be perverse of them not to look at it. They are charged to do things beneficially for the family, even if it is at their entire discretion. It was the most normal thing in the world, yet it has been turned into something strange.'

Robinson's scenario might have been credible had he not offered a similarly detached, third-person explanation for the use of Stenbell, his private company: 'The brokers said, "You have got this company, why don't you do it this way?" There had been no tax reason for doing so.' After his forty years in business, negotiating endlessly around the world, it was bizarre that Robinson's stockbrokers would have unilaterally conjured up a scenario using an off-the-shelf company. Similarly, Robinson's repetitious mention of his advisers or a detached, independent board of directors to justify his decisions, portraying himself as a hapless puppet, was, to an experienced journalist, fanciful.

Potentially, the most damaging criticism of Robinson was the transfer of 2.95 million TransTec shares to Orion just before the election. Robinson's defence was ignorance and his protestation that 'I have many faults, but hypocrisy is not one of them.' In his explanation, he had never owned the shares and he was uninvolved in the transfer. The transaction was blamed on the unidentified settlors of Joska Bourgeois's estate acting 'in early 1997' with Orion's unidentified trustees. An unknown and unnamed 'nonresident settlor', said Robinson, had deposited the shares into the trust and 'I did not even know it was happening.' The transfer to the trust by the anonymous settlors so close to the election, continued Robinson, was a 'coincidence', even though the legal ownership of shares was registered only after the election. Despite the coincidences and embarrassment, insisted Robinson, he had not asked either the 'settlor' or the trustees for an explanation. Instead, he attacked Hutton and his journalists: 'The implication the whole time is that I am telling lies.' That was precisely Robinson's dilemma.

Some were unconvinced by his explanations. Joska Bourgeois had never been a registered shareholder of TransTec shares and Sami Ahmed, Robinson's former employee, had heard her repeated insistence that, while she would lend Robinson money, she would not invest in TransTec. Moreover, Bourgeois had died three years earlier and Robinson had been an executor of her will. By 1997, all her bequests had been settled. As Robinson explained, he had resigned as an executor only two or three months before the election. To sceptics, it seemed Robinson was playing with words. Most likely, the shares had been owned by someone other than Joska Bourgeois. Robinson naturally resented the accusation that his innocence was doubted but his virtue seemed to be undermined by his own remarks.

To emphasise his detachment from Orion, his solicitors had stressed that Orion's trustees were not appointed by Robinson 'and act independently of him'. But Robinson conceded that he had 'suggested' deals to the trustees. 'I told the independent trustees that it would be rather helpful to the family if it bought the shares,' he said of Stenbell's purchase of TransTec shares.

Second, Robinson admitted 'suggesting' the investment in Coventry City. Robinson denied influencing Orion's trustees 'in any way', but he had negotiated the purchase with Derrick Robbins using Craigavon, an offshore company based in Guernsey, and, contrary to his suggestion, Orion's interest was not mentioned in the media.

Facing Will Hutton and other journalists, the politician

substituted confusion for his usual charm to argue his innocence: 'Honestly, these are just total coincidences . . . For the life of me I can't see what I've done wrong . . . Everyone is casting around for slurs, mudslinging. I ask you now: what have I done wrong?' Reticence was one accusation. Robinson was vague about the identity of Orion's beneficiaries. In December 1997, he suggested it was a 'family trust' with 'six' other beneficiaries, but he also – apparently mistakenly – 'let slip' he was the sole beneficiary. Three years later, he mentioned 'eight' beneficiaries. The confusion was compounded by his claim that 'I do not know what is in the trust. I have not received any balance sheets.' That would suggest unusual carelessness. The trustees, after all, could steal the whole trust without the beneficiaries' knowledge; and beneficiaries are usually entitled to scrutinise their trust's accounts although Robinson explained that he was barred from seeing the accounts. The paymaster-general was aggressively unwilling to offer detailed answers, nor permit the trustees to confirm his version. The trustees, he replied, did not want to explain. Pressed further, he exploded in familiar rhetoric, 'Are you calling me a liar?' Robinson was either remarkably naive or the cynical orchestrator of an unpersuasive performance. His line 'some recent media comment has been the most hurtful thing I have ever read' suggested remarkable isolation from politics. His explanations had worsened his plight.

The Sunday papers, quoting the authentic voice of their prey, roasted Robinson for his evasions. 'He's lied, lied and lied again,' the Tories chanted about Robinson's explanations. The damage limitation had failed. Ed Balls was outraged, and froze the Treasury's relations with Will Hutton.

Since neither Gordon Brown nor Ed Balls was willing to confirm, publicly or privately, prior knowledge of Orion, as Robinson suggested, the paymaster-general decided to rely on the record of his 'meticulous preparation' for the full disclosure of his interests. First, he invoked the reputation of Sir Peter Gregson, a retired permanent secretary at the DTI, as his confidant before the election about his blind trust. That was a distraction to the issue of Orion and Gregson resisted making a public statement. Next, during one of his rare appearances in the House of Commons, Robinson invoked the alleged endorsement of Terry Burns. The paymaster-general told MPs that Burns had 'completely vindicated' his trusts. 'So far as I was concerned he was fully satisfied. He dismissed the issue. I told him it was a family trust. I told him I was a discretionary beneficiary, and he said, "No, no that was not a problem".' Robinson sat down with the expression of a man begging to be taken off the front page. The Hotel Group applauded. Their attention focused on Burns to await his validation of Robinson's memory. New Labour expected civil servants, bound by an unwritten oath not to contradict their political masters, to support their project regardless of the truth.

Robinson later gave a considered description of the meeting on 21 May in the Treasury. 'I informed the Permanent Secretary of the existence of the offshore trust and of the reasons why it was not included in the blind trust. He seemed well satisfied.' Subsequently, Robinson insisted that he had 'repeatedly' mentioned the trust's location 'offshore', as witnessed by Brenda Price and Peter Davis who were both in the room, and emphasised Burns's negligence in not taking a contemporaneous official note of their discussion – a criticism which annoyed Burns because the permanent secretary had been unexpectedly summoned in the midst of Robinson's meeting and custom required the minister's office to organise any minutes of the discussion. Robinson's assertion about the mention of an 'offshore trust' had serious implications, not concerning Burns's approval, but about Robinson's veracity.

The pressure upon Burns was similar to Ed Balls's invective against Will Hutton, but the Hotel Group's ostracism of Burns hardly encouraged him to lie in Robinson's defence and he resisted the demand of total loyalty. In his firm recollection, Robinson had spoken of a 'family trust' but had not mentioned its location in a tax haven. Burns's version was published in a letter to Peter Lilley, who was leading the Conservatives' attack. 'During the course of the discussion,' Burns wrote, 'the Paymaster-General told me of the existence of a family trust. Since this vehicle already existed, and offered similar protection to that provided by a blind trust, there was no reason to consider it further.' Burns was curt. Despite Gordon Brown's expectations, he refused to authenticate Robinson's version that the 'family trust' was located in a tax haven; and he clearly understood the difference between a 'blind trust', a 'family trust' and an 'offshore trust'.

Those fundamental flaws were ignored in Downing Street. 'Vindication by Burns' was the headline, even if it was inaccurate. The prime minister's endorsement of 'highly successful business people, who come and work for the Government' remained valid. Geoffrey Robinson, Blair repeated, 'is doing an excellent job for the country without even taking a ministerial salary'. Without querying the evidence, he added that his 'brilliant minister' had 'done everything according to the rules' and abided by the ministerial code. 'He has not avoided UK tax,' Blair taunted the Tories. 'He has paid probably more UK tax than either you or me.' His paymaster-general would not be pushed out of office. The issue was no longer whether Burns had approved of the Orion Trust based offshore (which he had not), but the hypocrisy and concealment by a Treasury minister in a government dedicated to curtailing offshore trusts. Robinson's fate had become a disagreement between Old and New Labour.

Traditional Labour had never liked New Labour's relationship with businessmen. John Prescott spoke for many when he publicly conceded that Robinson was a hypocrite, prompting Robinson to mention to Gordon Brown the possibility of his resignation. Brown dismissed the notion of losing an ally and his 'Mr Fixit'. More than any other minister, Robinson was ideally suited to introduce ISAs, reform the PFI, negotiate with Sir Richard Evans, chief executive of British Aerospace, about government finance for an Airbus project, and discuss with Richard Budge, chief executive of RJB Mining, the government's commitment to the coal industry. Five thousand workers in seventeen coal pits risked dismissal unless Robinson could broker, by 15 December, a successful deal with the generating companies to use RJB's coal. In all these ventures, Brown valued Robinson's energy, expertise and ideological reliability. For personal and political reasons, Robinson was too important to discard. During that week, his survival was guaranteed by another suggestion of Labour phoniness.

Forty-seven Labour MPs had voted against the government's plan to reduce child benefits, and twenty-five had abstained. The vote on Wednesday, 10 December, to reduce benefits for Britain's poor children coincided with a party at 10 Downing Street hosted by the Blairs for the rich and famous, part of the government's £7.4 million celebration of Cool Britannia. The juxtaposition was embarrassing but easily dismissed. Only seven months had passed since the election and there was limited public reproach. Robinson could content himself that the nation was not demanding his head. An opinion poll reported that although 58 per cent were critical, only 47 per cent thought he should resign.

To try to terminate the crisis, Alastair Campbell, the prime minister's spokesman, solemnly declared on 15 December, 'He is staying.' A sympathetic journalist was recruited to explain the reason. 'Robinson's real crime,' wrote Peter Riddell in *The Times* on 16 December, 'is being a successful businessman and a multi-millionaire who is a member of a Labour government.' Charlie Whelan scoffed about a 'pathetic attempt to smear him. He has nothing to hide.'

Robinson persuaded himself that he was the victim of a vendetta orchestrated by the Murdoch organisation. He even found a mouthpiece in Polly Toynbee, a matriarch of zealots, who described Rupert Murdoch as 'so much nastier and less tolerant' than others for preaching puritanism and hunting for hypocrisy in 'an honest man'. Robinson, the 'honest man', hoped that the holidays would terminate the 'conspiracy' among journalists. After making 'a full statement which was proved to be entirely accurate', he believed the ordeal was over. Rather than spending the time reviewing all his past registrations in a belated hygiene exercise to forestall further revelations, he lazily assumed that his last public comment at the end of 1997 would terminate the inquiries. 'I have nothing further to add,' he pronounced. In his confused world of ruthlessness and make-believe, he expected

Whitehall to draw an iron curtain across his domain. The only irritation was Tony Blair's surrender to the pressure of Sir Robin Butler that Robinson be barred from any work on the new Capital Gains Tax. The civil service had struck its first blow against a minister whom they no longer trusted.

Unfortunately for Robinson, during the last days before Christmas the origins of a second round of the battle were laid. First, Sir Gordon Downey, despite his original ruling, agreed to a Conservative request to investigate Robinson's failure to declare Orion. Second, Orion's tax-free profits of £187,864 after Robinson's sale of Coventry City shares to Derek Higgs were revealed. Third, on 18 December, 600,000 TransTec shares were sold in six blocks on the stock market, causing the share price to fall from 86.5 pence to 67.5 pence, a 25 per cent crash. In March the price had been 119 pence. Although Robinson's investment had fallen in value, his income had not been reduced.

Helpfully, Bill Jeffrey, the finance director, and Richard Rimmington, the deputy chairman, spent £28,000 on shares, pushing their value up to 77 pence. A new company report did not mention the demand for compensation by Ford Motors. TransTec's uncertain finances were kept secret from the public. In the summer, the directors of TransTec had signed the company's accounts showing a 69 per cent increase in pre-tax profits to £7.6 million. The dividend had been raised by 15 per cent, paying Robinson and the Orion Trust £250,000. For the moment TransTec's problems were becalmed.

Geoffrey Robinson nevertheless believed that his troubles were under control and would pass.

7

SMOKING GUNS

Few could miss the public reappearance of Geoffrey Robinson on 10 January 1998. The occasion was the wedding of Ed Balls in Eastbourne, Sussex. Unusually, Robinson was accompanied by Marie Elena, his wife, determined to be noticed on such a rare outing to a New Labour fest starring the Hotel Group. She wore a gold Lurex trouser suit over a figure-hugging black bustier, and a black choker, fan and sunglasses; few hazarded an interpretation of the spectacle. If the intention was a show of confidence, Robinson's faith was disturbed shortly afterwards.

New Labour supporters had puffed that the worst Robinson represented was possibly hypocrisy, 'but not sleaze. That died in 1997.' Twelve Conservative ministers had been forced to resign during the five years of John Major's government, taunted during the election by Peter Mandelson: 'Sleaze will continue to dog the Conservative party in this campaign and rightly so . . . We have no intention of following their dismal example . . . Without openness and transparency in our dealings with the British people there will be no trust.' By the end of the year, the Conservatives were riled. Nobody like Bernie Ecclestone had been welcomed in

Downing Street by John Major to donate cash for changes in the
law, and no minister had been so elusive as Geoffrey Robinson.
The Conservatives sought to minimise their own culpability.

During the previous five years, Conservative MPs had been
found in bed with girls who were not their wives, but adultery was
not illegal; nor was it illegal to suck the toes of a goodtime girl,
enjoy three-in-a-bed sex or be a married homosexual. Those
scandals had attracted Labour jeers, not only about the MPs'
proclivities but about their undignified behaviour after exposure. Their torrid struggles for survival had ended in miserable
surrender. The more serious Conservative sleaze potentially
undermined targeting Robinson.

Conservative ministers had accepted directorships on the
boards of companies they had privatised; two MPs had been
caught by the *Sunday Times* willing to accept cash for questions;
Jonathan Aitken had committed perjury; the Scott inquiry
revealed the calculated dishonesty of ministers in parliament and
in court about selling armaments to Iraq; and Neil Hamilton and
four other Conservatives had not registered their receipt of money
from Mohamed Fayed for lobbying. That was a heavy handicap for
Conservatives seeking to pin a charge of sleaze on Geoffrey
Robinson. The criticisms by the Conservatives in the Commons
before Christmas had been damagingly rebutted by Blair: 'The
cheek of that lot there. We remember your record all through the
past years . . . for you to shield yourselves in robes of financial
probity is a joke. You have no credibility whatsoever.' Yet the
paymaster-general's self-destructive conduct provided the prize of
revenge for their obloquy as merchants of sleaze.

Robinson's failure to register Orion was the first chance for
retaliation.

The paymaster-general sought to blame his professional
advisers for the non-registration of Orion. In his defence, he
explained that since his appointment as a minister neither he nor
the other seven beneficiaries of the trust had received any money.
He did not explain why Orion's trustees had denied the other
beneficiaries any money, and that anomaly was ignored when the

parliamentary committee found him innocent of breaking parliament's rules but agreed that he had committed a 'mistake' by not declaring Orion. Significantly, in his letter to the Committee on Standards and Privileges, Robinson did not repeat that Burns had been told by himself that his 'family trust' was offshore, merely that it was a 'discretionary trust'. To his good fortune, the committee was impressed by the evidence he provided from a leading lawyer that any 'discretionary trust' was not registrable on the grounds that there was only a 'hope' and no certainty of any income for himself from the trust. In a mild rebuke, he was criticised for relying on his professional advisers rather than on Sir Gordon Downey, who had reported that Robinson's interest in Orion 'would have been better registered'. The first shot by the Conservatives had missed.

In a Commons debate on 22 January 1998 about offshore tax avoidance, the prime minister chided the Conservatives for their 'crude attempt' to smear Robinson who was absent. The paymaster-general, the prime minister continued, had not avoided tax nor, according to Downey, had he broken any Commons rules. The counter-attack was artlessly repeated by Charlie Whelan. The Tories, he declaimed, had made 'another pathetic attempt to smear Geoffrey Robinson', who 'has registered his interests and clearly has nothing to hide'. That was untrue.

Researching Robinson was delegated by the Conservatives to David Shaw, an accountant who, in the Commons, had probed Robert Maxwell's activities; Shaw lost his seat in the 1997 election. Shaw had discovered new vulnerabilities. Robinson's directorship of Agie UK had been registered in 1987, four years late. He had earned £131,846 from Agie during those years. Second, Robinson had not registered his directorship of TransTec between 1987 and 1990 although he had earned £108,000. Third, Robinson's directorships of three Maxwell companies – C&S, Hollis and AGB – had not been registered, which was obligatory if there was remuneration. Suspiciously, his entry in *Who's Who* also failed to mention those Maxwell relationships. Robinson's rebuttal of the latest allegations was handicapped by the truth.

Concerning Agie, there was no defence. His directorship should have been registered.

On the second allegation, his directorship of TransTec, he explained that he had loaned his income back to the company. However, he was a paid director, and had paid income tax and National Insurance on his income. Where he deposited that income was irrelevant.

His relationship with Maxwell was his Achilles' heel and the Conservatives' best opportunity for retaliation. 'There's a burning anger among my constituents,' discovered David Heathcoat-Amory, the Conservative spokesman on trade and industry, 'that Blair has elevated a business associate of Maxwell's as pristine while my constituents have lost their pensions.' At last there was a chance for the Conservatives to wreak revenge for their humiliation. For the second time, an allegation against Robinson was referred to Sir Gordon Downey and the Committee on Standards and Privileges.

Six years after Maxwell's death, the nature of Robinson's relationship with the tycoon remained unknown. To the mischievous, Robinson's pedigree – Labour politician, millionaire, publisher and football club director – were the familiar characteristics of Maxwell, but Robinson dismissed the comparison as 'complete rubbish I'm afraid'. Just before Christmas 1997, Robinson had said of Maxwell: 'We bought some companies from him. They were good companies.' Asked if he was embarrassed, he smiled, 'No. Not at all. My dealings with him were perfectly satisfactory and correct. There was nothing wrong with them.' To another inquirer he replied, 'I didn't have extensive business with Maxwell . . . We bought two companies off him. Am I not allowed to buy a company off Maxwell?' Robinson's belligerence did not inspire confidence. While assumed to be intelligent, he seemed oblivious of the impression he created.

Since 1991, retribution against those involved in the Maxwell frauds had been sparse. Kevin Maxwell had been acquitted by a jury and saved from a second criminal trial; a few accountants had been censured; several bankers and lawyers had suffered embarrassment; an investigation by IMRO, the investment regulator, had not been published; and two inspectors appointed by the DTI were far from completing their report. The appointment of Bernard Donoughue, Helen Liddell and Geoffrey Robinson as ministers confirmed widespread amnesia.

On 17 March 1998, Robinson posed for photographers with Gordon Brown and other Treasury ministers in Downing Street. The chancellor was about to present his budget, characterised as advancing 'enterprise and fairness', to the Commons. The paymaster-general smiled self-consciously. Although Brown had rebutted the attacks against him with a standard response – 'He has met all the rules on ministerial conduct; and he has paid taxes in the UK to the tune of £1.5 million' – there was unease about Robinson's insensitivity. His jeer at Middle Britain's savers with over £50,000 in PEPs – 'people who have done extremely well' – was unfortunate from a man with at least £12 million in an offshore tax haven. He was an easy target: 'the tax-dodger in charge of taking away tax relief from Middle Britain'. Labour's managers finally sensed that Geoffrey Robinson's past was not straightforward. Their cure was graceless: Robinson disappeared from the House of Commons. Other ministers answered the paymaster-general's questions and party managers considered organising his absence from committee meetings. The sentiment was protective of Robinson rather than suspicious until the next accusation was delivered.

Neither David Shaw nor David Heathcoat-Amory had under-stood Maxwell's importance to Robinson's fortune. Initially, Robinson explained that his directorships of Maxwell's companies were unpaid and therefore not liable to registration. That reply was inconsistent with Robinson's registration of his unpaid directorships at Meriden, his family furniture business and several similar directorships.

More pertinently, Robinson admitted his receipt of £150,000 from C&S which had not appeared on the Commons register. He explained that he had sought to register the payment in January 1991 but his notification was received 'too late' by the parliamentary official and 'missed the printer's deadline'. The

Conservatives suspected that Robinson had tried to conceal his relationship with Maxwell but their allegations led to an impasse until Heathcoat-Amory and Shaw examined the back-to-back transaction on 23 April 1991 transferring Lock and PSS from Hollis to Central & Sheerwood (C&S), which Robinson controlled. To the researchers, Robinson and Maxwell appeared to have benefited at the expense of the shareholders. Hollis's value had fallen from £118.8 million in June 1988 to minus £44.5 million in December 1991. The coincidence of that deal and Robinson's failure to register his payment from C&S was strange.

Another discovery was sensational. The last Hollis accounts, signed by Robinson as chairman, recorded the payment to him of £200,000. That income had not been registered in the Commons. The pattern appeared irrefutable, since neither the £150,000 payment from C&S nor his income of £239,000 from Agie and TransTec had been registered. Various excuses could not reduce the impression of conduct worse than carelessness.

For the first time, Robinson panicked. The non-disclosure of a £200,000 payment from Hollis in response to the Orchards invoice would lead to automatic suspension from the Commons and the end of his political career. He instantly expressed ignorance: 'I never asked for the money and wasn't paid.' After reviewing all his bank statements to ensure none revealed the payment, he telephoned Kevin Maxwell. 'Do you remember a £200,000 payment to me by Hollis?' he asked. Pondering the madhouse days of 1991 as his father's empire was daily, even hourly, rocked by earthquakes, Kevin Maxwell was nonplussed. Amid the thousands of complicated transfers he had master-minded, the possibility of recalling an isolated payment in an insignificant company was remote. Even if he could help, he was disinclined to do so after Robinson had reneged on his under-taking to appear as a witness for the defence in the fraud trial. But in all honesty Kevin could only recall his father dismissing Robinson's request for payment. 'Bugger him,' Robert Maxwell had snapped. 'He landed us in this.' Kevin gave Robinson that information, which pleased the politician.

Robinson's next call was to Michael Stoney, Hollis's finance director and accountant. 'There's a problem,' said Robinson in a noticeably nervous voice. 'I can't remember being paid £200,000 by Hollis. Can you remember anything about it?' Stoney was sympathetic towards Robinson. After Maxwell's death, Robinson had invited the beleaguered and unemployed accountant with his wife and children to lunch at the Commons. Stoney was grateful for that generous gesture. 'I can't remember anything like that,' replied Stoney supportively, but he added less helpfully, 'It was bedlam, chaos, there. I wouldn't remember something as small as that.'

Bad memory, Robinson knew, would not satisfy the political hounds. His requirement was for something irrefutable. Fortunately, Stoney had been employed after Maxwell's death by Arthur Andersen to unravel and organise the archives of the empire's private companies. 'I'll see if Arthur Andersen will let me look for the payment,' offered Stoney. 'Thanks very much,' replied Robinson.

By any reckoning, the scenario was contentious. Stoney, who had escaped criminal prosecution but had been struck off the register of the Institute of Chartered Accountants for his conduct on Maxwell's behalf in one transaction, obtained permission from Andersen's to search through twenty-five boxes of Hollis files barred to other inquirers. Seven years after the event, many of Hollis's original documents were missing. Some were lost and others had been deliberately destroyed. Nevertheless, Stoney eventually found in Andersen's archives his own memorandum dated 16 November 1990 requesting a £200,000 payment to Robinson for 'management fees'. Stoney was surprised by his discovery. 'Quite simply,' he admitted, 'I cannot recall writing that memo.' That was unsatisfactory for Robinson. He could no longer assert that the £200,000 payment was a complete surprise. After all, if Stoney had requested the payment, there would be an invoice. Fortunately, Robinson's invoice on the Orchards notepaper had not been found. Nor had any evidence of the payment been discovered. Robinson may have thought that the paper trail

had been destroyed. Nevertheless, the burden was upon Robinson
to prove a negative: namely, that the entry in Hollis's accounts was
mistaken.

In June 1998, despite a curt reminder from Heathcoat-Amory
that his complaint was four months old, Sir Gordon Downey was
still waiting for Robinson's replies. In Downing Street, the prime
minister and chancellor were impatient. Despite the absence of
information, Tony Blair decided to dismiss the allegations against
his prospective host for his third free holiday in Tuscany.
Reassured by Robinson's promise that he had never requested or
received £200,000 from Maxwell, Blair instructed Alastair
Campbell to anticipate Downey's report and the conclusions of the
select committee, and express his full confidence in the paymaster-
general. Dutifully, Campbell blamed Coopers & Lybrand for a
mistake. 'We can state categorically,' said Campbell, 'that
Geoffrey Robinson did not receive £200,000 or any money as a
result of his chairmanship.' He added with the knowledge of an
expert, 'I think you'll find there's an error in the accounts.'

Robinson was under pressure to deliver the documents and
statements substantiating the prime minister's exoneration. He
delayed but suddenly time was no longer available. On 5 July, the
Observer revealed that Derek Draper, a friend of Peter Mandelson
and a New Labour lobbyist, had been offering a journalist, who
was working undercover, access to the 'seventeen most important
people' in the government for cash. Draper's offer had been
partially recorded on tape and he did not dispute the allegations.
Aggravatingly, Roger Liddle, an adviser to Blair at 10 Downing
Street and former lobbyist, who was close to Draper, had also
offered information and access to the same journalist posing as an
American investor. 'Cash for secrets' was pure sleaze, redolent of
'cash for questions'. Blair's response was an absolute denial. 'Not a
single allegation in the *Observer* article is true,' he told the
Commons, a valuable guide to Blair's veracity in his defence of his
minister. Contemporaneously, the premier also denied intervening on Rupert Murdoch's behalf with Romano Prodi, the
Italian prime minister, for favoured treatment in a TV deal. His

denial was inaccurate. Protecting relationships with the rich appeared to justify Tony Blair's subterfuge. His endorsement of Robinson's denial of requesting or receiving £200,000 was unequivocal.

Robinson was fighting for his own and Blair's reputations. Gathering favourable testimonials was passing more smoothly than he might have anticipated. Robert Coe of Wilder & Coe, Robinson's personal accountants who negotiated on Robinson's behalf with Alan Chick, the Orion trustee, had written supportively to their valued client that 'we have no record of you receiving the £200,000 remuneration from Hollis'. The emphasis was on the receipt of the money from Hollis.

In addition, Stoney re-emerged from Arthur Andersen's archives to report that no paper trail had been found of his own memorandum. Principally, he had not found a £200,000 payment in Hollis's bank statements, nor had he found an invoice from Robinson. Robinson was relieved. His plight, he realised, could be resolved by a favourable statement from Stoney. The accountant, thankfully, was amenable. Since he could not find any further records, Stoney agreed, after Robinson's prompting, to recall sufficient circumstances surrounding the money to provide a helpful statement. 'I wrote to our accountants asking them to provide £200,000 for Mr Robinson,' wrote Stoney, but 'no money was paid and I forgot to inform the accountants. The subsequent (1990) accounts recording the £200,000 were incorrect and I must take the blame.' Stoney added obligingly, 'I do not know why the fee was not paid.' He concluded that Robinson 'never received the £200,000 from Hollis'. That statement was a relief for Robinson, prompting him to make an untrue public statement. 'It wasn't the intention that there should be any remuneration so it wouldn't have been an item to look at,' he said referring to the chairman's payment in the accounts. 'There was no need to check it.' Unknown to Robinson, new evidence which Stoney had understandably forgotten had been unearthed, undermining his veracity.

During June, Martin Fishman, an accountant at Arthur

Andersen, had found a memorandum dated 31 January 1991 with a handwritten comment, '£200,000 paid to G. Robinson (Recharged by Pergamon AGB)' referring to the cheque cashed on 21 December 1990. In a letter to Robinson on 7 July 1998, Fishman agreed that Hollis had not made the payment in January 1991 but he added, unaware of the cheque's fate, 'It is possible that further information may exist in the records of PAGB [Pergamon AGB].'

Potentially, the last sentence was dynamite. The failure to discover the Orchards invoice in the Hollis files gave Robinson confidence that it was lost. Since Michael Stoney had admitted the accounts were 'mistaken', there was every reason to persevere with that version to escape censure. Robinson grasped the threat boldly. 'I now propose,' he wrote to Sir Gordon Downey and the House of Commons Committee on Standards and Privileges, 'to commission a detailed examination of the Pergamon accounts and unequivocally assure the committee that this remuneration was not agreed by me and that no payment was ever made.' He also contacted Price Waterhouse Cooper, the administrators of those publicly owned Maxwell companies previously quoted on the stock exchange, and secured a reply which he hoped might be helpful. An assistant had found a £200,000 payment to a director in Pergamon's accounts for 1989/90 for the loss of office. That director was not Robinson. The flourish of that letter by Robinson may have been intended to confuse the investigation because a salient fact was ignored: the Pergamon payment was in the wrong year. Hollis's last accounts, based upon records censured by the auditors as 'unsatisfactory', were signed on 24 January 1991. The Pergamon payment to Robinson had been made on 21 December 1990.

Discovering the truth depended upon Arthur Andersen, the custodians of Pergamon AGB's archives, a company which had been privately owned by the Maxwells. Martin Fishman at Andersen's suggested it might take one month to sift through three hundred boxes of Pergamon's records. Robinson's fate depended upon Sir Gordon Downey's attitude. During that year,

Neil Hamilton, the MP who had not declared his receipt of cash and gifts from Mohamed Fayed, had criticised Downey's personal inadequacies and prejudices for thwarting an impartial inquiry, and he also complained that Labour's majority on the Committee on Standards and Privileges had denied him a fair hearing. Robinson hoped to avoid that grievance.

Martin Fishman's proposal to examine Pergamon's records did not appeal to Downey or to the committee of MPs. They were under pressure to report before the summer recess, and they preferred to ignore confusing discrepancies and a potential conflict of interest which might delay that timetable. Robinson was even left with the impression that Downey was well-disposed towards him. 'He seemed to me,' recalled Robinson, 'to develop a fastidious distaste for the Tories and their vendetta, as he called it, against me. His view was that "they were really scraping the barrel".' Downey disputed the veracity of Robinson's quotations and impressions but his report to the committee of MPs was tilted in Robinson's favour.

In his appearance before the MPs, Robinson deployed the charm that had persuaded men and women over the previous thirty years to extend their trust and bequeath their fortunes. Unlike Neil Hamilton and Robert Wareing, the latest witness oozed honesty and credibility. Robinson's offer to the MPs 'to commission a detailed examination of the Pergamon accounts' was rejected. Michael Fishman's offer to search Pergamon's archives was also declined. The existence of Robinson's invoice for £200,000 on Orchards notepaper remained unknown. All the MPs agreed that if proof had been discovered showing that Robinson had concealed the £200,000 payment, he would have been instantly suspended from the Commons. But the evidence, they agreed, did not exist. To doubt Robinson's word was to impugn the honour of Tony Blair and Gordon Brown.

Adopting a purely legalistic interpretation, the MPs agreed that since Robinson was not a paid director of Pergamon, it would be 'time-consuming and costly' to pursue a further investigation of Pergamon's records with 'no reasonable prospect' of finding new evidence. The MPs had not fully understood the unorthodox finances of Maxwell's empire whereby the cash in one company (namely, Pergamon) was regularly used to pay the debts of another. Since there were no eyewitnesses or documents to contradict Robinson's protestations of innocence that the £200,000 had been neither paid nor received from Hollis and Robinson's accountants had accurately reported, the complaint by Heathcoat-Amory was dismissed. 'We believe the relevant entry in the published accounts [of Hollis] is false,' concluded the parliamentary committee. Robinson was also excused for failing to register his directorships of the Maxwell companies because the positions were unpaid.

There were two caveats. Robinson was blamed for his responsibility for signing Hollis's inaccurate accounts; and criticised for failing to 'meet all the requirements' by the late registration of his directorships of TransTec Ltd [1987–90] and Agie [1984–7]. Despite those criticisms, Robinson persuaded the committee that, although he had broken the rules, his offences did not 'reach the threshold' to justify any penalty.

Robinson had been fortunate. With the prime minister's support, the Labour majority on the committee of MPs agreed to spare the minister humiliation like that of Robert Wareing and Neil Hamilton. The publication of the report on 14 July 1998 was marred only by the title: 'Complaints against Mr Geoffrey Robinson (No.2)'. On Blair's own test that ministers must be 'purer than pure', Robinson had not passed, but that was ignored.

Robinson ebulliently preached his outright vindication: 'Given the evidence, I could not see how they could come to any other conclusion.' Although the committee's acquittal was not unequivocal, he blamed 'political envy underlying the political vindictiveness' for a 'highly personal vendetta which has got out of all proportion. I have not grumbled about it because it does no good. I have been hurt by it but I have never openly complained. Nor will I now.' But he did add, 'The Tories cannot stomach the fact that a successful businessman can work successfully with business leaders in a Labour government.' Robinson spoke with

Blair's unconditional support. 'Every time,' said the prime minister, 'the Conservatives have made an allegation it has proved to be worthless.' The *Financial Times* agreed, judging that Robinson's behaviour 'amounted to little more than carelessness'. But the newspaper showed an unusual ignorance of Robinson's finances and relationship with Maxwell in 1991: 'He was rich enough not to need to abuse public office.' Robinson's apparent wealth was certainly true in 1998. He had just received £756,000 in dividends from TransTec, although the shares were languishing at 82 pence.

Beyond his public support, Blair had become uncertain about the paymaster-general. His summer host was a wounded man, too scarred and vulnerable to appear on 11 June 1998 at a committee hearing to scrutinise the budget. (Helen Liddell was his replacement.) Robinson had breached the Commons rules on registration and, on his own admission, he had as chairman of Hollis signed false accounts. The *Daily Express*, to Blair's surprise, although firmly committed to supporting the government, was publishing a series of critical accounts about Robinson and the rivalry between the chancellor and the prime minister. Within his own office, David Milliband, a political adviser in Downing Street, was complaining about Robinson's intolerable behaviour at the interdepartmental committee meetings. Regularly, Robinson arrived, without understanding the carefully written briefs, to offer his opinion on any subject, ignoring the details. 'Just like a wheeler-dealer,' complained one frustrated participant. Robinson praised his own contribution for getting the discussion 'moving along' but appeared unconcerned by the destination of his efforts. At the regular meetings of the Treasury's Management Committee, Terry Burns was constantly noting complaints by his officials about the 'chaos and methods' in Robinson's office.

A wiser man might have digested the opprobrium and moderated his attitude. With some percipience, he would have exhaustively reviewed his commercial history to forestall the recurrence of yet another indictment. Robinson found that too difficult. His ruthlessness, contempt or myopic folly precluded a

considered strategy. Rather, he revelled in the epithet of a 'shrewd
and clever' Dom Pérignon socialist. Bullishly, he proclaimed, 'I
failed to register one interest for a certain period, and this is
fourteen years ago. It was an omission, there wasn't anything
deliberate about it.' He trusted to luck that the Conservatives
would find nothing more and he could continue to rely on the
support of Labour MPs. 'Why don't you just tell them to get
stuffed and go back and make another million?' asked one Labour
MP. 'I've made enough already,' replied Robinson, adding, 'but in
any case, I understand these economic policies in a way that no one
does. I can still make a contribution.' Neither Robinson nor his
Labour sympathisers appreciated the dangers.

By contrast, civil servants inhabiting the warren of offices
around Downing Street spoke about Robinson's relationship with
the Maxwells as 'murky'. Richard Wilson, the new cabinet
secretary, had brought to Tony Blair's attention a sensational article
in the February issue of *Business Age*, falsely alleging a profoundly
criminal conspiracy between Robinson and Maxwell which had
continued for the Maxwell family's benefit after the tycoon's death.
Blair did not understand the detail but the headline, 'Maxwell's
Paymaster in Death', inflamed the doubts raised by two Downey
inquiries. Although the allegations in the article were ludicrous,
there were new fears that Robinson's relationship with Maxwell
might have been closer than previously understood despite his
attempts to minimise it. 'I hardly knew Maxwell,' he had told
inquirers, including the journalist Francis Wheen. 'I only met
him once.' The impression he cultivated was of a detached
acquaintanceship without any financial consequences. 'The proof is
that I wasn't even invited to his birthday parties in Oxford.'
Business Age suggested the contrary but despite his denunciation of
its allegations as a farrago of lies, Robinson was unwilling to
threaten a writ. That would be a counter-productive gesture, he
calculated, forcing his resignation, and he had no intention of
submitting himself to cross-examination in a courtroom.

Richard Wilson had little good to say about the paymaster-
general. Contrary to Robinson's assertion of having been 'cleared

twice by Downey', his involvement with Robert Maxwell was dubious. Although the cabinet secretary did not know about the Orchards invoice, his experience of smoking guns was mature. There was a jaded resonance to the paymaster-general's patter about the 'privilege and pleasure' of serving in government; and his cavalier, trader's mentality aroused unease. Wilson knew from Terry Burns, whose resignation had finally been announced, to Gordon Brown's glee, on 3 June 1998, that Robinson was distrusted by many Treasury officials. For his part, Robinson had little good to say about Wilson, describing the Cabinet Office as 'the repository of every fizzled-out runt initiative that's been thought up. I've never seen such a mess in my life.' Unpleasant tension between politicians and Whitehall's officials is not uncommon, but only a heedless politician, delighting in Blair's politicisation of the civil service, could have ignored the invariable survival of Whitehall's natives in those contests. Geoffrey Robinson, the cabinet secretary observed to the prime minister, was blinded by a short-sighted view of his own mess.

The moment had arrived, Blair concluded, to clear up the mess and bid Robinson farewell. That removal, Blair knew, would be difficult, because he was indebted to the paymaster-general. The businessman had financed his private office and the research before the election, and had twice provided a holiday home. But the minuses were too overwhelming. Robinson was tarnished and distrusted. He was beginning to represent sleaze. As a preliminary step, Blair decided to cancel his summer visit to Robinson's house in Tuscany. Since he and Cherie were, as usual, unwilling to pay for their holiday, he required an alternative free invitation. Fortunately, Prince Girolamo Strozzi, a neighbour of Robinson's in San Gimignano, was persuaded hastily to offer his own home. Although he barely knew Strozzi, Blair accepted without apparently expressing concern about his host's inconvenience.

The cancellation prompted Robinson's fear of dismissal. Despite the personal reassurances of Gordon Brown and the briefing to Peter Riddell, the loyal journalist from *The Times,* that the chancellor regarded Robinson as a 'test case' of an informal, unconventional businessman enjoying a prominent role in government because he brought experience and insight to solve problems, Robinson knew about damaging rumours concerning his probity. The *Business Age* article had not been ignored. Even Gordon Brown had asked Robinson about 'a personal cheque' from Maxwell. Expunging the Maxwell legacy had become a priority for the government. Robinson understood the drift but expected Brown to provide protection.

The prime minister, a man who loves to be loved, hated his task as a butcher. A reshuffle of the cabinet was imminent, a perfect moment to move Robinson with the explanation of 'ill-health', a genuine reason since he was on the eve of entering hospital for abdominal surgery. In the midst of preparations for the 28 July reshuffle, Robinson was summoned to meet Blair. Shortly afterwards, on Brown's instructions, the meeting was cancelled. The consequences of dismissing Robinson, the prime minister appreciated, threatened his relationship with Gordon Brown. Too embarrassed to inflict pain himself on Robinson, the prime minister asked Richard Wilson to perform the deed which he recommended. Wilson could have refused to perform a party political chore but instead obliged.

During the same day, Wilson called on Gordon Brown and explained that the prime minister expected the chancellor to deliver his paymaster-general's resignation. The reason, explained Wilson, was the bad press, especially the allegations in *Business Age*. In anticipation, Brown had already obtained from Robinson a full rebuttal. Pages of detail, countered Wilson, were too late. The prime minister was impatient to announce his cabinet changes and among them was Robinson's resignation. Brown refused to perform Blair's task. Haplessly, Wilson bowed to the prime minister's request and confronted Robinson. 'Rough old game, politics,' said the emissary as he entered Robinson's office to explain his mission. Maxwell and the *Business Age* allegations, said Wilson, were the reason for the prime minister's demand, regardless of Robinson's insistence that the article was 'a pack of lies'. Robinson refused to be cowed. Wilson's involvement, he scoffed, was 'distasteful'. Calmly, Wilson ignored Robinson's protest, suggested that 'it's rather more dignified to resign than to be sacked', and departed. Sensing his isolation, Robinson heard that the newspapers were reporting Geoff Hoon, the spokesman for the lord chancellor in the Commons, as his successor.

Both Gordon Brown and Ed Balls remained stoutly loyal. Brown, according to Robinson, was 'distraught'. Balls talked about the paymaster-general as a 'fucking brilliant minister'. Bolstered, Robinson refused to resign 'under a cloud. No one, not even my severest critics,' he later wrote, 'had ever suggested that I was less than competent.' He was clearly deaf to the senior officials in the Treasury; and was unaware that honesty rather than his competence was the issue. Brown understood the stakes. Robinson's replacement by Geoff Hoon would be a tactical victory for Blair and the betrayal of a friend. In the midst of renewed publicity about the Brown–Blair feud, the chancellor, despite the evidence of shadiness, could not afford to lose an ally. The wheeler-dealer had become the latest fulcrum in the battle between the prime minister and chancellor. A meeting was arranged with Blair for the chancellor to plead Robinson's case.

Brown deployed two arguments to keep Robinson. The paymaster-general offered original ideas; and he was an effective operator with valuable City contacts. While the first reason was possibly true, the second, selling Robinson as a skilful tycoon, was a myth which Brown and Blair still failed to dispel. Half convinced by Brown, Blair agreed that he should meet Robinson at eight o'clock that night. To smooth Robinson's path, Brown and Whelan arranged for that evening's television news to include Robinson in the photocall of the 'new' Treasury team.

Sitting with the paymaster-general in his living-room, the prime minister was compromised. Accusations of sleaze festered, injuring the government. The *Observer*'s sting against Derek Draper and Roger Liddle, who had offered access to ministers for cash, smouldered; Jack Cunningham's appointment as 'cabinet enforcer' was accompanied by reports of his overindulgent living expenses in hotels and on air travel, and his eager acceptance of hospitality; there were arrests for corruption of Labour councillors in Wakefield and Rotherham; and the suicide in 1997 of Gordon McMaster, Labour Co-op MP for Paisley South, had aroused accusations of corruption in the city. Robinson was an unwelcome addition to the list of unscrupulousness. Thoughtlessly, some would say greedily, Blair was speaking to another tainted man who, rejecting any blame, refused to depart quietly.

After an hour's conversation about the paymaster-general's battles on behalf of New Labour against the civil service, Blair was too confused to execute the fallen angel. He had plunged the dagger in, but was undecided whether to pull it out. Blair was too indebted to curtail Robinson the salesman chanting his defence of his ambitions and reputation. Civilly, they agreed to 'sleep on it'. After daybreak, Blair bowed to Brown's wishes and Robinson remained. The only certainty was the predictions of senior officials in Whitehall. They spoke openly about the paymaster-general's slender hopes for survival, repeating Blair's parting words to him that, as a target of the media, he would be allowed only one more chance.

'A chance' had been the words also used in discussing the principal beneficiary of the cabinet changes: Peter Mandelson's appointment as secretary of state at the DTI. Among the many responsibilities of the new minister, who earned £90,000 per annum, was the regulation of the nation's corporate life. A myriad of letters awaited Mandelson's attention, including a copy of a provocative submission written on 15 July 1998 by David Heathcoat-Amory to the registrar of companies seeking an investigation of Geoffrey Robinson and urging his possible removal as a director for signing the last Hollis's accounts showing the 'error' of the £200,000 payment. Heathcoat-Amory had sent the copy of his letter to the DTI, not anticipating that a reply would be among Mandelson's first chores.

Peter Mandelson had been welcomed by Sir Michael Scholar, the DTI's respected, academic permanent secretary. Over the previous twenty years, the average tenure of the senior DTI minister had been little more than one year. Scholar had little reason to place his latest minister among the accident-prone but, as Richard Wilson had said on the same day to Robinson, 'Rough old game, politics.' Mandelson was certainly not renowned as a conviction moralist. Before the election he had been aware of Bernard Donoughue's proximity to those organising Maxwell's pension-fund frauds but had remained silent. He also knew about Helen Liddell's relationship with Maxwell and said nothing. As the DTI minister, he had become responsible for the continuing DTI inquiry into Maxwell's affairs. The Maxwell legacy refused to be buried. The recent revelations of Robinson's relationship with the Maxwells, which threatened the paymaster-general's position, had anchored Mandelson's ministerial involvement in his bene-factor's history. This was sensitive territory, especially for Mandelson, who before the election had magnified sleaze into a dominant issue.

As a professional politician, Mandelson was aware of paragraph 123 of the *Ministerial Code*, which advised all ministers to consult their permanent secretary about 'any action which they are considering, to avoid any actual or potential conflict of interest' and to inform their senior civil servants or even the prime minister in 'cases of doubt'. Under that paragraph, Mandelson was obliged to inform Scholar of the £373,000 he had received from Robinson as a loan in 1996 for his house; the British system of govern-ment requires ministers to volunteer all relevant information. Mandelson chose to avoid that embarrassment. To admit his own vulnerability to the paymaster-general, Mandelson feared, would not remain a secret for long. A conversation with Scholar, just hours after Robinson had been asked to resign, was not appealing to a politician who had just won a cherished prize. David Heathcoat-Amory's letter listing Robinson's alleged breaches of the law was best ignored until an escape from the conflict of interest could be considered.

In September, Mandelson's predicament worsened. Robinson's relationship with Maxwell and the management of Hollis, Mandelson was told by Scholar, required investigation. Among the topics to be examined would be false accounting, the sale of

Hollis's assets to Robinson and the alleged £200,000 payment to Robinson by Hollis. Politically and legally, Mandelson was responsible for the investigation. Although Mandelson later said that he had agreed with Scholar 'not to be involved in this process', suggesting that the decision was taken by his departmental officials, the responsibility was his. In the public interest, Mandelson could have ordered the inquiry to produce a public report. Instead, he approved an internal, secret investigation which would protect Robinson. As it was an internal inquiry, the identity of the investigator, Hugh Aldous, also remained secret. Aldous, a senior partner at the accountants Robson Rhodes, had a controversial record as an investigator and expert witness, but he was admired by the DTI as reliable.

The letter from Peter Mandelson to David Heathcoat-Amory on 23 September reporting the Hollis inquiry sought to be sterile and beyond reproach: 'The matter which you raised is being considered. As I am sure you will understand, I shall not be able to comment further on any action which the Department might take.' In signing that letter without declaring the loan from Robinson, Mandelson compounded his conflict of interest. As a member of the government, Robinson was also compromised. Aware that he was under investigation, he should have sought advice from the Treasury's permanent secretary about his financial relationship with Mandelson. But, having narrowly escaped dismissal, Robinson preferred to remain silent. The loan, he wrote later, was a secret between the two ministers, 'because we had both mutually agreed that it was a private arrangement that concerned no one else'. That was precisely why, as government ministers, they were obliged to breach the bond of secrecy they had concluded as backbenchers. After July 1998, the loan did concern others.

Mandelson said that Robinson requested secrecy. Whenever asked about the source of the money for his house, Mandelson lied. 'I got an inheritance from my father through my mother,' he told friends. He blanched when told during a dinner party that his inheritance was open to scrutiny since his father's will was a public document, but he perpetuated his lie.

That summer, the financial relationship between Robinson and Mandelson was known to several of the former's intimates in the government. Gordon Brown, Ed Balls and Charlie Whelan were aware of the loan, probably from Robinson. None considered raising the impropriety of the conflict of interest. Elsewhere in Whitehall, Michael Wills, a newly elected member, had been told by the Brown camp about the loan. During his holiday in Spain, Wills revealed the secret to Charlie Falconer, the barrister who was appointed first solicitor-general and then a minister in the Cabinet Office. On hearing the news, Falconer, a lawyer and a former government law officer, might have been expected to understand the conflict of interest. Instead, he listened to Wills and made no comment. Not a flicker of concern registered on his face. Subsequently, Falconer might have said to his friend the prime minister during one of their many meetings, 'A problem of morality has arisen', but he remained silent. The lawyer resisted any obligation to be a guardian of honest government.

During autumn 1998, the relationship between Mandelson and Robinson – thin in its heyday – became marginally strained. The loan and the DTI investigation of Hollis were not the cause. Rather, Robinson's political survival depended entirely upon Gordon Brown, and the chancellor's feud with Mandelson was constantly resurfacing. In that cause, Robinson criticised Mandelson's antagonism to socialism. 'You're too sure about the importance of markets,' he warned Mandelson. 'You believe that capitalism can do no wrong.'

Like all New Labour's ministers, Mandelson did not understand capitalism and wrongly assumed that Robinson's wealth, based on industry, proved the paymaster-general's expertise about markets. Others in the party and elsewhere understood that the origins of Robinson's wealth were suspicious. In the Treasury, the paymaster-general prided himself on cutting through bureaucracy. In commercial life, he was renowned for cutting corners. In government, Robinson married the two.

In October 1998, despite the rules against ministers' involvement in private business, Robinson had not quite isolated himself from the fortunes of Coventry City FC. His investment, he knew, would be enhanced by the development of a forty-thousand-seat stadium to be built at Foleshill, an abandoned gasworks outside Coventry. The estimated cost for Arena 2000 was £150 million, and Robinson was lobbying Coventry Council to invest public funds in the scheme, which would include a shopping develop-ment. Like all developers, Robinson's consortium hoped to obtain building permission without an expensive public inquiry which would undoubtedly attract opposition and jeopardise the project. To avoid that risk, Robinson wrote in autumn 1998 to Richard Caborn, minister for planning, seeking support for building the stadium without an inquiry. His letter, Robinson explained, was on behalf of an interested constituent. The politician revealed surprising insensitivity about the impression he risked creating just as the Conservatives asked Sir Gordon Downey to investigate new discrepancies in Robinson's register of interests.

Conservative Party researchers had discovered that Robinson registered Stenbell in October 1997, although he had become a director in February 1996. At the Conservative's request, Downey agreed to begin a third report. In the Commons and Downing Street, there was bewilderment that the saga could not be killed. Robinson's 'laziness' was remarkable. An additional complication was a complaint by the Belgian tax authorities that the Inland Revenue, contrary to EU laws, was refusing to co-operate in their investigation to discover whether Robinson had benefited by Joska Bourgeois's evasion of Belgian taxes. The embarrassment was compounded by the paymaster-general's constant negotia-tions with the Inland Revenue about ISAs and corporate taxation. Conflicts constantly recurred. To protect the government, Robinson avoided oral or written questions in the Commons and abandoned, without explanation and at short notice, lunches and speaking engagements in the City. His salvation partly depended upon establishing his value as a minister.

In a blitz of activity, the paymaster-general launched an initiative to improve financial management in small businesses and to improve the training of managers; he chaired a new public

incite any of Brown's entourage to pose honest questions about their benefactor in public. For two years they had wilfully ignored Robinson's business methods and the source of his wealth. While enjoying his champagne at the Grosvenor House Hotel, or watching football from the directors' box at Coventry City, none had questioned the pedigree of the money financing their comfort. The three principal ministers of the government were paralysed by their indebtedness to the paymaster-general. Brown agreed with Whelan that Robinson should not be isolated but he would no longer be wholeheartedly embraced by the spin-master's protection. The Treasury's immobility was shared by Mandelson and Tony Blair's office. Their sole preoccupation was Robinson's presentation of his apology to the Commons that afternoon. 'As far as the Prime Minister is concerned,' Alastair Campbell told the public, 'this afternoon will be the end of the matter.' In the Commons, Tony Blair defended the paymaster-general: 'He accepts it was an oversight on his behalf and I think the Commons should listen to what he has to say.' Fifteen minutes later Robinson rose to speak, his first solo appearance on the front bench for eleven months.

In drafting his statement, there were many precedents and sages whom Robinson might have consulted to achieve the correct tone. Any of those passing through his office could have been asked for advice, or he might have called on friends in the party. Instead, those whom he encountered during the morning witnessed a casual parliamentarian who was remarkably unfazed about his predicament. His apparent indifference to the attacks suggested either an inept personality who was genuinely unaware of the crisis or a standard-bearer of New Labour's credo never to apologise.

Gordon Brown sat nearby as the paymaster-general rose. Not a semblance of self-doubt was visible during his fifty-four-second statement. As if reciting a railway timetable, he rattled through his announcement without a hint of humility. There was an apology for failing to register his directorships of Agie UK and TransTec and, to everyone's surprise, an apology for failing to

register 'Roll Center Inc., which I owned between February 1988
and January 1992'. Even the Conservatives had not spotted that
omission. 'The House will want to be reassured,' he said in the
voice of a mechanical menu, 'that these shareholdings and
directorships were matters of public record. No attempt was made
by me at any time to use my position in the House to advance any
commercial interest.'

That last statement was not strictly accurate. At the outset of
TransTec, he had obtained the patents from the University of
Birmingham without charge after introducing himself as the local
MP, and he had applied for DTI grants mentioning his political
status. His employees at TransTec, like the academics at Warwick
University, distinctly recalled Robinson's use of his status in
Westminster to advance his commercial interests. 'Hello. I'm the
MP for the area,' he said in phone calls to suppliers who were
refusing deliveries because of non-payment, 'and I'm trying to
help out this company. I'd be grateful if you could assist.' He was
never heard to declare his interest.

Conservative members of parliament, still unaware of those
performances, were surprised by the paymaster-general's unexpected admission about his ownership of the American company
Roll Center. The sale of the company to TransTec for £100,000
was as odd as his unexpected declaration soon afterwards about a
loan he had provided to R J Engineering, a small hi-tech company
in the Midlands, in return for shares. His past never ceased
unravelling.

In self-interest, Robinson believed that Labour MPs were
'genuinely complimentary' about his statement to the Commons.
To friendly MPs he confided, 'I am under siege. I am trying to
plug leaks in a dam with my fingers, but then something else leaks
and the water floods through.' They nodded, he assumed, in
sympathy. Detached from reality, he persuaded himself that no
one suggested 'anything more was required'. With contempt, he
fumed about the front-page headline in the *Daily Express*, 'Who
does he think he is?' and 'Has he no shame?' That was evidence,
he persuaded himself, of the media witchhunt initiated by Rupert

Murdoch and inspired by 'Tory jealousy'. The traducer of Michael
Edwardes, Terry Burns, Derrick Robbins, Alastair Ross Goobey
and so many more loathed receiving his own treatment but, not
unnaturally, he did not recognise the similarity. His colleagues, he
told himself, were supportive.

Robinson had misjudged the backbenchers' response to his
laments. The demands for his resignation were as widespread as the
blame of Blair for not dismissing a tarnished minister. Every
newspaper reported calls for his resignation. In the tea rooms and
bars, Ian Pearson, his parliamentary private secretary, heard Labour
MPs complaining about the paymaster-general. Backbenchers
disliked his uncontrite statement, which failed to acknowledge the
gravity of a third report. 'Too much drip-drip,' Pearson heard from
the same Labour MPs who one year earlier had laughed about the
paymaster-general 'shagging' a rich woman for a multimillion-
pound inheritance. Their tolerance had turned to displeasure. 'We
don't need this,' said politicians fearing the scourge of sleaze.

Robinson dismissed Pearson's report as meaningless grumbles.
The paymaster-general could even quote the *Daily Mirror*'s condemnation of the Tories' smear as 'a disgrace [which] must not be
allowed to succeed'. That precisely reflected Gordon Brown's new
strategy.

Robinson had become the symbol of the government's resolve.
To concede his guilt would equate New Labour with the sleaze-
ridden Conservatives. To avoid the impression that Robinson was
a 'lame duck' minister, the paymaster-general was promoted with
Gordon Brown's agreement as a 'supremo'. In a photocall, he was
placed on the grand sweeping stairway within the Treasury,
pronouncing his intention to change Whitehall's culture and give
government departments the 'incentives to operate efficiently'.
Robinson, the 'successful industrialist', was rejuvenated as the
standard-bearer of increased productivity in the public sector. No
one noticed that TransTec's shares were again falling.

Few in Westminster were deceived. The Conservatives scented
blood. On 23 November 1998, David Heathcoat-Amory wrote to
Peter Mandelson listing thirteen examples of Robinson's 'wilful

disregard' of company laws between 1988 and 1992, relating mostly to Maxwell's companies. The list included approving false accounts, failing to keep proper records and the non-disclosure of directorships. Heathcoat-Amory asked how Mandelson intended to 'proceed', since the allegations 'involve one Minister investigating criminal law matters involving another Minister'. Privately, he recalled Robin Cook's outburst in 1994 mocking Michael Heseltine's declaration that 'no further action' was necessary after reading the report of a DTI inquiry into Lord Archer, a former deputy chairman of the Conservative Party, for insider dealing. 'One Tory politician,' intoned Cook in a prepared statement, 'should not sit in judgement on another Tory politician.' Heathcoat-Amory suggested that rather than the internal inquiry, Mandelson should appoint independent inspectors under Section 432 of the Companies Act 1985 to report about the sale of two Maxwell companies (Lock and PSS) to Robinson shortly before Hollis's bankruptcy.

Mandelson delayed replying to Heathcoat-Amory's letter. Although he had officially isolated himself from the investigation of Robinson, other government ministers were not similarly barred. The paymaster-general's uncertain relationship with Maxwell created more fear than his non-disclosure of directorships. After successive conversations between ministers at the DTI, Treasury and Downing Street, it was agreed that Jonathan Powell, the prime minister's chief of staff and a political appointee, should ask Robinson about the allegations in *Business Age* and about his management of Hollis. Their conversation was short. Robinson curtly denied any wrongdoing and Powell, like his political masters, was too ignorant about commerce and Maxwell's empire to challenge those denials. But sentiment towards the paymaster-general had irrevocably changed. Robinson, everyone agreed, was a perpetual sore who was best removed. Alastair Campbell was no longer directed to speak of the prime minister's unequivocal support. Rather, inquirers understood that the prime minister had lost patience and regretted not dismissing Robinson in July. Blair's dilemma infected the Treasury and the

DTI. After two weeks, Heathcoat-Amory had still not received a reply to his letter. 'The delay,' he wrote in a third letter to Mandelson on 11 December 1998, 'raises questions of its own about your ability or desire to act decisively in this matter whilst Mr Robinson remains a Government Minister.'

Mandelson's riposte was immediate. Heathcoat-Amory's complaints, he pledged, 'will be considered'; however, 'I should make it clear for the avoidance of doubt that, in line with the practice of successive administrations, I shall not be able to comment further on the substance of the issues.' Mandelson's suggestion that a serving Conservative minister had ever been under investigation by the DTI was erroneous; and for the investigation in 1994 of Lord Archer, a former deputy chairman of the Conservative Party, the government had appointed independent investigators. For still unknown reasons, Mandelson was equivocating.

Unknown to Mandelson, an accountant had by then found Geoffrey Robinson's invoice on Orchards notepaper for £200,000 issued on 24 October 1990 to the Maxwells. The discovery disproved Robinson's contention that he never 'requested . . . any compensation'. The belated discovery was explicable. Since Robinson had issued the invoice on Orchards notepaper, his Surrey home, not on TransTec's, the invoice had been misfiled. For the moment, its history, including any evidence of payment, remained unclear. Finding the answer depended upon Hugh Aldous, the accountant hired by the DTI.

Peter Mandelson, while unwilling to compound Robinson's woes, could do nothing more to protect his benefactor, not least because of Tony Blair's equivocation about the paymaster-general. While the prime minister repeated that he would not be pushed into sacking his summer host, he no longer expressed his confidence in the minister. Four days later, Mandelson knew that Robinson's demise was imminent.

On the evening of Wednesday, 16 December 1998, Mandelson was told that a book written by Paul Routledge, a journalist close to the Brown camp, would be published shortly and expose Robinson's loan. Routledge's source, many would assume, was

Charlie Whelan, the laddish spokesman for Gordon Brown. In the bizarre relationships characterising the Brown–Blair feud, Routledge was aligned with Robinson, yet was prepared to destabilise his ally to destroy a hated enemy. Whether Mandelson and Robinson discussed their plight that evening is unknown, but both feared a common fate.

Sitting in his office the following morning, 17 December, Mandelson invited Sir Michael Scholar, his unsuspecting permanent secretary, to recite the history of the department's reaction to Heathcoat-Amory's letters and the decision to inquire into Robinson's relationship with Hollis. Mandelson extracted what he thought was necessary – Scholar's agreement that his minister had not influenced the policy in any way. Then Mandelson announced, 'Even if I had not had a loan to buy my house from Geoffrey, I would have still stood aside from the investigation.' After a long pause, Scholar said, 'I didn't know you had a loan to buy your house. We'll have to look into it.' Scholar was bemused by the revelation and the manner of its delivery. His professional calm was not echoed in Downing Street. Tony Blair exploded on hearing the news from Alastair Campbell. The decisions he took over the following hours reflected on his pledge to be 'purer than pure'.

Properly, Blair telephoned Sir Richard Wilson, the cabinet secretary, to ask whether Mandelson's financial relationship with Robinson jeopardised his impartiality as the minister responsible for the DTI's investigation of the paymaster-general. Officially, the prime minister did nothing more. After Mandelson arrived that evening in Downing Street, the prime minister and Campbell vented their anger about their friend's stupidity. In self-defence, Mandelson replied that he had not done anything 'fundamentally wrong'.

By the following day, the prime minister knew from Wilson that Mandelson's concealment of the loan was undoubtedly a conflict of interest, yet Blair appeared unconcerned by the dishonesty. He was focused entirely on the prospect of the publicity. Mandelson, the creator of sleaze as the issue to destroy the Tory government, would be a prime target, and the *Guardian*, aware of the loan, was certain to publish the facts early the following week. Any rational analysis of the crisis was impeded by Blair's insouciance towards the pedigree of wealth, especially Robinson's. His warm welcome over the previous years to so many rich Britons at formal dinners, receptions and discussions reflected his worship, shared by Mandelson, of financial success and corporate power. His excitement about money, including Robinson's millions, precluded any interest in its genesis and integrity.

During Saturday, Blair was smitten by a desire to mitigate the political damage rather than dismiss two culpable ministers. His advocacy of principle was compromised by his personal debt: a debt of friendship to Mandelson and a financial debt to the paymaster-general. His indebtedness to Robinson compromised his criticism of Mandelson accepting money from the same source. Consequently, during that weekend Blair did not ask Mandelson to explain his personal finances. The answer would have revealed remarkable imprudence.

Mandelson had borrowed £373,000 from Robinson to buy a house which cost £475,000. He also committed himself to spending over £40,000 on renovation. He had met the shortfall by raising a mortgage of £150,000 from the Britannia Building Society. At the same time, he remained the owner of his original flat in Clerkenwell, which was mortgaged for £40,000, and he owned a house in Hartlepool, his constituency, which was mortgaged for £35,000. In total, when Mandelson's parliamentary income was £53,000, including a housing allowance, his debts had been £598,000.

Though unaware of Mandelson's recklessness, Blair did grasp the fact that the paymaster-general's money had spread like a cancer within the government. Radical surgery was required. Without realising the enormity of the task, he urged Mandelson to repay the loan rapidly to Robinson and agreed that they would seek to brazen out the storm that would certainly erupt on Monday, 21 December 1998. Contrary to his pre-election pledge that New Labour would strike remorselessly against sleaze, he would react only because the loan was about to become public knowledge. He never contemplated Mandelson's failure to register the benefits of the loan – saving about £10,000 of interest payments – in the Commons. The consequences of Mandelson's benefits were no different from Neil Hamilton's, and the Tory had been hounded for his deception. Blair's strategy would be determined not by principle but by the public's reaction.

On 21 December, ten days after sending a stonewalling reply to Heathcoat-Amory about the DTI's investigation of Robinson, Mandelson signed a similar letter. Again he denied any 'unreasonable delay' and warned that the department 'does not expect to comment further'. But he added, 'I decided in September, in line with the advice of the Permanent Secretary, that I would not be involved in any consideration of this matter, and neither before nor since then have I or any of my ministers played any part in it.'

At the Treasury, Robinson was surprised by the arrival of Charlie Falconer in his office. The lawyer announced, 'The press have the details of your loan to Peter Mandelson and the *Guardian* will be breaking the story tomorrow.' Falconer had known about the loan since the summer but sought to understand the details only because the government was facing public embarrassment. Why, he asked, was the loan made? Robinson explained that he had known Mandelson for twenty years and considered him a 'sound investment prospect' who, with his future inheritance, could be expected to repay the money in the distant future. In Robinson's opinion, 'Falconer was evidently relieved at this explanation.' Like so many of Robinson's recollections and quotations of conversations, this seems faulty. Falconer, a man of undefined ideals, was visiting as a lawyer with a brief, rather than as a politician espousing integrity. There must have been a motive, Falconer suggested to Robinson, for such extraordinary generosity. Had Mandelson borrowed the money from any minister other than Robinson, an acceptable excuse might have been conjured up. But the paymaster-general, regardless of his nebulous charm and endless champagne, had become notorious for concealment and skeletons in the cupboard. Naturally, in vigorous self-defence, Robinson snapped that the insinuation of 'some hidden truth' was insulting. How, he wondered, could a minister be punished for being 'on the give'? In his relations with politicians, Robinson could often not grasp that his self-justification was unpersuasive. 'I can't understand the fuss,' he exclaimed. With pride, he recalled saying, as Falconer left his office, 'I'm not going to be done in because of this. It was a perfectly correct arrangement between Peter and me and that's an end of it.' Robinson understood better than most the single issue about the loan. The crisis was not about his loan or its chronology during that fateful dinner, but about Mandelson's failure to declare his conflict of interest at the DTI.

His own immediate fate, Robinson knew, depended upon Mandelson's survival. The Downing Street machine would be utterly devoted to saving the prime minister's friend regardless of propriety. Tony's friends would never be sacrificed because of accusations of sleaze, however true. 'People help out friends,' Robinson told the curious staff in his private office. 'This is not a resigning matter.'

That afternoon, Alastair Campbell prepared the words he would deploy to signal Blair's vindication of Mandelson: 'The prime minister does not consider it a hanging offence.' Blair ignored the official advice that Mandelson had broken the ministerial code by concealing his financial interest from Scholar. He reassured himself that his ally had not interfered in the Robinson investigation.

That night, in their joint self-defence, Mandelson exercised, as his critics noted, his mastership of the black art of a spin-doctor. He denied to the *Guardian* any wrongdoing and told *Newsnight* on BBC TV, 'There is no conflict of interest so the question of resignation does not arise.' Some would say that only after seeing Mandelson's performance on the evening news did Blair read the official report explaining that Mandelson, regardless of his 'insulation' from the investigation, had broken the ministerial code. That was untrue. Tony Blair did not require a report to reveal the obvious.

Tuesday morning's newspaper headlines were frenzied and furious. The target was Mandelson: could his word be trusted when he said he had wholly avoided the DTI's investigation of the paymaster-general? His opening gambit on Tuesday morning was robust. In a whirlwind tour of every TV and radio studio issuing an invitation, Mandelson repeatedly rejected calls to resign, because 'I've done nothing wrong.' He claimed that he had 'insulated' himself from the DTI investigation and said, 'at all times I have protected the integrity and professionalism of the DTI'. The secrecy, he explained, was at Robinson's request. 'Geoffrey Robinson is a friend of mine of twenty years' standing. He asked for confidentiality and I respected that.' Even Sir Michael Scholar, he said later, cleared Mandelson of any conflict of interest. That appeared to be inaccurate. Following the money trail determined Mandelson's fate.

Asked about his application for the mortgage, Mandelson at first replied, 'I filled all the forms in properly,' and added that Robinson's loan had been mentioned on the form. Later that day, realising that the application still existed, he equivocated: 'I can't remember the details of the form.'

On the application form, Mandelson had been asked, 'Do you propose to borrow any other money upon the security of the property to assist in the purchase?' He had answered, 'No.' By nightfall, he had changed his story again. After admitting that the completed form 'may not reflect the final financial arrangements as these were undecided at the time', he explained on *Newsnight* that complete disclosure was not necessary because the loan was 'a non-political, confidential arrangement between two friends'. Having paid back £40,000, he intended rapidly to repay the outstanding £333,000 with his mother's help. Mrs Mandelson did not volunteer to endorse that suggestion. Mandelson's final words that night reflected his ethics: 'I do not think there are any moral aspects.'

Those words were the shared judgement of Tony Blair, Geoffrey Robinson and New Labour's spokesmen. Tory corruption, said Blair's spokesmen, was worse than Mandelson's mistake. The

spectre of Neil Hamilton and Mohamed Fayed's cash in brown
envelopes was resurrected. A crucial distinction was ignored.
After his appointment as a junior DTI minister, Hamilton
declared a non-financial relationship with Fayed to the permanent
secretary and himself announced hostile decisions about Fayed.
Mandelson had concealed his relationship. At midnight, as Blair
read the following morning's newspapers, he was disappointed
that his morality was not universally shared.

'So how the hell can Mandy stay?' asked the *Sun*. 'Mandelson,
the master of deception,' snapped the *Daily Mail*. Mandelson,
according to the *Mirror*, was engaged in 'sordid politics' and was
'greedy, arrogant and having delusions of grandeur'.

In the Treasury, Robinson acknowledged an unpleasant irony.
Two years earlier, Mandelson had accepted his offer of an enormous loan and promised friendship. During the ensuing months,
the paymaster-general had grown to dislike his debtor.
Mandelson's interference, secret briefings, plotting and trouble-
making were destabilising. Mandelson's passion for Europe was
positively dangerous. He was the opposite of an asset to the
government. His lifestyle, dressing in expensive suits, socialising
with *Hello!*-style multimillionaires, and flying in private jets for
holidays, irritated the Brownites. Yet, Robinson reflected, his own
fate, which was hanging by a thread, depended on the contortions
of a politician he preferred to shun. At those moments, the central
character rarely reflects on his own contribution to the suffering of
others: the former Jaguar executives, Fawzi el-Menshawy and,
more recently, the civil servants castigated as hopeless. Regardless
of his stated habit of voraciously reading Shakespeare, Robinson
failed to appreciate the delight of a selected audience poring over
the self-inflicted wounds of Robinson and Mandelson. The ironies
eluded him. Both Robinson and Mandelson blamed their fate on
the media, which, as Mandelson complained, 'present my motives
in the worst possible light' and 'distorted' his behaviour.
Robinson was equally angry, 'I'm allowed to lend money to
whoever I want. It's a free country, for God's sake.'

Disabusing Robinson depended upon Blair's regard for honesty.

Peter Mandelson had once said to his patron, 'We can't be like the last lot.' Blair's request for Mandelson's resignation reflected his reluctant agreement, except that he made a sharp distinction between Tory sleaze and Peter's mistake. Others saw another distinction. All the culpable Tories were low-level politicians. By contrast, Mandelson and Robinson were at the heart of New Labour.

At daybreak on 23 December, six days after hearing about the loan, Blair decided that Mandelson would have to resign. Subsequently, he excused his prevarication by explaining his pre-occupation with the RAF's bombardment of Iraq, but those hostilities had ended four days earlier. Contrary to his pre-election promise to act swiftly against sleaze, he had reluctantly bowed to public opinion.

Mandelson agreed to resign. Blair telephoned Gordon Brown and insisted on Robinson's departure. In turn, Brown telephoned Robinson with the news. Robinson believed that the chancellor was 'genuinely upset' about failing to protect his friend. Others convincingly suggest that Brown was relieved to be rid of an embarrassment.

During the morning, Blair telephoned Robinson. The pay-master-general was aggrieved. In Robinson's opinion, he had been acquitted by Downey and had become the necessary stooge for Mandelson's folly. His self-justification was echoed, in his opinion, by Blair's expressions during the dismissal. 'The PM did not convey,' he wrote subsequently, 'any sense that he blamed me for what had happened. Rather he was annoyed and dismayed at the press reaction to the private arrangement.' If true, it reflected precisely the confusions within Downing Street. Blair had apparently mused, to Robinson's approval, 'Someone like Peter could easily earn in the private sector a salary that would justify a house like this.' Both misunderstood the principle of public service. Volunteering for office in government explicitly excluded pecuniary advantage and conflicts. Robinson's insistence – and Blair's agreement – that 'Peter was good for the money' reflected further muddle about impeccable integrity. Even gangsters – and

Mandelson was certainly not among those ranks – are often 'good for the money'.

Just two years earlier, before the general election, Robinson had hosted successful parties as the man with money seeking power, blind to any vulnerabilities. For nineteen months he had enjoyed power. Suddenly, he was returned to his original status.

The traditional exchange of letters marking a minister's resignation was perfunctory this time. Blair's phrases of gratitude and praise for Robinson's business acumen, his list of Robinson's achievements, and his commiseration – 'I know that you have felt these past months hounded by the campaign against you' – failed to gloss over a dismissal for unacceptable conduct. 'There comes a time,' wrote Robinson, 'when after more than twelve months of a highly charged political campaign, the point has been reached when I feel that it is no longer right that you or your government should be affected by or have to contend with these attacks.'

Robinson's protestations of innocence, after three Downey reports and a continuing DTI investigation, were his last ministerial words: 'I have done nothing wrong in any of these areas and I will vigorously defend myself against any allegations. In the case of the loan to Peter Mandelson, I merely considered myself in 1996 as someone in a position to help a long standing friend, with no request for anything in return.'

In Surrey, Marie Elena, his unconventional wife, confirmed the MP's resignation several hours before the official announcement: 'You accept it one way or another, don't you? It's sunny when it's sunny, it's rainy when it's rainy. As for plans for the future we'll be spending Christmas as we always do here at the house.'

At the Treasury, the ex-minister did not have the opportunity to contrast the cold, official tone of his letters with those arranged for Mandelson's resignation. 'I do not think I have done anything wrong or improper,' wrote Mandelson in the agreed version drafted by Alastair Campbell, before stating in self-contradiction, 'but I should not, with all candour, have entered into the arrangement.' Blair and Scholar, he acknowledged, should have been told. 'I am sorry about this situation. But we came to power promising to uphold the highest possible standards in public life. We have not just to do so, but we must be seen to do so.' The deliberate disorientation and the high moral tone, so different than his media interviews the previous day, allowed Blair to exonerate his friend: 'It was a silly thing to do but there was nothing illegal about it . . . This is nothing more than a moment of madness.'

Blair's pardon reflected New Labour's particular interpretation of integrity. Mandelson's 'moment of madness' had lasted two years; describing a minister who accepted a loan ten times more than his annual income as 'silly' demoted recklessness to irrelevance; and while Mandelson's concealment of the loan was not 'illegal' it was unethical. Mandelson's interview that night with ITN reflected Blair's Gospel. Mandelson lamented his failure to 'take precautions against the time when this became public knowledge'. His sorrow was about appearances. At that moment, few drew the parallel with Mandelson's passion for the Dome. The project was a grandiose symbol whose construction and sustainment could succeed only by guile.

That night, Robinson reflected upon an absurdity: could the sanitisation of Mandelson have begun? The insidious Downing Street spin machine was fostering speculation and slurs. Robinson's resignation, whispered one anonymous official, was expected in any event to have occurred over Christmas; while Alastair Campbell officially damned him with questionable praise: 'Geoffrey is not a leper. Geoffrey is somebody who has been a Labour MP for a long time and is very generous.' On reflection, Robinson might have realised that his own statement that afternoon uttered to the reporters clustered outside Grosvenor House seemed lame: 'My future is very bright. I have got plenty to do and I will continue to do many things, as I have done in the past.' Sages of Old Labour recognised that Robinson was being cast as the villain compared to Mandelson. The departure of the Prince of Darkness, wrote Barbara Castle, a senior minister in Harold Wilson's cabinet, 'is being presented by Downing Street as something akin to a spontaneous and noble act of self-sacrifice by a fellow who is voluntarily laying down his career to save the Government he loves. It is nothing of the sort.' Blair did nothing to assuage Castle's anger. He invited Mandelson and his boyfriend to spend the night at Chequers and minimised the concealment of the loan as 'not earth-shattering'.

Over Christmas, Blair realised that he had misjudged the nation's reaction. His conviction of the irrelevance of Mandelson's deception was not shared by most Britons. Mandelson was distrusted. Mindful that a book written by Margaret Cook, the foreign secretary's estranged wife, would soon expose her former husband's serial infidelity, Blair interrupted his holiday to acknowledge the wrongdoing. The loan, he agreed, was a 'misjudgement' and 'not a wise thing to have entered into'. When the DTI inquiry was first announced, he admitted, 'it would have been wiser to have disclosed it'. Mandelson had 'made a mistake' and 'paid a very high price for it'. On one issue, there would be no retreat. Mandelson had not breached the code and, as Alastair Campbell declared after the dismissal on 4 January 1999 of Charlie Whelan, the whole matter was 'closed'. The notion of a 'cancer at the heart of government' was mocked.

8

CONCEALMENT

Martin Fishman's reply to David Heathcoat-Amory was distinctly unhelpful. The auditor was adamant. He seemed unwilling to resolve the riddle of the £200,000 payment to Geoffrey Robinson.

Fishman was Arthur Andersen's administrator responsible for the Maxwell archives in a warehouse in Sittingbourne. In his letter to Sir Gordon Downey, the auditor had mentioned three hundred boxes of Pergamon records. Among those papers might be the evidence of the payment to Robinson. Downey had not favoured devoting a whole month to sifting through the boxes and the MPs on the Standards Committee had agreed. Instead of the time-consuming effort with no guaranteed result, they preferred to accept Geoffrey Robinson's assurances, supported by his accountants and Michael Stoney, that, despite Hollis's accounts, no payment had been made. That credulity did not satisfy David Heathcoat-Amory who, although unaware of the Orchards invoice and payment, was unhappy with Fishman's refusal to allow him access to the Maxwell archives.

Before the election, Arthur Andersen had established a special relationship with Robinson and other Labour ministers. Whatever the truth, this could have explained Andersen's apparent reluctance to search for evidence which might endanger Robinson. Even Andersen's rejection of Robinson's offer of £20,000 to finance the search, pledging their services free 'to ensure total independence', could not dispel the suspicion.

David Heathcoat-Amory was prepared to devote time to the hunt. The justification for granting him access, he believed, was unanswerable. Michael Stoney, on Robinson's behalf, had searched through Andersen's archives and Sir Gordon Downey would have been granted permission. There was a public interest in knowing the truth. But Fishman resisted Heathcoat-Amory's request as 'not appropriate', and wrote to him that 'we have concluded that such access will only be permitted where either we are legally obliged to do so or where there is a demonstrably justifiable interest in so doing'.

Fishman's reply rekindled Heathcoat-Amory's interest. The latter suspected that the agreement in 1991 between Robinson and Maxwell passing Hollis's assets to C&S may have been a 'strip-out', benefiting Robinson at the expense of the public shareholders. He was puzzled by Hollis's unreliable financial accounts. Above all, the financial relationship between Robinson and Mandelson, concealed by so many in the government, cast doubt on the DTI's decision to commission an internal inquiry by an unknown investigator whose report would remain secret. To allay suspicion, Heathcoat-Amory had expected Stephen Byers, the new secretary of state at the DTI, to approve a public inquiry.

Stephen Byers was a New Labour apparatchik. Like so many of that unworldly class, the former law lecturer at Newcastle Polytechnic enjoyed no experience beyond the classroom and the political caucus. Without a ministerial appointment, Byers could not hope for similar high profile employment. Planted inside the DTI as a reward for his political loyalty, he was ignorant of business, industry and finance, but was a reasonable propagandist. In those circumstances, faced with a choice between the public interest and the interests of New Labour, Byers would unhesitatingly care for his party.

That choice was presented to Byers on 10 January 1999. Within days of inheriting Peter Mandelson's office, Byers received a protest from Heathcoat-Amory about the DTI's 'secretive' internal inquiry into Hollis. The complaint questioned whether in the context of the financial relationship between Mandelson and Robinson, the internal inquiry was 'sufficient': '[it] raises the suspicion that the Government is unwilling to risk further embarrassment by revealing the source of Mr Robinson's fortune'. Two months later, on 11 March 1999, Heathcoat-Amory reminded Byers that no reply had been received. The delay was suspicious. Byers, he suggested, was awaiting a directive from the Treasury and Downing Street.

Unlike Peter Mandelson, Stephen Byers did not intend to isolate himself from the inquiry. On the contrary, he intended to manage the embarrassment into its grave. The investigation of Hollis and Robinson, he told Heathcoat-Amory at the end of March, was to remain secret. Geoffrey Robinson had good reason to feel protected. The DTI report would be locked up until long after he died, and the Maxwell archives would be protected by Arthur Andersen until their eventual destruction. Once again, Robinson decided to focus his energies on Coventry City and TransTec, the principal repositories of his wealth.

TransTec's fate was precarious. In his absence, in September 1998 the company's board had approved the previous year's accounts, which showed that, despite a fall in the forecast of profits from £26 million to £22 million, the dividend had been increased by 12 per cent. Robinson's income had grown but since May 1997 the value of his shares had halved. The more recent, unpublished accounts revealed the company's deteriorating plight. The actual losses on falling sales were £7.6 million, the company's accumulated debts were £66.5 million, and that did not include the undisclosed settlement of Ford's claim; Richard Carr, the chief executive, had not publicly announced the £12 million of credits to Ford. Ford's non-payment for supplies was reconciled by a debit note fixed to the invoice, recorded in the sales ledgers. That procedure was not disclosed to Price Waterhouse, the company's auditors, who failed to request the ledgers. Price Waterhouse relied entirely on the general accounts, where the debit was unmentioned.

During summer 1999, Robinson apparently undertook no detailed inquiries about TransTec's accounts, despite the clues to a potential disaster. The share price had fallen to 17 pence and the board announced that there would be no dividend. That decision was a sharp blow to Robinson. Over the previous two years he had received £1 million in dividends and he had expected at least £300,000 in 1999. His shares, once worth £36 million, were valued at only £5.3 million. Richard Carr blamed the 'worst economic conditions'. Apparently, Robinson believed Carr's excuse although the shares had underperformed the engineering sector by 80 per cent. That 'laziness' reflected Robinson's chequered record. The politician hailed by Tony Blair as a 'high-calibre' businessman and 'an exceptionally able minister', recently famous for castigating the civil service and British industry, was failing to monitor the management of his own small company. 'I felt inhibited because of the DTI inquiry into Hollis,' he unconvincingly explained.

Robinson's personal finances were deteriorating and the French government had served a writ to recover £3.6 million of Joska Bourgeois's unpaid taxes; he was contesting it. Years earlier, he had been accustomed to perform as a vastly rich tycoon when in fact he had little money. Reviving that feat was irksome. To reduce his overheads, he decided to sell Marsh Court, the Lutyens house in Stockbridge that had been mortgaged in August 1998 to cover his costs. In July 1999, on the eve of the house's sale for about £6 million, he hosted a party in the ballroom so that his friends could admire his meticulous renovations, which had transformed a derelict into a stunning house. Most visitors were especially impressed by the gardens, which had been restored to their original Victorian glory designed by Gertrude Jekyll. He earned over £2 million profit on the sale.

The contents of Marsh Court, all Joska Bourgeois's possessions from her flat in Geneva, were auctioned by Sotheby's at

Billingshurst. Robinson told James Miller and Harry Delmany, the auctioneers, that he expected record prices, reflecting the high insurance values he had stipulated on Bourgeois's behalf. The auctioneers were sceptical. The Buhl furniture was not genuine eighteenth-century but nineteenth-century Italian reproductions; and the birds, fish and other ornaments bought as antiques for large amounts in the Far East were enamel on copper. Lacking any hint of an old collection from a historic house, the furniture found few bidders in the saleroom. After failing to reach their reserve prices on 16 September 1999, many lots were withdrawn.

Those disappointments coincided with another blow to his political fortunes. During the summer, the Blair family were again enjoying a free holiday in Tuscany, the guests on that occasion of the local governor. In San Gimignano, Robinson was being shunned by those who only two years earlier had eagerly taken his money and hospitality. He might even refuse, he suggested, to contribute to the Labour Party's funds. Mournfully, he complained that he was suffering the consequences of Peter Mandelson's deceit and, unexpectedly, the hurt was compounded. Tony Blair disclosed that Mandelson was to mastermind the next general-election campaign, and the publication was announced of a substantial biography of Mandelson, written with his co-operation, by Donald Macintyre, a journalist.

Until that moment, no authoritative account had been presented describing the circumstances of the loan for the house. The version offered by Macintyre/Mandelson appalled Robinson. The paymaster-general was caricatured as an intriguer, persuading a hapless ingénue to accept his money. Macintyre/Mandelson's gloss described the older man's 'distinctly avuncular interest in Mandelson's affairs, rather as, sixteen years earlier, he had helped to sort out the trade union funds to pay Mandelson's salary'. Robinson was portrayed as urging Mandelson to buy 'something substantial' because, once he was a cabinet minister, 'you should have somewhere in London where you can have a good home, where you can relax, where you can bring people round, and have a proper base'. In Mandelson's version, his regret for lacking the finance was rebutted by the older man: 'Well, one day you'll write your memoirs.' After Mandelson volunteered that he would eventually inherit half a million pounds from his mother, Robinson allegedly said, 'Fine. I'll tide you over.' To emphasise Robinson's initiative, the book quoted Robinson's sales pitch: 'helping out his friend would be "as easy as falling off a log"'. In the hunt for his home, according to Macintyre/Mandelson, Robinson 'exhibited shrewdness and exacting standards'. Taking the lead, he dismissed as 'unsuitable' some flats they had visited, and suggested a house. With the promise of a loan, Mandelson was persuaded to buy something beyond his means.

Robinson felt traduced. Despite his generosity to Blair and Brown – including his silence since his dismissal – Mandelson's version was widely accepted. The scapegoat, portrayed as a villain who had corrupted Mandelson, sensed a vicious disparity. While he, the innocent loyalist, languished in the wilderness, protesting that 'He asked for the loan', Mandelson, the knave whose congenital meddling destabilised the government, was on the verge of rehabilitation, thanks to Blair's loyalty.

In hindsight, Mandelson's words of contrition nine months earlier were widely seen as mere pretence. His resurrection had started on the same day as his resignation. On 22 December 1998, he had suggested to Elizabeth Filkin, the successor to Sir Gordon Downey, that there had been no reason to register the loan, 'as it was not a gift or gained through my being an MP'. In truth, he had saved £10,000 in interest and the loan was offered by Robinson only because Mandelson was an MP and expected to be a member of the cabinet. By the end of the first week of 1999, Mandelson had extracted from the Britannia Building Society a helpful declaration that his application had been 'accurate at the time', despite his concealment of the loan. Although the building society manager refused to publish the 'accurate' application form, Mandelson gushed about 'a clean bill of health', exclaiming, 'I wish my critics had waited to find out the real position before reaching hasty judgements.' The masterstroke of publicity diminished what followed.

Six months later, Elizabeth Filkin agreed that Mandelson had not broken any rules, since loans between friends were not registrable. But Mandelson's mortgage application, she reported, had been 'incomplete' and 'incorrect'. By withholding 'three material facts' he had 'breached the MPs' Code of Conduct' which required their honesty. Mandelson was dismissive. Filkin's report, he complained, suffered from 'sleight of argument, inconsistency and illogicality'.

Unlike Robinson, Mandelson had been nurturing his pitch to the members of the Committee on Standards and Privileges. His plea of innocence and his accusations against Filkin fell on fertile ground. Unanimously, the Labour majority echoed Mandelson's defence of having 'acted without dishonest intention'. Not wishing to impede Mandelson's return to the cabinet, all the committee members ignored Elizabeth Filkin's report, explaining that she was exceeding her powers, cleared Mandelson of wrongdoing and blamed Stephen Wegg-Prosser, the solicitor who had negotiated the conveyance, for not informing the Britannia Building Society. Wegg-Prosser, the father of Mandelson's personal assistant, could not protest. He was dead. On 11 October 1999, Mandelson returned to the cabinet as secretary of state for Northern Ireland. The interruption in his income as a cabinet minister had been minimised by his claim for £12,912 in severance pay and, after the sale of the house, he had repaid his loan to Robinson. Mandelson's resurrection confirmed the suspicion that sleaze was a weapon with which to attack the Conservatives but could be ignored among New Labour's ranks.

In Park Lane, Robinson fumed. His normally sparkling eyes were cold and hard. 'They've made a big difference between the man who lends the money and the man who takes it,' he told one of his parliamentary friends. As a man who always expected to be the winner, he could take rebuffs but not humiliation. Mandelson's folly had robbed him of the job he loved. Mandelson had been exonerated, while he faced the continuing DTI internal inquiry into Hollis. He was uncertain of the inquiry's outcome and had reason for concern.

During his conversations with Hugh Aldous, the investigator appointed by the DTI, Robinson had heard that new evidence had surfaced concerning the payment of £200,000 by Hollis. Despite the destruction and loss of documents, Aldous had looked through the list of Pergamon's payments compiled by Arthur Andersen in 1992, after Maxwell's death. Andersen's list featured a payment made in December 1990 by Pergamon to Orchards. Andersen's accountant had assigned that payment a code number, 99-7976. Six years later, no one at Andersen's had associated Orchards or payment 99-7976 with Robinson. However, Aldous had dug further into Pergamon's cash books, the very papers that Martin Fishman of Andersen's had forbidden David Heathcoat-Amory to inspect. Among those Pergamon papers, Aldous had found a citation of a payment in December 1990 for £200,000, which had prompted the issuing of a cheque numbered 1751. There could be no doubt that the cheque for £200,000 had been issued by Pergamon. All that remained was to find the cancelled cheque or Pergamon's bank statements reflecting the transfer of £200,000.

Aldous had asked NatWest, Pergamon's bank, for proof of the payment, but nine years after the transaction, the bank had destroyed all the statements and the photocopies of the cheques. In October 1999, the cancelled cheque could not be found in Andersen's warehouse. There could be no doubt that the payment had been made against the Orchards invoice but the identity of the account where the cheque had been cashed was uncertain.

The new evidence gave Robinson cause for serious concern. He telephoned Michael Stoney, and invited Hollis's finance director to come to Grosvenor House, explaining, 'I want you to swear an affidavit that the £200,000 was never paid.' The affidavit, he said, would be presented to the DTI. 'I'll think about it,' replied Stoney, unaware of Hugh Aldous's discoveries. Robinson had every reason to begin persuading the government to bury Aldous's eventual report beyond anyone's view.

Authoritative stories began appearing in national newspapers, mentioning Robinson's grievances, especially his isolation as a 'non-person'. Quoting his 'friends', the reports mentioned Robinson's threat to explode a 'thermonuclear device' in retaliation against Mandelson. By then, Robinson had shown literary agents in London a sample of the handwritten manuscript of his memoirs. He promised substantial revelations but was undecided about a precise publication date. As the story of Robinson's tour spread, a new rumour arose. Mandelson's friends, it was suggested, were leaking Robinson's threats to pre-empt the danger of the new book. In that bizarre mood, Downing Street feared the incineration of a new feud. A telephone call to Robinson from Anji Hunter, Blair's private secretary, confirmed that he was writing a book to rebut Mandelson's 'lies'. Why, he reasoned, should Mandelson be allowed to father an authorised book, while he was expected to remain silent? After all the hospitality in London, Cannes and Tuscany, his generous retention of Sarah Macaulay's public relations company and contributing £400,000 to Blair's and Brown's private offices, Robinson felt 'betrayed'.

Downing Street's unfairness aggravated Robinson's anger. Everyone, he believed, ought to be reminded that his discretion should not be taken for granted. If he were pushed, the money trail could reveal embarrassments. His contribution of £200,000 to Brown's office was not a secret but other payments were unknown. His substantial donation to Blair before the election, he hinted, had always been denied. His insinuation was alarming. In early 1997, Robinson had been approached by Jonathan Powell, Blair's chief of staff, to solicit funds. At Powell's request, Robinson's donation for Blair's private office had been paid through the Labour Party's fund. Subsequently, that approach had been publicly denied by a party spokesman. The money's eventual destination – either a 'blind trust' for the Labour leader's office fund or the Labour Party – was deliberately vague, but stirred suspicions of Labour deceit. Margaret McDonagh, the deputy general secretary of the party, had denied on 13 May 1998 that the party's funds were used to finance Blair. 'The leader's office has never been funded by the Labour Party in our history,' she told the Neill Committee. The implication was that Blair was unaware of the contributors, to avoid any conflicts of interest. Margaret Jay, a trustee of the 'blind trust', had denied accurately that Robinson had contributed anything to that fund. Robinson threatened to embarrass the party's bankers. He had been told that his donation to Blair's office would be channelled through the Labour Party. Eventually, Margaret McDonagh admitted that she had 'accidentally misinformed the Neill committee'. Blair had known about Robinson's favours.

Having incited the rumours, Robinson made a rare appearance in the lobby of the House of Commons. 'It's all rubbish, rubbish,' he told every journalist in sight. 'I'm not bitter and I'm not twisted.' In conversations with fellow MPs, he blamed Mandelson for the leaks and smears, and quipped 'He shall reap what he sows.' Everyone was encouraged to believe that Robinson was considering the government's request to omit embarrassing material from his book.

The coincidence was remarkable. In what appeared to be a decision to deter complacency among those ministers who controlled the fate of Aldous's report, a sensational story suddenly appeared in newspapers from a 'friend' of Robinson. The former minister, it was suggested, possessed a 'compromising' but not 'explicit' photograph of a cabinet minister in an embrace with a teenager. The sex of the teenager was not mentioned but the innuendo was that 'It's not the sort of picture you would want to be made public.' To stir fear in Downing Street, the 'friend of Robinson' allegedly commented that 'He's heard the pictures are about but I am sure Geoffrey doesn't have them and he is not the sort of person who would ever try to blackmail the government.'

Robinson's threats provoked new fears among the prime minister's staff. Rich men's money was never delivered without complications. Despite Robinson's telephone call denying any intention to cause embarrassment, he could, if minded, reveal colourful details of the feuds between Brown, Blair and Mandelson. Unlike books by journalists, Robinson's would be the first by an eyewitness of Labour in government. Telephone calls from Gordon Brown, Anji Hunter, Sue Nye and Fraser Kemp all urged Robinson to desist. He seemed obdurate. The latter three suggested to Robinson a lunch at the Grosvenor House Hotel to revive their pre-election friendship. 'Your book will just re-open old wounds,' urged Hunter during the meal. Robinson, she could see, was torn between his loyalty to Brown and his fury with Mandelson. 'I want to put my point,' he replied, anxious to defend his reputation. Nothing could be more threatening than Aldous's report on Hollis. The government, he reasoned, needed to protect itself from his anger, and the unmentioned price was to suppress the Aldous report.

During October 1999, Stephen Byers became obstructive towards David Heathcoat-Amory's repeated inquiries about the fate of Aldous's thirteen month inquiry into Hollis and whether its conclusions would be published. Byers had refused to answer four detailed letters from Heathcoat-Amory and had ignored his reminders. His eventual reply was circuitously sarcastic. Instead of a considered answer, Byers merely repeated his statement to the Commons in January, ten months earlier.

Disclosure, he wrote, 'depends on the nature of the case itself and other considerations such as the applicable law and commercial confidentiality. Subject to these constraints I would wish to be as open as possible on these matters.' With unconcealed irony, Byers concluded his letter on 31 October 1999, 'I hope that this is helpful.' The minister was being markedly unhelpful. Nearly eight years earlier, the DTI had started an investigation of Robert Maxwell's flotation of the Mirror Group. That report was also far from completion.

On 9 November 1999, Michael Stoney at last obliged Geoffrey Robinson. After several meetings at Grosvenor House, the accountant swore an affidavit that the £200,000 had not been paid. Three weeks later, Stoney was invited by Hugh Aldous to visit his office at Robson Rhodes near the City. 'I'd just like you to answer some questions,' said Aldous. The request puzzled Stoney. After all, Aldous had been appointed fourteen months previously.

In the course of their conversation, Aldous told Stoney that, during his intensive search through Arthur Andersen's warehouse in June 1999, he had found the original Orchards invoice that

Robinson had presented to Stoney in October 1990. On the invoice, Stoney saw his scribbled 'Paid'. Aldous continued: NatWest had destroyed the records and he had been uncertain whether the payment had been made until he found Pergamon AGB's computer cash book. The cash book showed that, during Arthur Andersen's reconstruction of Maxwell's labyrinthine transactions, the payment on cheque number 1751 had been credited to Orchards – 6933 rather than to Robinson. Subsequently no one at Arthur Andersen associated Robinson with Orchards and Arthur Andersen's code number, 99-7976. 'The cash book,' Aldous told Stoney, 'shows a £200,000 payment to G. Robinson,' and he added, 'Even if we can't find Pergamon AGB's bank statements, the cash book is conclusive.' The £200,000 had been paid. The mystery was the identity of the account into which the cheque had been paid. Without the records, there was evidence that a £200,000 cheque for Robinson's benefit had been cashed, but the final destination might be unknown. At that stage in their conversation, Aldous delivered his final bombshell. He revealed to Stoney that although Shirley Caddock, his secretary, had written on the Orchards invoice that the money was to be paid to Robinson 'personally', the £200,000 cheque had been made payable to a company. Bewildered by the succession of revelations, Stoney did not recognise or remember the company name that Aldous mentioned. 'I feel a bit of a tit,' sighed the accountant.

On his return home, Stoney telephoned Bernard O'Sullivan, Robinson's solicitor. 'I've just been told that Geoffrey was paid the £200,000,' said Stoney.

'Oh, didn't Geoffrey tell you?' replied the lawyer.

Later that day Robinson telephoned Stoney. 'I'm sorry, I should have told you,' said Robinson. 'It seems that the papers were discovered but I knew absolutely nothing about it.' And he added prophetically, 'But there's no evidence of the account into which the money was paid.' Stoney could not cite the company's name to contradict him. On that slender omission, Robinson could plead innocence.

On 12 December 1999, Stephen Byers received Hugh Aldous's

report. The auditor explained the circumstances of the £200,000 payment to Robinson and offered conflicting conclusions about the alleged conspiracy between Robinson and Maxwell to strip out valuable assets from Hollis just before it went into liquidation. An honourable politician would have laboured with a dilemma. Six weeks earlier Byers had said, 'I would wish to be as open as possible.' The alleged asset-stripping of Hollis had occurred eight years earlier. There was no legal or commercial reason to prevent the publication of Aldous's report. But disclosure was tempered by party interest. Publishing a report which suggested that Robinson had, despite his denials, received the £200,000 and reawakening interest in Maxwell's frauds would provoke a firestorm. Far better to bury the whole issue. Consistent with that furtiveness, Byers hoped to terminate the imbroglio and protect Robinson by stealth. Robin Cook's stricture in 1994 about the investigation into Lord Archer, that 'One Tory politician should not sit in judgement on another Tory politician', did not apply to New Labour.

On the last day of the parliamentary session before Christmas, 21 December 1999, Byers arranged to insert into *Hansard*, parliament's official record, a written answer announcing the conclusion of the Hollis inquiry. His statement was timed and drafted to terminate any further interest in Robinson's affairs. After 'thorough inquiries' under the department's normal procedures, Byers stated, 'solicitors acting for the honourable member for Coventry North West have been informed the department does not propose to take any further action'. Byers refused to provide any details. Officially, Robinson had been neither blamed nor exonerated. The absence of comment could have been ominous but Robinson chose the positive interpretation. 'I am pleased,' he announced, 'that this proper scrutiny has shown the allegations were unfounded.' After the holidays, Stephen Byers expected, the affair would be entombed and forgotten. That met precisely the requirements of Blair, Brown, Mandelson and Robinson.

Three days later, on Christmas Eve, the stock exchange

announced the suspension of TransTec shares. Shortly afterwards, the company announced it was bankrupt, owing its creditors £129.5 million. Robinson's fortune, worth £32.6 million two years earlier, had evaporated. He was shocked. During the previous year, he had ignored all the warnings. Margaret Lancaster, his constituency agent, spoke on his behalf: 'This won't affect him at all. He will bounce back. Geoffrey is Geoffrey – he is an excellent businessman and he will recover. He always does.' Lancaster's optimism was delusory.

The collapse of TransTec affected Robinson badly. Over Christmas, he repeatedly telephoned Colin Cooke, the non-executive chairman of TransTec, and asked, 'Just what happened?' The politician never mentioned his loss of £30 million, but frequently complained about the publicity. 'I'm all over the newspapers and it's nothing to do with me. Will you issue a statement that I wasn't involved?' Cooke refused, but agreed that Robinson had 'walked away from it' and relied on Richard Carr. The irony was lost on Robinson. Emulating most politicians, Carr had not disclosed the payments to Ford, believing that he was serving the best interests of the shareholders. Unfortunately for Robinson, the shareholder, his interests had not been well served. He had lost the bulk of his fortune; he had lost his credibility as a businessman; and he had reawakened all the suspicions he hoped had been suffocated only three days earlier. The coincidence aroused mistrust. By stealth, he had been declared innocent by the DTI of any wrongdoing at Hollis, just when the DTI might have been expected to know that TransTec was on the verge of bankruptcy. That coincidence could not be explained by Byers who made two decisions arousing further doubts.

The receivers appointed to administer TransTec were Arthur Andersen. In particular, John Talbot and Murdoch McKillop, who had both been administrators of Hollis in 1991, returned to deal with Robinson's assets. Considering Andersen's recent refusal to help the Conservatives discover the truth about Robinson and Hollis, the partnership's re-appointment appeared a little too cosy.

The second coincidence followed David Heathcoat-Amory's

protest to Stephen Byers. Hollis and TransTec, both at one time under Robinson's chairmanship, had been declared bankrupt, and both were part of the legacy of Robert Maxwell. That required a public inquiry, suggested Heathcoat-Amory. Byers, adrift in financial matters, asked his political mentors for advice.

The pattern of Robinson's conduct had become incomprehensible to any ordinary entrepreneur. After 1981, he had used patents without payment and permission; during the 1980s, he had earned a huge income as the chairman of Agie UK, although the company had incurred losses; in 1991, Robinson's company had avoided near bankruptcy by an advantageous deal with Maxwell; in the same year he had signed Hollis's unreliable accounts which awarded him a payment of £200,000; in 1994, he had been ejected as an executive director from TransTec; in 1997, he was forced to admit his interest in a secret offshore trust whose financial activities were secret; in 1998, he had been censured three times for failing to register his commercial interests in the House of Commons; and in 1999 he was the principal shareholder of a company which was declared bankrupt. At the beginning of the new millennium, he once again was relying on Labour ministers and MPs for protection.

Stephen Byers had no intention of meeting the Conservatives' renewed demands that he publish the DTI's internal report on Hollis. In reply to Heathcoat-Amory, he wrote that his answers to the Conservative request for the publication of the Hollis report would be given to the House of Commons. 'I believe,' he wrote, 'it would be a discourtesy to the House if I answered in a private letter to you.' His statement to the Commons said, 'These were confidential inquiries and in accordance with established practice and legal constraints I have no proposals to publish the findings of the investigation.' The same sarcasm and obfuscation marked Byers's next decision.

David Heathcoat-Amory demanded a public inquiry into the relationship between Hollis and TransTec, especially the possibility of fraudulent trading before the collapse of the Maxwell empire and TransTec. 'Anything less than this,' he wrote on

6 January 2000, 'will amount to a cover-up and add to the suspicion that Labour ministers are blocking a full, proper and public examination of the business affairs of Mr Geoffrey Robinson . . . Since your government repeatedly boasts of its commitment to openness, transparency and high standards, I look to you to put some of this rhetoric into practice.' Byers had every intention of frustrating the Conservative's demand, but found himself undermined.

Since TransTec's directors had not disclosed their debts, the creditors and shareholders had a right to know the circumstances of their losses of over £200 million. Reluctantly, the minister found that he had little alternative but to appoint two independent DTI inspectors, under section 432 of the Companies Act, to deliver a report on TransTec's collapse, suitable for publication. Yet Byers's appointment on 20 January 2000 of the inspectors was curiously characterised by restrictions and dissembling.

The two inspectors were Hugh Aldous of Robson Rhodes and Roger Kaye, QC. No one beyond the DTI was aware that Aldous had been responsible for the internal Hollis inquiry. Aldous's unwillingness earlier to reveal any of the adverse findings against Robinson suited Byers. The reliable accountant understood the value of a full DTI inquiry. His partnership would benefit from generous fees and the kudos of being appointed an inspector under the Companies Act, as he had discovered during his similar duties investigating Mohamed Fayed's purchase of the House of Fraser after 1985. That report had been criticised by some Conservative ministers because the inspectors had not shown impartiality. More recently, in January 1999, Aldous had been criticised by those who had witnessed his testimony during a complex fraud trial in London. Aldous, testifying as an expert witness, appeared bogged down in the detail. Aldous was liked because, as an Establishment figure, he could be relied upon not to cause embarrassment.

Roger Kaye, QC, had been appointed by the DTI to investigate Jeffrey Archer's purchase of Anglia TV shares in 1994. Archer was accused of insider dealing because his wife, a director of Anglia, was aware of price-sensitive decisions. Kaye had failed to unearth sufficient evidence to prosecute Archer, which pleased the Conservative government.

In the TransTec case, the senior officials advising Byers could be sure that Aldous and Kaye would adhere to the proper procedures for inquiries whose results might be politically sensitive. Byers approved suitably restricted terms of reference for them to examine 'the accounting treatment [i.e., the concealment] of a claim against the company for $18 million and the extent to which the claim and other matters were disclosed to shareholders and the public – and on the reasons for the downfall of the Group'. The inspectors were not asked to investigate the company during the period of Robinson's management. In those limited circumstances, Robinson was understandably optimistic. 'I am quite sure that we will be found totally blameless in these situations,' he bubbled. He even foresaw his return to government, admitting, 'I can see it isn't on the cards yet' but after 'the problems surrounding me' were resolved. His optimism was shared by Tony Blair. His spokesman, Alastair Campbell, derided all the allegations against Robinson as 'Tory-inspired' and worthless. Not all agreed.

Max Ayriss, the former bookkeeper of TransTec, was prompted by the *Sunday Times* to renew his allegations that applications and use of about £470,000 of grants by TransTec were dishonest. Ayriss's assertion was unequivocal: 'Robinson's instructions were to maximise the claims up to the quarterly amounts available and he indicated how to make up any possible shortfall. The invoices were not forged but existing invoices for other unrelated work were booked against the DTI project. We were knowingly deceiving the DTI.' The deception of overcharging for costs and underperforming on production was crude, suggested Ayriss. Just before the DTI inspectors arrived in Coleshill, the machinery developed with DTI grants was taken out of mothballs, dusted and displayed. His account was supported by Fawzi el-Menshawy, who admitted that the money obtained from the DTI was not spent on the approved projects. 'I know I could incriminate myself,' said Ayriss, 'but it's time the truth came out.'

The government could no longer resist an investigation. The DTI and the fraud squad of the West Midlands Police were ordered in late January to launch inquiries. In Birmingham, the police case was assigned to Inspector David Churchill and two detectives. Their success depended entirely upon the policy dictated by their superiors and also, in particular, by Robert Wardle, assistant director of the Serious Fraud Office in London. Their attitude dictated the investigators' sentiments.

Although fifteen years had passed since the grants had been awarded, some DTI documents had survived from a previous investigation in 1994. Churchill's team reviewed each grant in the DTI folders and gazed at each invoice written by Ayriss and submitted by TransTec. Methodically comparing each invoice with each grant, the police observed that individual DTI officials recorded in their files their satisfaction with TransTec's compliance with the rules. Not surprisingly, the DTI's records did not reveal anything improper. The grants would never have been awarded if the DTI officials had discovered grounds for suspicion. Accordingly, Churchill's team could find no evidence of fake invoices. In the opinion of the police, the DTI's records demonstrated that Robinson was doing 'the best for his business'. At that stage, Churchill's investigation headed into the sand.

The alleged irregularities could be properly investigated only by scrutinising TransTec's bank statements and records, and comparing them with the completed forms that Ayriss had been directed to complete to satisfy the civil servants. On his own admission, Churchill did not comb through TransTec's records. After a conversation with Robinson revealed that no TransTec documents relating to the grants survived, the police officer did not undertake on his own initiative any scrutiny of TransTec's records. After relying entirely on the DTI's own documents, the police approached Ayriss to produce the evidence of the fraud.

Ayriss's co-operation could be unconditionally assumed. Not only had he made the allegations but he had retained the documentary evidence and named other employees who would corroborate his account. His was not an isolated accusation. If the police had been determined to prosecute, they would have researched TransTec's history and discovered from Professor Kumar Bhattacharyya, Michael Shattock and others the details of Robinson's unauthorised use of Birmingham University's patents. Instead, the police were directed by Robert Wardle to treat Ayriss as a suspect rather than a witness. The whistleblower whom Inspector Churchill later derisively labelled 'my star witness' was not to be given immunity to tell the truth but was to be formally cautioned by the police before his interview and warned that anything he said could be used as evidence in his own prosecution.

On 20 July 2000, Ayriss sat in an interview room in Livery Street, the headquarters of Birmingham's fraud squad. In the first telephone call inviting Ayriss for the interview, the police officer had not mentioned the intention to issue a caution. Only after a warning from a journalist did Ayriss ring Churchill's office and discover that threat. Accordingly, he consulted Stephen Jonas, a solicitor, who advised utmost caution. Before the interview, Jonas had drafted a statement and advised his client to say nothing more.

The two police officers in Livery Street were irritated. 'Their body language and their actions were really, really angry,' recalled Ayriss. After reading his five-page statement listing Robinson's allegedly false claims and mentioning five others who could corroborate his version – Fawzi el-Menshawy, Peter Dickinson, John Harrison, Lorraine Upton and John Haley, an accountant – Ayriss sat silently in the interview room. Fearful of prosecution, he refused to answer any questions. Much that he knew remained unspoken. After ninety minutes, Ayriss left the police station. The investigation, he was convinced, was dead.

Geoffrey Robinson shared that opinion. Inspector Churchill was impressed by the confident politician, sitting with his solicitor and presenting himself as the multimillionaire owner of a fast-expanding company. Whatever decisions were taken, soothed Robinson, he had always relied on professional advice. Unfortunately, he agreed, TransTec's own documents were incomplete but the police could certainly rely on the DTI's documents, which were wholly accurate. Ayriss's allegations, scoffed Robinson, could be blamed on a grudge.

In retrospect, Inspector Churchill believed that the investigation could have been completed in nine weeks. The inquiry lasted nine months. In October 2000, a spokesman for the West Midlands fraud squad announced that, because of 'insufficient evidence', Robinson's prosecution would be unjustified.

Once again, Robinson escaped censure. After Sir Gordon Downey's inquiry into the £200,000 payment by Hollis he had been protected by the indolence of MPs and Downey; after the internal DTI inquiry, he had been protected by Stephen Byers and his political friends; concerning the DTI grants, he was protected by a bureaucrat's decision to subdue the key witness.

All that remained was to rebuild his bridges with the Labour Party. Even some loyal constituency members in Coventry, he knew, were nervous. After twenty-two years, he enjoyed close relations with men and women whose admiration and affection for him were unconditional. However, during a recent, rare walk through Coventry, he had met with some hostility. The disaffected whispered that his popularity was bought with favours, houses, school fees and entertainment, although absolutely nothing had ever been proved. His friends, especially Labour councillors, defensively spoke of a maligned man of impeccable qualities who was always helpful. To allay their disquiet about the newspaper reports, he summoned a meeting at the Hen Lane Club to offer an explanation. 'Ask me anything you like,' he challenged. Unanimously, his audience was impressed that their friend did not 'shy away' from their pertinent questions. At the end, they applauded, 'putting our fears to rest'. Their MP had done 'a blooming good job' and, they agreed, was 'suffering crucifixion by the media'. Their reply to the critics was robust. 'Geoffrey Robinson,' said Margaret Lancaster, his constituency agent, 'is so generous that there's absolutely no reason for that nasty campaign. It's odd that such a nice man, liked by everybody, has attracted so much bad publicity.'

The members of his Coventry constituency were easier to woo

than the parliamentary Labour Party. In Westminster, Robinson was stained by Gordon Downey's three reports and so much more. Regardless of his exoneration by the DTI and the West Midlands fraud squad, the headlines had been unattractive even among his friends. If Robinson had been more sensitive to his predicament, he might have resolved to wait in the shadows and patiently create opportunities to rehabilitate himself gradually. But that belied the nature of a self-made millionaire devoid of self-doubt, accustomed to smothering criticism. Little rankled more during that year than Peter Mandelson's version of the loan and then his speedy rehabilitation. In January 2000, Robinson had swooned, 'I'm delighted' about Mandelson's return, but in truth he was sour. Despite the pressure from his friends, Robinson would not allow his reputation to be trashed. Although prepared to restrain his anger and withhold some damaging information, he would not suppress his book and lose the opportunity to record his personal success at the Treasury.

The serialisation contract with the *Daily Mail* for his book, *The Unconventional Minister*, undermined his assertion that his intention was to 'do the government a good turn, to heal the rivalries and bury the bitterness'. Choosing a newspaper that was hostile to the Labour government cast doubt on his pious claim to be seeking to help Blair and Mandelson. Though he kept repeating, 'I have nothing but the greatest of respect for Peter', his book listed all the damage Mandelson had done, restated the rivalries and re-heated the bitterness. 'The public hates to see politicians squabbling,' he said launching his book on 19 October. 'I didn't set out to create damage.' The *Mirror*'s headline caught the mood: 'Robbo's Revenge – How Mandy Asked for It'. The loan dominated the headlines but Robinson pretended to ignore the tumult he had created. 'Why write the book?' he was asked. 'It's obvious,' he replied, sipping champagne. 'I wanted to give an account of how we prepared for government.' To another inquirer he explained, 'I wanted to be constructive. I wrote the book to make the government more effective.' How his description of Mandelson as a 'destabilising' influence and his hints about

Mandelson's unpublished letters to himself about the loan could be 'constructive' was as baffling as Robinson's protestations of innocence and benevolence. By the time Mandelson resigned from the government amid extraordinary rancour three months later, Robinson's barbed warnings had been forgotten. 'I'm giving the proceeds of my book to The Royal College of Music,' Robinson benignly announced. The college could expect about £300,000.

Rather than using his book as an opportunity to prepare for a graceful return, Robinson behaved in an unvarnished manner: a politician hawking his grievances around TV and radio studios, and snapping irritably at interviewers welcomed to the Grosvenor House for an interview over a glass of champagne. 'I don't want to get into that,' he replied to pertinent questions about his motives, money and machinations. Throughout his career, he had focused on self-aggrandisement, shielded from scrutiny thanks to his insignificance. His downfall had been his desire for stardom. His reluctance to give a straight answer, when asked if he had sought to buy influence in the infamous eighth-floor suite, meant that his guests reported question marks and mystery. None could understand the rules of the ex-paymaster-general's game. Geoffrey's terms were incomprehensible.

At the end of five days of interviews to promote his book, Geoffrey Robinson appeared angry and puzzled. His book had been variously called 'interesting', 'wretched' and 'crushingly boring'. He was damned for breaching secrets and damned for offering 'no smoking gun'. Universally, there was agreement that his book caused damage, not to his targets but to himself. 'Before the publication of this book,' wrote one critic, 'Geoffrey Robinson had a pretty poor image. Now he has an even worse one.' Another critic commented, 'Every jilted courtier has a poisoned dart to shoot, and he has now shot his.' At the end of the week, his bid for reacceptance as an insider and not as a man buying influence looked doomed, although there seemed no outstanding, irrefutable charge which he could not answer. Had his detractors examined his book carefully, the reasons for his undoing would have been glaring.

For reasons of laziness or deceit, Robinson's book contained numerous mistakes which the suspicious might categorise as evasions and distortions. Few were more important than his statement on page 239 about the £200,000 payment from Hollis, the threat to his political career. He wrote:

I neither requested nor received any compensation as non-executive chairman, nor was any payment made to me, despite an erroneous entry in the 1988/89 accounts showing the chairman, myself, receiving £200,000 – a mystery (to myself).

He continued, 'It is also possible to show that neither Hollis nor its holding company Pergamon has made such a payment.'

Within those fifty-four words lie the proof of Geoffrey Robinson's dishonesty. The £200,000 payment was entered in the accounts of 1990, not 1988/89. In 1990, he was an executive chairman. He had been the non-executive chairman in 1988/89, when he was not entitled to any income. By juxtaposing the unrelated events, he sought to confuse the reader about his receipt of the £200,000. Most important of all, by October 2000, Robinson knew that Hugh Aldous had discovered his request on Orchards notepaper for the payment of £200,000.

A trail of disingenuous excuses over the previous twenty-eight years had prepared Robinson to answer any allegations of hypocrisy and dishonesty. The list of transgressions was considerable: the socialist breaking exchange controls at Innocenti; the huge costs and bribery scandal surrounding the paint-shop at Jaguar; the chaos of Meriden's accounts; his refusal to register and pay for the use of patents; his alleged dishonest use of DTI grants at TransTec; the unexplained finances of Agie UK; his strange deals with Robert Maxwell which enriched Robinson at the expense of others; all the interests which were unregistered in parliament; and finally his failure to disclose his invoice for £200,000 from Hollis. The list was awesome when the author met Geoffrey Robinson at his London home.

Over breakfast on Thursday, 7 December 2000, at the Grosvenor House Hotel, Robinson was asked whether there was a deliberate deception on page 239 of his book. 'It's a mistake,' he reluctantly agreed.

'But did you submit an invoice for £200,000?' he was asked.

'Yes,' he replied. 'For my work at Lock.'

'So you did request compensation?'

'Yes,' he replied, acknowledging he had presented the Orchards invoice to Michael Stoney. 'I was soliciting payment but I don't know why it was on Orchards paper,' he said. 'I did ask for payment for my work at Lock. There was an exchange of letters.'

There was no reconciliation of that admission with his emphatic denial to cabinet ministers, civil servants, Sir Gordon Downey and the parliamentary committee of having requested the payment.

'And you know that there is proof that the cheque was issued?'

'Yes,' he admitted. 'But no one knows into which account it was paid.' He looked at his interviewer. 'Do you know the account?' he asked.

Robinson's smile had disappeared. He appeared determined. The final humiliation, he appeared to hope, could still be avoided.

Robinson had been neither wise nor careful. His personal catastrophe was concealed by the calmness of his flaccid features. To his misfortune, those features matched his reality. The standard-bearer of New Labour's flagship of economic competence had been revealed as an uncertain adventurer prone to ignoring inconvenient rules, antagonising rather than dazzling his peers.

As an aspiring tycoon, Robinson had assumed that money would secure his protection from criticism and retribution. Thoughtlessly, the buccaneer had not anticipated the dangers of emerging from the shadows. He had failed to appreciate that fortunes created by mavericks, gambling on intuition, occasionally neglecting government controls while acknowledging the laws of the jungle, hardly matched the qualities required of a socialist member of parliament. Human weaknesses and vanities had smothered his judgement of his fellow politicians and the public's reaction to suggestions of sleaze. At the end, he appeared to be a man without steel, difficult to overestimate. Possibly behind the image of a false Geoffrey Robinson, there was no real Geoffrey Robinson.

As a businessman, Robinson had gambled, had earned millions of pounds and witnessed the evaporation of his fortune. As a politician, he had yearned for the public spotlight for twenty-five years, only to witness the premature termination of his life's ambition. The master of confusion, having failed to understand the requirements of parliament, sought exculpation as a victim. Like genuine tycoons faced with bad news, Robinson fought aggressively to survive, uttering threats calculated to cause alarm. In defeat, he was a petulent rather than fearsome adversary. His past was unflattering.

Contrary to his proffered self-portrait, the manufacturer of unglamorous aluminium moulds and rubber seals lacked the ruthlessness and talent to beome a powerful and rich player. The narrow range of relationships enjoyed by the trader, deprived of alliances among City bankers and institutions, could not create or sustain a private empire. Without a recognised commercial jewel, he remained an ambitious but unexceptional aspirant unable to sustain his losses.

In politics, his plight during his extended downfall was unusual. Although he was an unclubbable freelance, a king without courtiers, his hospitality had won powerful allies.

Shielded as an insider, Geoffrey Robinson's significance was the relationship, support and protection he enjoyed from Tony Blair, Gordon Brown, Peter Mandelson and Stephen Byers. Among those politicians pursuing an uncertain ideological crusade, Robinson's fate was the litmus test of the prime minister's pledge that a Labour government would be 'purer than pure', the righteous champions of probity and truth, the exterminators of sleaze.

Pouring champagne into the glass of Gordon Brown and allowing Tony Blair to stay at his Italian home had infused

Robinson with fantasies of intimacy and the illusion of power. His fortune, earned from government grants, the abuse of the patents and an extraordinary inheritance, had sustained his promotion as an entrepreneurial clairvoyant and Labour's agent of Britain's industrial regeneration. The truth destroyed the paymaster-general's dream and New Labour's chastity.

While other tarnished celebrities, after fluttering across the stage, slip into obscurity, the legacy of Geoffrey Robinson remains as the symbol of a prime minister's judgement. The paymaster-general, averred Tony Blair, was a 'high-calibre' businessman and a 'brilliant minister' who had 'done everything according to the rules'. He has never disavowed that acclamation.

In reality, Geoffrey Robinson had sought to create and control an international industrial giant but was left with worthless share certificates; he had sought glory as Britain's prime minister but instead had been dismissed as a junior Treasury minister; he aspired to become a broker between Labour and the City and instead found himself ostracised as a stricken politician, famous only for a dubious inheritance from a Belgian. The paymaster-general has been repaid in his own coin.

Acknowledgements

I owe several people an incalculable debt for their generosity in providing information and research to write this book.

First, Geoff Atkinson and Jack Cheshire of Vera Productions were magnanimous in providing innumerable files concerning Geoffrey Robinson's business career.

I am also immensely grateful for the files of information provided by Michael Crick and by other journalists who prefer to remain anonymous.

Barrie Penrose undertook valuable and long-term help in the book's research, and I am also grateful for the assistance of Bob Cole, Nick Fielding, Geoffrey Wansell, Leaf Kalfayan, Will Hutton, Dan Atkinson, Chris Blackhurst, Valerie Elliott and Matt Born. Many others requested that their help should not be publicly acknowledged.

In an unusual decision, based upon the advice of the lawyers who vetted this book, it has been decided that no interview sources will be provided or individually thanked. Nevertheless, the reader should be assured that every fact stated in this book has been sourced and for obvious reasons has been verified to the satisfaction of the lawyers who have vetted this book. I do, however, want to thank the many people who provided information and advice.

The legal chores were undertaken, with good humour as usual, by David Hooper of Pinset Curtis Biddle. Michael Shaw of Curtis Brown was steadfast in his support and as always an inspiration to complete a rapid undertaking. I owe a great debt to them both.

At Simon & Schuster, I am grateful to Helen Gummer and Katharine Young.

As always, my principal gratitude is to my family – Veronica, Nicholas, Oliver, Sophie and Alexander – who, with my parents, have endured yet more arduous months.

NOTES

Prologue

9 'so nobody could be jealous': *Daily Mail*, 16 December 1997.

9 Robinson says he received £9 million: *Sunday Express*, 14 December 1997.

Chapter 1: The Butterfly

21 with a record return on capital: *New Scientist*, 28 October 1976.

25 'I am not bad at leading people': *Birmingham Post*, 1 May 1974.

25 'confident it will work at Jaguar': *Coventry Evening Telegraph*, 25 October 1973.

25 no further strikes during his management: *New Scientist*, 28 October 1976.

26 all Labour's competing ideologues: Tony Benn, *Against the Tide: Diaries 1973–76*.

28 ration petrol for motorists: *Coventry Evening Telegraph*, 3 March 1976.

33 'star in British Leyland's firmament': *Observer*, 23 June 1974.

33 'the most exciting thing since the war': Philip Whitehead,

The Writing on the Wall: Britain in the Seventies (Michael Joseph, 1985), p. 142.

34   in return for Jaguar's order: *Guardian*, 20 May 1975.

35   the original £4 million: *New Scientist*, 28 October 1976.

37   'I prefer to leave': *The Times*, 12 May 1975.

37   'few profitable overseas subsidiaries': *Guardian*, 13 May 1975.

37   unhappiness with BL's business strategy: *Evening Standard*, 14 June 1993.

38   'line management of British Leyland': *Guardian*, 18 August 1975.

40   'cloud-cuckoo-land' at Innocenti: *Sunday Express*, 22 February 1976.

40   it was too close to the truth: *Guardian*, 13 December 1997.

40   'everyone else is happy': *Sun*, 6 March 1976.

41   'I can't say yes or no about divorce': *Independent*, 6 December 1997.

43   'we weren't playing games': Whitehead, *The Writing on the Wall*, p. 357.

43   Labour's abandonment of the industry: *The Times*, 8 February 1977.

44   'than all the strikes put together': *Daily Telegraph*, 16 April 1976; Robinson, speech in House of Commons, *Hansard*, 15 April 1976.

44   Whittaker remained silent: *Observer*, 6 March 1977.

45   'an industrial disaster area': *The Times*, 25 February 1980.

45   'is at an all time low': *Daily Express*, 11 January 1978; letters to *The Times*, 29 November and 3 December 1979.

46   under discarded laws: *The Times*, 18 December 1997.

46   and urged 'mediation': letter to *The Times*, 30 October 1981.

46   'We have a long way to go': *The Times*, 27 September 1980.

46   appear before Cardiff magistrates: *Coventry Evening Telegraph*, 19 April 1983.

47   'due propriety and fairness': letter to *The Times*, 29 January 1981.

Chapter 2: The Patents

57   a multi-purpose EDM generator: *Sunday Telegraph*, 14 December 1997.

59   'every day another factory went': *Coventry Evening Telegraph*, 16 March 1996.

62   pursuing a television career: Geoffrey Robinson, *The Unconventional Minister: My Life Inside New Labour* (Michael Joseph, 2000), p. 2.

63   Hattersley as party leader: *Guardian*, 24 December 1998.

66   speeding on the M25: *Daily Star*, 21 December 1985.

66   'dressed up as new': *Guardian*, 31 January 2000.

68   or by false invoicing: *Sunday Times*, 23 July 2000; Michael Crick, interview with Max Ayriss, from notes.

68   TransTec employees subsequently admitted: *The Times*, 23 January 2000; Michael Crick, interview with John Harrison, from notes, pp. 47–8; Michael Crick, interview with Max Ayriss, from notes, p. 16.

69   'I'm really going to be in trouble': Michael Crick, interview with John Harrison, p. 33.

69   more than 60 per cent of his time on other work: Michael Crick, *Newsnight*.

69   'This is the way the government helps small companies': Michael Crick, interview with Max Ayriss, from notes, p. 14.

69   he was the company's chairman: *Sunday Times*, 7 December 1997; Michael Crick, interview with Max Ayriss, pp. 25–6.

69   'A very hard man': Michael Crick, interview with John Harrison, pp. 38–9.

Chapter 3: The Profitable Relationship

74   'the only problem I haven't got': Geoffrey Robinson, *The Unconventional Minister: My Life Inside New Labour* (Michael Joseph, 2000), p. 234.

74   'I wasn't turned off by him': *ibid.*

78   the best tactic to win that prize: *ibid.*, p. 236.

83   salary of £200,000 'is fair': *Daily Express*, 29 June 1998.

84   appear in the official record: letter to House of Commons

Standards and Privileges Committee, 18 June 1998.

85 included in Hollis's 1990 accounts: House of Commons Committee on Standards and Privileges, 18th Report, 14 July 1998, p. 23.

86 'give a true and fair view': Coopers & Lybrand qualified Hollis accounts, 24 January 1991.

87 'which has become a big industry': *Coventry Evening Telegraph*, 14 March 1988.

88 to the offshore family trusts: *The Times*, 9 December 1997; Titmuss Sainer, letter to *Sunday Times*, 5 December 1997.

88 redundant on grounds of 'restructuring': TransTec, letter to Diane Shaw, 10 January 1991.

89 Labour could penalise the rich: *Observer*, 3 January 1999.

92 kept £1.153 million of PSS's cash: the balance was paid by C&S issuing shares worth £2.9 million at 200 per cent premium.

93 sold his 27 per cent stake for £8.24 million: *The Times*, 11 October 1991.

Chapter 4: Fulfilment

96 profits of £50 million: *The Times*, 15 December 1997.

97 'Neil Logue, the finance director': *Evening Standard*, 14 June 1993.

98 although he criticised smoking: *Coventry Evening Telegraph*, 27 February 1997.

98 he lived like a tycoon: *Evening Standard*, 14 June 1993.

100 projected to be £13 million: *Sunday Telegraph*, 13 June 1993.

100 'unique' in the House of Commons: *Evening Standard*, 14 June 1993.

101 less than the previous year: *Independent*, 9 October 1994.

101 'below market expectations': *ibid.*, 5 November 1993.

102 'if you don't mind': *Today*, 10 February 1994.

103 avoided the issue: *Sunday Telegraph*, 14 December 1997.

104 Bourgeois's jewellery were copies or 'fake': Geoffrey Robinson, *The Unconventional Minister: My Life Inside New Labour* (Michael Joseph, 2000), p. 21.

106 resignation as chief executive: *Independent*, 6 November 1994; *Sunday Express*, 26 February 1995; *Daily Mail*, 20 December 1997.

106 'I volunteered to split the roles': *Independent*, 9 November 1994.

108 'rights without responsibilities': *Coventry Evening Telegraph*, 16 March 1996.

110 'should be fully disclosed': *Observer*, 15 October 1995.

112 'the trustees of my family trust': Robinson, *Unconventional Minister*, p. 143.

112 'a long-standing Spurs fan': *ibid.*, p. 144.

112 the identity of only one trustee: *Observer*, 14 December 1997.

113 of the sender's sincerity: *Sunday Times*, 4 January 1998.

113 'No one seemed to bother much': Robinson, *Unconventional Minister*, p. 147.

114 'None of it will be taken out': *Coventry Evening Telegraph*, 7 February 1997.

114 'support for my local team': *ibid.*, 15 December 1997.

114 'has been as an investor': *ibid.*, 7 February 1997; 3 March 1997.

114 Robinson's offshore trust: Robinson, *Unconventional Minister*, p. 209; *ibid.*, 26 February 1996.

115 'evolution of Labour Party thinking': *Daily Telegraph*, 9 February 1996.

116 'get some beer as well': *Sunday Times*, 16 January 2000.

117 'had nothing and was no one': Robinson, *Unconventional Minister*, p. 5.

121 'looking for a loan': *ibid.*, pp. 6–7.

121 'belies a very sharp mind': *Observer*, 30 November 1997.

122 He merely made an offer: Robinson, *Unconventional Minister*, p. 8.

122 'well be placed to do so': *ibid*.

122 'I gave no more thought to the loan': *ibid*.

123 'operate like that in practice': *ibid.*, p. 7.

123 Mandelson's house-warming party: *ibid.*, p. 8.

124 appointed to the cabinet: *Independent*, 28 August 1996.

124 a 'complete fabrication': *Observer*, 1 September 1996.

124 and 'malevolent': *Guardian*, 30 August 1996.

124 Spain, Russia and South Africa: *Daily Mail*, 27 September 1995.

124 contract was £26 million: *Independent*, 31 March 1996.

124 allocation of 9.8 million shares: *Financial Times*, 23 April 1997; 27 February 2000.

128 guest of honour abruptly departed: 'City Diary', *Daily Telegraph*, 31 October 1996.

129 'Labour's industrial policy': *Observer*, 26 January 1997.

130 'just total coincidences': *Sunday Telegraph*, 14 December 1997.

Chapter 5: 'Purer than Pure'

135 facing a discredited opposition: *Sunday Telegraph*, 22 October 2000.

135 'wrong in the recent past': Robinson, *The Unconventional Minister: My Life Inside New Labour* (Michael Joseph, 2000), p. 57.

135 'a series of unforced errors': *ibid.*, p. 56.

135 'optimism . . . and monetary laxity': *ibid.*

135 'clear and firm direction': *ibid.*, p. 54.

136 'which I didn't like at all': *Sunday Times*, 19 July 1998.

140 'deliver value for money': *The Times*, 3 July 1997.

140 not 'if' but 'when': *Observer*, 18 May 1997.

141 'easy money again under Labour': *The Times*, 3 July 1997.

143 triple the original estimate: *Guardian*, 24 December 1998.

143 signed by the end of 1999: *ibid,*, 24 June 1997.

143 'making this work,' he admitted: *Daily Telegraph*, 24 June 1997.

144 to Robinson's mirth: Robinson, *Unconventional Minister*, p. 173.

145 'ruined their normal life': *The Times*, 27 May 1997.

145 with unconscious irony: Robinson, *Unconventional Minister*, p. 173.

146 'has not avoided tax': *Hansard*, 16 August 1997.

147 Blair pouted, 'and I am': Andrew Rawnsley, *Servants of the People* (Hamish Hamilton, 2000), pp. 91ff.

147 not on the government's integrity but on its competence: Donald Macintyre, *Mandelson* (HarperCollins, 2000), pp. 435–6.

148 'catch you out': *Financial Times*, 28 October 2000.

Chapter 6: Earthquake

150 'as a bolt out of the blue': Geoffrey Robinson, *The Unconventional Minister: My Life Inside New Labour* (Michael Joseph, 2000), p. 209.

150 'the Orion Trust was 'widely known': *ibid.*

150 'has shares in Coventry FC': *Sunday Times*, 21 December 1997.

150 'more than their fair share': *Observer*, 14 December 1997.

150 'legal arrangements to incur tax': Robinson, *Unconventional Minister*, p. 212.

154 'for tax or any other purposes': *ibid.*, p. 211.

154 'She left me £9 million': *Daily Mail*, 15 December 1997.

156 'an asset for the government': *The Times*, 3 December 1997.

156 'passed without hostile questioning': Robinson, *Unconventional Minister*, p. 179.

156 'I made no secret of the existence of the trust': *ibid.*, p. 212.

158 'he has revealed everything': *Guardian*, 6 December 1997.

159 'He's a pretty tough character': *The Times*, 13 December 1997.

160 'the rules have been carried out': Press Association, 8 December 1997.

160 'an exceptionally able minister': *Daily Mirror*, 9 December 1997.

160 to minimise his taxes: *Evening Standard*, 9 December 1997.

160 Robinson had avoided tax: *News*, Channel Four, 8 December 1997; *Hansard*, 10 December 1997.

161 'something like that': *Sunday Express*, 14 December 1997.

162 Orion's unidentified trustees: Titmuss Sainer, letter to the *Observer*, 9 December 1997.

163 'that I am telling lies': *Observer*, 14 December 1997.

163 'suggested' deals to the trustees: *Sunday Telegraph*, 14 December 1997.

163 not mentioned in the media: *Sunday Times*, 14 December 1997.

164 the sole beneficiary: *Observer*, 14 December 1997.

164 mentioned 'eight' beneficiaries: Robinson, *Unconventional Minister*, p. 212.

164 'not received any balance sheets': *Observer*, 14 December 1997.

164 barred from seeing the accounts: House of Commons Committee on Standards and Privileges, 10th Report, 20 January 1998, p. 10.

164 'Are you calling me a liar?': *Sunday Telegraph*, 14 December 1997.

164 chanted about Robinson's explanations: *Hansard*, 21 January 1998; *The Times*, 22 January 1998.

165 'that was not a problem': *Observer*, 14 December 1997; Robinson, *Unconventional Minister*, p. 210.

165 'He seemed well satisfied': Robinson, *Unconventional Minister*, p. 210.

165 about Robinson's veracity: *Sunday Times*, 30 November 1997.

165 the demand of total loyalty: Andrew Rawnsley, *Servants of the People* (Hamish Hamilton, 2000), p. 148.

165 'to consider it further': *Independent*, 13 December 1997.

166 an 'offshore trust': Press Association, 13 December 1997.

166 'than either you or me': *News*, Channel Four, 8 December 1997.

166 pushed out of office: *Independent on Sunday*, 14 December 1997.

166 that Robinson was a hypocrite: *Daily Telegraph*, 15 December 1997; *Frost* interview, BBC TV.

166 possibility of his resignation: Robinson, *Unconventional Minister*, p. 226.

167 thought he should resign: *Sunday Times*, 21 December 1997.

167 'an honest man': *Independent*, 26 December 1997.

167 the ordeal was over: Press Association, 23 December 1997.

168 to Derek Higgs were revealed: *Sunday Times*, 21 December 1997.

168 value up to 77 pence: *The Times*, 20 December 1997.

Chapter 7: Smoking Guns

169 'That died in 1997': *Independent*, 26 December 1997.

170 'no credibility whatsoever': *Hansard*, 17 December 1997.

170 had received any money: House of Commons Committee on Standards and Privileges, 10th Report, 20 January 1998, Para. 7.

171 'would have been better registered': House of Commons Committee on Standards and Privileges, 10th Report, 20 January, Conclusions, p. 4.

171 'clearly has nothing to hide': *Independent*, 22 February 1998.

172 'There was nothing wrong with them': *Sunday Telegraph*, 21 December 1997.

172 'buy a company off Maxwell': *Express on Sunday*, 14 December 1997.

173 'to the tune of £1.5 million': *Hansard*, 15 January 1998.

173 'tax relief from Middle Britain': *ibid.*, 3 March 1998.

173 several similar directorships: House of Commons Committee on Standards and Privileges, 18th Report, 14 July 1988, pp. 13ff; *The Times*, 20 June 1998; *Daily Telegraph*, 31 January 1998.

175 'recall writing that memo': House of Commons Committee on Standards and Privileges, 18th Report, p. 23.

176 'an error in the accounts': *Daily Telegraph*, 20 June 1998.

177 'no need to check it': *Coventry Evening Telegraph*, 29 June 1998.

178 Pergamon's accounts for 1989/90 for the loss of office: House of Commons Committee on Standards and Privileges, 18th Report, p. 23, Appendix 10, Annex B.

179 'really scraping the barrel': Geoffrey Robinson, *The Unconventional Minister: My Life Inside New Labour* (Michael Joseph, 2000), pp. 230–31.

179 of finding new evidence: House of Commons Committee on Standards and Privileges, 18th Report, p. 6.

180 positions were unpaid: House of Commons Committee on Standards and Privileges, 18th Report, p. 10.

180 'in a Labour government': *Daily Mirror*, 16 July 1998.

181 'has proved to be worthless': *Daily Telegraph*, 23 July 1998.

181 'to abuse public office': *Financial Times*, 16 July 1998.

181 languishing at 82 pence: *Guardian*, 24 March 1998.

182 Dom Pérignon socialist: *Daily Mail*, 18 July 1998.

183 serving in government: *ibid.*, 18 July 1998.

183 'many Treasury officials': Robinson, *Unconventional Minister*, p. 226.

183 'such a mess in my life': *Sunday Telegraph*, 22 October 2000.

183 his host's inconvenience: *ibid.*, 26 July 1998.

184 concerning his probity: *The Times*, 7 July 1998; Robinson, *Unconventional Minister*, pp. 221–2.

185 'to be sacked', and departed: Robinson, *Unconventional Minister*, pp. 221–2.

185 a 'fucking brilliant minister': *ibid.*, p. 224.

185 'less than competent': *ibid.*, pp. 224–5.

186 and Robinson remained: *ibid.*, p. 228.

187 'Rough old game, politics': *ibid.*, p. 222.

188 the responsibility was his: *Daily Telegraph*, 22 December 1998.

188 'that concerned no one else': Robinson, *Unconventional Minister*, p. 10.

188 Mandelson said that Robinson requested secrecy: Donald Macintyre, *Mandelson* (HarperCollins, 2000).

190 the training of managers: *Sunday Times*, 18 October 1998.

191 worth £4.25 billion: *Guardian*, 22 October 1998.

192 following day, 18 November: House of Commons Committee on Standards and Privileges, 20th Report, November 1998, p. 4.

192 triviality of the complaint: Robinson, *Unconventional Minister*, p. 232.

193 'the end of the matter'; *Daily Telegraph*, 19 November 1998.

194 never heard to declare his interest: *Sunday Times*, 7 December 1997.

194 in return for shares: *Guardian*, 3 March 1999.

194 statement to the Commons: Robinson, *Unconventional Minister*, p. 232.

195 'be allowed to succeed': *Daily Mirror*, 23 November 1998.

195 'incentives to operate efficiently': *Independent*, 11 November 1998.

196 'another Tory politician': Michael Crick, *Stranger Than Fiction* (Hamish Hamilton, 1995), p. 411.

196 before Hollis's bankruptcy: David Heathcoat-Amory, letter to Peter Mandelson, 26 November 1998.

196 dismissing Robinson in July: *Daily Telegraph*, 3 December 1998; *Financial Times*, 5 December 1998.

197 'requested . . . any compensation': Robinson, *Unconventional Minister*, p. 239.

198 'look into it': Macintyre, *Mandelson*, p. xxvii.

198 on hearing the news from Alastair Campbell: Andrew Rawnsley, *Servants of the People* (Hamish Hamilton, 2000), p. 222.

198 anything 'fundamentally wrong': *ibid*.

200 'breaking the story tomorrow': Robinson, *Unconventional Minister*, p. 9.

200 'relieved at this explanation': *ibid*.

201 'that's an end of it': *ibid*., pp. 9–10.

202 conflict of interest: *Independent*, 19 April 1999.

202 'undecided at the time': *Daily Mail*, 24 December 1998.

203 'distorted' his behaviour: *Sunday Telegraph*, 20 December 1998.

204 bowed to public opinion: *Daily Telegraph*, 26 December 1998.

204 to protect his friend: Robinson, *Unconventional Minister*, p. 13.

204 'the private arrangement': *ibid*.

205 'here at the house': *Daily Telegraph*, 24 December 1998.

207 the loan as 'not earth-shattering': *News*, BBC Radio 4, 26 December 1998.

207 'a very high price for it': *Independent*, 28 December 1998.

Chapter 8: Concealment

209 dispel the suspicion: House of Commons Committee on Standards and Privileges, 18th Report, 14 July 1998, p. 25; *Guardian*, 16 July 1998.

209 'justifiable interest in so doing': Michael Fishman, letter to David Heathcoat-Amory, 1 March 1999.

210 remain secret: Stephen Byers, letter to David Heathcoat-Amory, 26 March 1999.

210 his shares had halved: *Daily Telegraph*, 22 September 1998.

211 engineering sector by 80 per cent: *Financial Times*, 23 September 1999.

211 'an exceptionally able minister': *Daily Mirror*, 9 December 1997.

211 he was contesting it: *Guardian*, 24 June 2000.

213 'reaching hasty judgements': *The Times*, 8 January 1999.

214 required their honesty: *Daily Express*, 2 July 1999.

214 'inconsistency and illogicality': *ibid.*, 17 June 1999.

215 isolation as a 'non-person': *Evening Standard*, 20 October 1999.

216 through the Labour Party's fund: *Sunday Telegraph*, 22 October 2000.

217 anything to that fund: *Daily Express*, 22 October 1999.

217 'the Neill committee': *Daily Mail*, 19 October 2000.

217 'I'm not twisted': *Sunday Times*, 24 October 1999.

217 material from his book: *Daily Telegraph*, 25 October 1999.

217 'blackmail the government': *Daily Express*, 25 October 1999.

218 conclusions would be published: David Heathcoat-Amory, letter to Stephen Byers, 12 October 1999.

218 ten months earlier: *Hansard*, 20 January 1999.

218 'I hope that this is helpful': Stephen Byers, letter to David Heathcoat-Amory, 31 October 1999.

220 did not apply to New Labour: Michael Crick, *Stranger than Fiction* (Hamish Hamilton, 1995), p. 411.

223 'some of this rhetoric into practice': David Heathcoat-Amory, letter to Stephen Byers, 6 January 2000.

224 'these situations,' he bubbled: *Daily Express*, 27 January 2000.

224 'Tory-inspired' and worthless: *Daily Telegraph*, 10 February 2000.

224 'deceiving the DTI': *Daily Express*, 24 January 2000.

224 dusted and displayed: *Sunday Times*, 31 March 1996.

228 in truth he was sour: *Daily Express*, 27 January 2000.

228 'set out to create damage': *Financial Times*, 28 October 2000.

228 'prepared for government': *ibid*.

229 'Now he has an even worse one': *Independent*, 27 October 2000.

229 'he has now shot his': *Guardian*, 17 October 2000.

230 'Pergamon has made such a payment': Geoffrey Robinson, *The Unconventional Minister: My Life Inside New Labour* (Michael Joseph, 2000), p. 240.

INDEX